Gender, Theory, and the Canon

GENDER, THEORY, AND THE CANON

James A. Winders

The University of Wisconsin Press

The University of Wisconsin Press
114 North Murray Street
Madison, Wisconsin 53715

3 Henrietta Street
London WC2E 8LU, England

5   4   3   2   1

Printed in the United States of America

Winders, James A., 1949–
    Gender, theory, and the canon / James A. Winders.
    208 pp.   cm.
    Includes bibliographical references and index.
    1. Feminist criticism.   2. Feminist literary criticism.
I. Title.
HQ1190.W56   1991
305.42'01—dc20
ISBN 0-299-12920-9   90-50655
ISBN 0-299-12924-1 (pbk)   CIP

For Becky, Jacob, and Ben

Contents

Acknowledgments

I am acutely aware of the debt I owe to so many persons who helped make this book a reality. I owe the most to my family for their love and patient support and encouragement, especially to my wife, Becky, whose own scholarly accomplishments serve always to inspire me. Nietzsche observed that a marriage partner should be someone with whom you would wish to have a lifelong conversation. Thank you, Becky, for excellent conversation, and for long hours of proofreading.

The following persons read the entire manuscript: Dale Bauer, Betsy Draine, Daniel O'Hara, and Mark Poster. My debt to them for the care and intelligence of their critical readings is enormous. Thomas McLaughlin, whose friendship and fine scholarly example have sustained me through my twelve years at Appalachian State, read nearly all of the manuscript and supplied many of the best ideas and insights this author might be tempted to claim. Moreover, it was Tom who, in response to a paper I gave in 1985, wondered aloud whether a book such as this might be incubating. I also remember an important conversation in 1984 with David Schalk, who posed some richly speculative questions about the relations obtaining among intellectual history, gender, and theory. Carl Pletsch read the principal chapters in their initial form, and helped me considerably in the "talking stages" of this book. He also suggested the title, or, more specifically, distilled the three key terms of the title from a wordier, more unwieldy version. Several colleagues read portions of the manuscript-in-progress, and I benefitted greatly from their suggestions and criticisms: Michael Beard, Jefferson Boyer (intellectual comrade and racquetball opponent *par excellence*), Fuat Firat, Michael Moore, Clayton Morgareidge, Karen Offen, Winifred Woodhull, and Jonathan York. Douglas Kellner provided helpful suggestions on the subject of Marx's early writings. I thank Michael Sateia, a psychiatrist, for some memorable conversations generated by my earlier work with Freud and psychoanalysis. I also thank a lifelong friend and ardent reader, Robert McClung, for his unflagging interest and good conversation. Conversations and correspondence with Martin Jay, Dominick LaCapra, and Elaine Showalter proved most valuable in the earliest stages of writing this book.

Barbara Hanrahan of the University of Wisconsin Press believed in this book from the very start, and unfailingly provided intelligent suggestions, sound critical judgment, and much-appreciated encouragement. My thanks to her and to Raphael Kadushin for their editorial skills, and also to Susan Tarcov for outstanding copy editing. For several years, the Center for the Development of Social Responsibility, based in Boone, North Carolina, has offered me a forum for my ideas, an atmosphere of intelligent, critical interdisciplinary discussion, and a collective example of political practice and concern. The Program in Women's Studies at Appalachian State provided several opportunities for me to present this work in its early stages, and its able leader, Margaret McFadden, has contributed a great deal to my education in women's history and feminist theory. I must also thank Patricia Beaver for her extensive knowledge of feminist anthropology and for the stimulating experience of team-teaching a course in 1988 on "Gender, Race, and Culture." Appalachian State University provided support in the form of release time and scholarly leave. I particularly thank George Antone, Chair of the Department of History, and J. William Byrd, Dean of the College of Arts and Sciences from 1984 to 1990. Temporary reassignment to the ASU New York Loft in New York City provided a writer's haven at a crucial point. My thanks to Clinton Parker, among others, for this opportunity.

Access to New York University's Bobst Library during the summer of 1988, and the fall of 1989, was very helpful, as was the support of Dartmouth College in the form of a full tuition fellowship at the 1986 School of Criticism and Theory. Martha Kreszock, world-class interlibrary loan expert, helped me many more times than she may realize. My thanks also to many friends and colleagues who offered suggestions or mentioned titles of books and articles new to me, or simply provided excellent intellectual companionship. I wish I could mention all of them by name.

I wish it were possible personally to thank (and name) each of the many fine students who has contributed in myriad ways to the ideas expressed herein. I doubt that my editors would want to attach an acknowledgments section that long to this book. I hope those students will recognize themselves in its pages, and perceive the gratitude thus conveyed. Many times their willingness to work patiently with challenging writers like Freud or Derrida or Irigaray has kept me going, and their enthusiasm for the insights and perspectives of recent cultural theory has sustained my effort to relate such reputedly obscure, difficult topics to basic themes of undergraduate education in the Humanities.

Finally, though our intellectual collaboration has involved topics distinct from, though related to, this book, I want to recognize my colleague Melissa

Barth, whose writing, teaching, political commitment, and boundless energy command my admiration and provide continual inspiration to me. She knows that no line should be drawn between "high" culture, and mass or popular culture. She also makes me laugh. To you, Melissa, I offer these two words: *Spa fon!*

Tribeca, New York City
Boone, North Carolina
Athens, Georgia
1989–1991

Gender, Theory, and the Canon

CHAPTER ONE

Introduction: Gender, Theory, and the Crisis of the Canon

Être à la fois un universitaire et un intellectuel c'est essayer de faire jouer un type de savoir et d'analyse qui est enseigné et reçu dans l'université de façon à modifier non seulement la pensée des autres mais aussi la sienne propre. Ce travail de modification de sa propre pensée et de celle des autres me paraît être la raison d'être des intellectuels.

—Michel Foucault

By feminist, one understands a way of reading texts that points to the masks of truth with which phallocentrism hides its fictions.

—Peggy Kamuf, "Writing like a Woman"

Reading as a lesbian is not necessarily what happens when a lesbian reads . . . The hypothesis of a *lesbian* reader [is what] changes our apprehension of a given text.
  —Jean E. Kennard, "Ourselves behind Ourselves: A Theory for Lesbian Readers"

I'm not denying the pleasures, or value, of Keats, or Joyce, or Chaucer—but authors are merely the nice leafy trees. The canon is the forest. Like its military homonym, the canon is a machine: a form. Its main function is to place, to order, to establish things (texts) in relation to one another . . . Like Spam, the canon is resilient and, for planners of curricula, cheap. It is much easier to reprint 30 books than to choose every year from among 30,000 or 300,000.
  —Stacey d'Erasmo, "You Could Look It Up: Digesting the Canon à la Mode"

I've introduced three very loaded terms ("gender," "theory," and "canon") into the title of this book, and since, to borrow a phrase from Stéphane Mallarmé, a roll of the dice will never abolish chance,[1] I owe the reader some explanation. By the time this chapter has concluded, setting the stage for the textual forays that follow, I hope to have clarified exactly what these terms mean to me and how I am using them. First, however, some prefacing is in order. In the late 1980s and early 1990s we have found ourselves in the midst of urgent debates about the plight of humanities education. These debates rage within a climate whose political and economic currents are by no means unconnected to educational issues, including theoretical ones.

As accusations are hurled as to whose fault the perceived lapse in educational "excellence" (that dreadful, heavily coded word) is, persistent questions include the following: What should be taught (and how)? Should the claims of a (particularly Western, largely white male) canon be vigorously reasserted? Should students instead be introduced to the perspectives, i.e., female, gay, non-Caucasian, of those previously excluded from civilization's center stage? Should theoretical discussions of these and attendant issues of textual interpretation be confined to advanced graduate seminars, or introduced as well into the undergraduate classroom? These are far from abstract questions safely confined within campus walls. In an era of increasing "accountability" for faculty, declining minority enrollments, and growing indifference to affirmative action, the political import of these debates can easily be grasped, as apologists for sexism, white racial superiority, class privilege, and American imperial hegemony present themselves as the objective, neutral guardians of humanist values defending the integrity of the academy against those (e.g., feminists, African-Americans) who would dare to "politicize" the teaching of the humanities. These latter constituencies are the ones major political party leaders, thus defenders of corporate American privilege, deride as "special interests."

The generation of scholars thus under attack has come of age in a climate of interdisciplinary cultural theory emanating from French structuralism and poststructuralism, and adapted in this country by persons working in literature, women's studies, history, and anthropology, among other fields. Postmodern cultural theory, focused as it is on signs and texts, represents a critique of the autonomous subject standing apart from language and other social codes. This subject is dear to the hearts of traditional humanists, and they are understandably scandalized by the privilege accorded signifiers and sign systems at the expense of the hypostasized individual postulated by liberal democratic theory and political economy. Accordingly, some of the most vigorous debates concerning the fate of the humanities have involved as participants persons associated with new theory and criticism, who frequently find themselves at odds with those who would, to pick up speed on their helter-skelter ride "back to the basics," toss overboard the heavy baggage of theory.

Intellectual history, the subdiscipline I have worked in for more than a decade, has been increasingly engaged with efforts to understand and come to terms with such postmodern theorists as Michel Foucault, Jacques Derrida, and Jacques Lacan, also of course debating the implications for the field of a strong emphasis on language as theorized by these heirs of the tradition of Saussure.[2] Intellectual history, both because of its inherently interdisciplinary orientation (which has always included being conversant with developments in literary theory and criticism) and because of its function, within history, of historiographical and theoretical inquiry (including attempts to define "history" as a mode of intellectual inquiry), was the first historical subdiscipline to feel the impact of the new theory. Women's history and social history have since followed suit. I do not mean to imply that these theoretical shifts have taken place in an atmosphere of unanimity or without controversy.

Despite the challenge poststructuralism posed to the institution of authorship that had always been central to intellectual history, by 1980 there was a growing consensus among those in the field who had begun to work during the late 1960s and 1970s that the issues raised by Foucault, Derrida, and others who concentrated on language more than on individual users of language were transforming the field. The 1980 Cornell University conference on the future of European intellectual history produced the influential anthology *Modern European Intellectual History: Reappraisals and New Perspectives,* edited by Dominick LaCapra and Steven Kaplan, which captured this mood. Most of the contributors to that volume would certainly have agreed with Catherine Belsey, who, surveying the theoretical upheaval in literary studies at approximately the same time, wrote that "we are in the midst of a Copernican revolution in theory."[3] Her use of imagery inspired by Thomas S. Kuhn's studies of scientific revolutions and paradigm crisis would also be congenial to these same historians.

Exciting transformations of intellectual history were under way in the early 1980s. For some, it must have seemed that the field was brought back from the dead. Most historians appeared to regard "intellectual history" as an outmoded field, and probably resented the very name, which unfortunately implies that other historians are not "intellectual." A narrow definition of "intellectual" would accord well with the traditional emphasis on celebrated thinkers. As long as intellectual history clung to an elite perspective, it would increasingly lose out to the "new history," with its emphasis on everyday life and popular consciousness. To some extent, bridges began to be built between intellectual and social history by, among others, Robert Darnton, Lynn Hunt, and Natalie Zemon Davis, who appeared to be in sympathy with Antonio Gramsci's observation in *The Prison Notebooks* that anyone, regardless of class background, can be considered an "intellectual." Only a relative few are called upon to play the role of one.[4] Their emphasis, carried out in studies of the ancien régime and the cultural climate of the French Revolution, complemented the broad sense of culture studies practiced by Raymond Williams and Edward Said, to cite only the most conspicuous of scholars whose interdisciplinary outlook and significance were rooted in literature.

Much of the recent work of these historians would seem to have direct bearing on so-called "intellectual" history. Both Robert Darnton, who announced his intention to inaugurate a "history of reading,"[5] and Natalie Zemon Davis, in her 1987 book *Fiction in the Archives*,[6] adapt the interpretive strategies of recent textual criticism to a greatly expanded sense of authorship and readership. Their work, however, gets discussed under the rubric of *histoire des mentalités* or the "new history," rather than as "intellectual history," whose boundaries with social history it tends to blur. Intellectual historians' receptivity to this crossing of boundaries depends upon their willingness to dispense with a distinct domain known as "intellectual" history. And yet some historians, the most notable example being Dominick La-Capra, have exhibited a fascination with postmodern textual theories (in La-Capra's case, his enthusiasm, though not unqualified, is greatest for Jacques Derrida and Mikhail Bakhtin, the latter being postmodern in the sense of having been recently "discovered" as a cultural theorist), even while retaining an allegiance to intellectual history.[7] Indeed, he is the Goldwin Smith Professor of European Intellectual History at Cornell University. For La-Capra, "intellectual history" becomes a designation for an inquiry into texts, contexts, and history that is broad enough to encompass most of contemporary theory and criticism.

LaCapra and most of the intellectual historians (e.g., Martin Jay, Keith Baker, Mark Poster) who contributed to the volume of essays edited by LaCapra and Kaplan have worked to modify intellectual history along lines suggested by the new emphasis on language, signs, and texts. For Hayden White, however, "intellectual history" cannot contain the burgeoning realities and implications of new critical theory. Out of the ashes of the old field rises the "history of consciousness," a phrase more obviously inviting of history's alignment with anthropology, linguistics, psychoanalysis, and other human sciences. The "History of Consciousness" program at the University of California at Santa Cruz bears out this promise. If (and these are crude oversimplifications) LaCapra has been known for his mediation of the theories of Derrida, White reserves greater enthusiasm for the example of Michel Foucault, and was certainly one of the very first American historians to comment critically and carefully on Foucault's work.[8]

No doubt Foucault's genealogical interrogation of academic disciplines and institutions has influenced Hayden White's stance vis-à-vis history, i.e., his willingness to anticipate its eventual dispersion into related human sciences (see below, Chapter 7: "Cultural Criticism—Interdisciplinary and Global"). Much more energetically than Foucault, White has focused attention on rhetoric and the tropes that inescapably mediate both the writing and the reading of history.[9] Much of this emphasis derives from the example of Kenneth Burke.[10] Accordingly, White's most radical claim is that historians face insurmountable obstacles in their use of sources and their written accounts based on original sources because of the inherent rhetoricity of prose narrative, something stubbornly ignored or underestimated by most historians, with their disciplinary antipathy to theory. LaCapra, by contrast, calls for an end to the needless distinction between what historians prefer to call "sources" (or "documents") and what literary scholars and critics like to call "texts." Unlike White, he retains an optimistic insistence that historians can learn to do this. Much more attuned than LaCapra to Foucault, White offers a breathtaking vision of a historical discipline (not just intellectual history) that, having been around for little more than a century or so, has now almost run its course and must make way for new disciplinary formations arising in response to changing historical circumstances. In an important essay with the punning title of "The Burden of History," White concludes:

> It may well be that the most difficult task which the current generation of historians will be called upon to perform is to expose the historically conditioned character of the historical discipline, to preside over the dissolution of history's claim to autonomy among the disciplines, and to aid in the assimilation of history to a higher kind of intellectual inquiry which, because it is founded on an awareness of the *similarities* between art and science, rather than their differences, can be properly designated as neither.[11]

My own sympathies lead me to incline toward White as to the label to be given what for me is a necessarily interdisciplinary affiliation. In other words, I have no particular affection for the phrase "intellectual history," and, despite my fondness for historical inquiry, over which the discipline of history seeks unsuccessfully to maintain a monopoly, I would not particularly regret the "dissolution of history's claim to autonomy among the disciplines." But, despite my impatience with LaCapra's need to shore up the discipline of intellectual history, I am more impressed by the actual readings and the critical synthesis he brings to specific texts, particularly with regard to fiction,[12] a genre some intellectual historians have found daunting (see below Chapter 4, on Flaubert), than I am by the uses White makes of them. Thanks to LaCapra's example, intellectual history has increasingly made room for the advanced textual criticism that scholars in comparative litera- ture or English have embraced in greater numbers (at least partly because, with relatively more university requirements in English than in history, there are far more academic literary specialists than there are historians, let alone intellectual historians). But, we should ask: what has actually *changed* as a result? As many suspect of literary theory,[13] have the basic outlines of the field and the objects of study within it remained the same, with only differ- ent methodologies available for the amusement of the members of the guild?

Once every decade or so, that august journal the *American Historical Re- view* tips its hat in the direction of intellectual history, the wayward stepchild of the family of history. The most recent such gesture came in the form of a long review article by John E. Toews in the October 1987 issue. It is certain to be cited by intellectual historians for some time to come. Toews comments upon the LaCapra/Kaplan volume, as well as on similarly theoretical works by LaCapra, Allan Megill (author of a book on Nietzsche, Heidegger, Fou- cault, and Derrida), Martin Jay, and Mark Poster. He also discusses more specific studies in cultural history that show the influence of recent theory. Toews presents a view of intellectual history in the 1980s as a subdiscipline struggling, in its postmodern theoretical phase, not to be overshadowed by the achievements of new social historians. Picking up on the title of Martin Jay's essay in the LaCapra/Kaplan anthology on the prospects for intellec- tual history's "lingusitic turn," Toews's review article, "Intellectual History after the Linguistic Turn: The Autonomy of Meaning and the Irreducibility of Experience," argues forcefully that, after all this theoretical ferment, "meaning," as mediated by texts, remains unreconciled with the "experi- ence" of events and contexts.[14]

Toews synthesizes an impressive amount of material in order to take stock of a field he clearly believes has reclaimed the right to survive and flourish. Selecting four key theoretical perspectives on language, meaning, and his- tory afforded by Gadamer, Habermas, Foucault, and Derrida, he sees each of them as exemplars of "a peculiar combination of intellectual historian and cultural critic," and comments sensibly, "None of these responses can be theoretically or empirically grounded, of course, without falling into the illusions of a bankrupt metaphysics; they can only be justified in practice."[15] Typically for an essay by an intellectual historian, and despite its otherwise impressive range and theoretical sweep, Toews's essay contains the glaring omission of feminism and feminist theory, as if it never existed and the failure of the historians he discusses to engage feminist perspectives were no failure at all. This is partly the result of the list of historians Toews surveys: as was the case at the celebrated Cornell conference and in the subsequent book edited by LaCapra and Kaplan, not a woman among them. Ultimately, I think, this omission of feminist perspectives is explained by Toews's strong need (and that of others in this male-dominated field) to assert the prerogatives of a discipline that can retain its place only through avoiding the implications and claims of feminist theory and criticism.

At one very memorable point in his essay, Toews approaches the radical interdisciplinarity, if I may be permitted such an ungainly word, of theory in the humanities today in a way that underscores his need exhibited elsewhere in the essay (after all, he is writing *as* an intellectual historian *for* the leading American historical journal) to assert the prerogatives of his subdiscipline:

> The critical question is not whether theories, models, or methods developed in one discipline can be effectively applied in another but whether a general shift in perspective has occurred regarding the production, reproduction, and transmission of cultural meanings that impinges on all of the disciplines in the human studies and provides the basis for a genuine interdisciplinary dialogue in which intellectual history will have a distinctive voice.[16]

Something I find increasingly irritating and frustrating is the tendency of writers throughout humanities and social science disciplines to proclaim the interdisciplinary implications of the theoretical issues that confront them while continuing to conduct business as usual within their departmental enclaves. (A differing/deferring example of the Derridean "trace" at work in the word *enclave:* change one letter and you have *enslave;* change one letter of the equivalent French word *enclave* and you have *esclave.*) Several times a year, scholars receive stacks of university press book catalogs featuring new theoretical works nonetheless listed within conventional academic categories. Students keenly interested in feminist theory or deconstruction experience disillusion when forced to opt for standard kinds of departmental majors. Scholars write manifesto-like books declaring the interdisciplinary import of new interpretive practices and then turn around and form new departments of English, for example, where "literary theory" will find a home. At a 1988 conference organized by scholars seeking to counter the influence of cultural conservatives on discussion of the humanities curriculum, Stanley Fish was asked by a reporter employed by the MacNeil-Lehrer television program what, exactly, had changed at Duke University. He shot back the comment that the English Department had much nicer, newly renovated offices.[17] Business, in other words, can go on as usual. Psychoanalysis, whose inherently interdisciplinary energies are now in danger of being redomesticated within departments of literature, provides a perspective from which we can say that the suggested dissolution of disciplinary boundaries is one of the most thoroughly repressed insights in contemporary theory in the humanities. Call it repression or more conscious reluctance, but I contend that it has to do with the crucial problem of the canon.

The entire field of intellectual history has traditionaly been structured by its relation to a canon of "great" texts. Nancy Fraser, in her essay "On the Political and the Symbolic: Against the Metaphysics of Textuality," raised this important issue of the intellectual history canon and its exclusion of texts by women, but her mistaken judgment that Dominick LaCapra, who admitted in his response his relative neglect of feminism (a flaw he had earlier cited in the work of Fredric Jameson), stands for a defense of the high culture canon at all costs robbed her argument of much of its force (and her jargon-ridden, convoluted prose compounded the theft).[18] Whatever his affection for an intellectual history canon, one of LaCapra's most interesting observations about the overall field of history and its relation to theory is that

> historians at present do not have a canon (or even competing canons) of shared textual reference points, and the absence of such reference points may even further archival fetishism; a reliance on tacit, craftlike procedures; and a marked resistance to theory. One may even question whether historians as a group have anything approximating a shared "historical culture" in contradistinction to certain limited features of professionalism.[19]

That passage would cause many a historian to squirm, especially those susceptible to the arguments of E. D. Hirsch, Jr., about the peril that awaits our very republic in the absence of a shared national culture that affords the "literacy" that makes life together as citizens possible.[20]

LaCapra's argument about the absence of a historical "canon" (others might argue that the conventional chronological procession of historical "periods" constitutes a canon of sorts) depends upon the assumption of a canon of great works at the heart of English or other literary disciplines (and, for our culture, "literature," more often than not, is equated with "English"). And yet, as perusal of the publications of LaCapra, White, or virtually any other intellectual historian for that matter (as this book's selections demonstrate) reveals, European intellectual history is very much wedded to a canon. "Canon" here designates what academic professionals, critics, or other institutional authorities have judged to be great writings by exemplary figures (nearly always male, nearly always privileged) of the past. The interdisciplinary range and ambitiousness of the field can be measured in the tendency to incorporate the list of "greats" both from the history of philosophy *and* from literature, and, as time allows, from a number of other fields. The history of science, considered by some to be a branch of intellectual history, was at least until recently bound by this sense of a chronological ordering of great scientific texts.

Certainly a lot of very interesting work can still, in the wake of the recent theoretical importations, take place (and this book is, among other things, an attempt to demonstrate that there is still some life in well-worked-over canonical texts, although it could be a life the canon's defenders might prefer to have aborted), just as theorists working in literature are performing significantly new and ground-breaking readings of canonical texts, at least slightly modifying the literary canon in the process. Quite often, such work in literature has been accomplished by theorists who have reasserted the claims of history and a historical context for literature without sacrificing the sophistication of such formalist perspectives as structuralism and semiotics. "New historicism" is the catchphrase some attempt to apply to this critical movement. Whatever the value of that phrase, critics working in this direction are difficult to distinguish from the intellectual historians who have brought "literary" theory and criticism into the field of history. I, for one, am glad for the blurring of boundaries. Taken together, White and LaCapra have served to forge a sensibility that merges history and literature and that harmonizes well with that of such "historically minded" contemporary "literary" theorists as Terry Eagleton, Fredric Jameson, Frank Lentricchia, Stephen Greenblatt, Mary Poovey, Eve Kosofsky Sedgwick, and Catherine Gallagher.

Yet there is not much in the theoretical syntheses effected by the intellectual historians discussed above that would dislodge the canon itself, or that would redirect the field away from its longstanding focus on intellectual elites. Just as the sense that certain kinds of writing deserve the distinction "literature" stubbornly persists, so also does the sense that certain persons in history whose writings we can study deserve to be called "intellectuals" prove to be deeply rooted. But there is a direction from which a sustained critique of the canon, including in many cases an argument for its abolition, has been coming for years. It is a direction toward which the male scholars discussed briefly above, by far the most exemplary names in their fields, only begin to nod, for all their brilliant theoretical syntheses. I am talking about feminism, particularly as expressed through theory and criticism. Feminism, often only grudgingly tolerated in literary studies (where there might be room for a course here and there on women writers, to appeal to a limited audience drawn from the English majors or Women's Studies students), has been the great unmentionable in intellectual history. I am convinced that the repression, rather than overt suppression, occurs because to take feminist arguments seriously would be to say farewell to the canon that has been the heart, soul, and viscera of the field of intellectual history.

Far too many men in this and other humanities fields continue to behave as if such questions should be permanently relegated to "Women's Studies," as if feminist scholarship had little to do with a field like intellectual history. Jane Gallop has written with characteristic wit of the pitfalls of that phrase "Women's Studies," e.g., whether, with its problematic apostrophe, it suggests the object of study or the persons doing the work.[21] Familiar to even a casual observer of feminism is the realization that women have historically been excluded from activities of writing and publishing. Yet one of the most profound lessons of feminist theory is that the very criteria of taste and judgment that have determined the books that are taken seriously (true also of prevailing academic notions of what constitutes acceptable or appropriate scholarship and scholarly writing) have themselves been compromised by considerations of gender. Canon formation in literature or history should thus be seen as one of the processes in the ongoing construction of the "sex-gender system."[22]

It is easiest to see processes of exclusion or mere tokenism at work in conservative settings. Roland N. Stromberg's staunchly conservative *European Intellectual History since 1789,* just out (1990) in a new edition, is, almost by default, the leading textbook in the field. In it, one finds scant mention of women or of feminist thought. Two photographs of notable twentieth-century women writers appear in the book: Virginia Woolf and Simone de Beauvoir. The caption under the latter's picture tells us that she was "associated in the popular mind with Jean-Paul Sartre . . . was herself a prolific writer and, among other things, a pioneer feminist."[23] Before her own literary production comes her relationship to a famous male intellectual, and feminism is but a leftover "thing" to be found among other extraneous "things."

Unable to ignore it any longer, Stromberg devotes a last chapter ("After Everything: The Present State of Thought") to postmodern thought. Noting specifically the influence of "deconstruction," that persistent term that has finally invaded the intellectual historian's lexicon, Stromberg complains of "extreme" sorts of academic feminists, who, as he sees it, use deconstruction to impugn great thinkers for their patriarchal sins. He sounds a shrill alarm to bring contemporary scholarship back to its senses:

> The whole canon of Western thought, from Plato to Hegel and beyond, was accused of a disqualifying "patriarchal" bias. Every "great" thinker and writer must be deflated from a feminist perspective! "Everything one looks at assumes a different appearance," a feminist scholar observed.[24]

In other words, feminist issues for Stromberg get in the way of what should be an orderly process by which male scholars sort out the problems associated with deconstruction and other postmodern monstrosities. One problem in all of this is that intellectual historians to the left of Roland Stromberg have been less energetic in the production of textbooks, and this has not been the result of a repudiation of the field's raison d'être. One wonders whether the new generation of intellectual historians surveyed by John Toews, if it turned to the activity of writing textbooks, would provide much more visibility to feminism than even Stromberg does.

In my experience, no one who makes the effort to study feminist theory, criticism, and politics can remain unchanged. Once you realize the vast range of feminist cultural criticism, nothing—society, history, art, ideas— ever seems the same again. This can be more than a little threatening to the guardians of cultural tradition so many historians fancy themselves to be. Many historians and critics, I think, realize this at some level, and this could well account for their reluctance to do more than briefly acknowledge feminism at best. Of course, certain kinds of male attention to feminism may do more harm than good. I am thinking here of Elaine Showalter's often-cited essay "Critical Cross-Dressing: Male Feminists and the Woman of the Year,"[25] in which she comments on a certain type of masculinist writing about feminism that smacks of gloating mastery and seems to embody an "anything you can do I can do better" attitude, analogous to those tired clichés about the greatest chefs having been men. Feminist exasperation with this attitude may be compounded by the ambivalent sense of wanting men to study feminist criticism from the inside, while nevertheless feeling resentful that men may now be following the lead of feminist scholars who first stormed the fortress of the traditional academy and endured its fiercest resistance.

I would also like to avoid the prolonged equivocating and embarrassment that sometimes mark writing by would-be male feminists, such as the bizarre, convoluted statements that preface the essays by Stephen Heath, Paul Smith, Terry Eagleton, Cary Nelson, and others in the collection *Men in Feminism,* edited by Alice Jardine and Paul Smith.[26] They all begin in these essays to sound like Samuel Beckett's "Unnamable" ("I can't go on. I'll go on.")[27] It may be of some interest that, when first writing the sentence above that refers to *Men in Feminism,* I carelessly (?) typed Smith's name in first, ahead of Jardine. As syndicated humor columnist Dave Barry says, I am not making this up. I would say, simply, that any man whose intellectual and personal life (and feminism teaches us not to separate the two) has been transformed by feminism will want to continue to find ways to apply these perspectives to his work, and had better be ready to have his mistakes and blunders pointed out to him by feminists who may have a wide variety of reactions to his activity, and to learn from those encounters how to proceed more intelligently and helpfully.

I have been using the words "feminism" and "feminist," whereas the word "gender" appears in the book's title. Why this discrepancy? It is not, as might reasonably be feared, a shying away from a highly charged term in a "postfeminist" age. Nor is it an attempt to wrest control of discussion of sexuality away from feminism. Just as, above, I described what I have in mind when I say "theory" or "canon," here I must explain what I mean by gender. I personally believe very strongly that "feminism" speaks to masculine as well as feminine experience. Feminist efforts to reveal the complex processes of the construction of what is culturally assumed as "femininity" can work as well to demonstrate the construction of "masculinity." Moreover, at its best, in league with work by lesbian and gay male theorists, feminist theory takes us well beyond the binary logic of masculine/feminine. The word "gender," as I use it, is intended as a shorthand means of conveying that; of indicating a broader continuum of human sexualities than might otherwise be suggested. The words "feminism" and "feminist" certainly appear in the text that follows many times more than "gender." In any case, I derive my use of "gender" from feminist theorists who, by and large, use it to refer to the social and cultural categories constructed for and imposed upon the biological fact of human sex differentiation. My debt to Gayle Rubin for her concept of the "sex-gender system" will be readily apparent. And here I am beginning to sound apologetic and anxious like the critics I scoffed at earlier.

I have no startling new theory of gender to propose, so, in laying my cards on the table, I take them from the deck of Teresa de Lauretis. In her essay "The Technology of Gender," she carefully formulates a series of exemplary propositions concerning gender. She herself takes a page from Michel Foucault in her use of the word "technology," but takes his sense of social and political technologies deployed through discourse much further than he into the realm of gender. Foucault's books on sexuality were oddly and disappointingly silent on topics of women or feminism (which has not deterred recent feminist theorists from seeking some convergences with his ideas—see Chapter 3). I wish to quote the portion of de Lauretis' text in which she presents her propositions in full:

(1) Gender is (a) representation—which is not to say that it does not have concrete or real implications, both social and subjective, for the material life of individuals. On the contrary,

(2) The representation of gender *is* its construction—and in the simplest sense it can be said that all of Western Art and high culture is the engraving of the history of that construction.

(3) The construction of gender goes on as busily today as it did in earlier times, say the Victorian era. And it goes on not only where one might expect it to—in the media, the private and public schools, the courts, the family, nuclear or extended or single-parented—in short, in what Louis Althusser has called the "ideological state apparati." The construction of gender also goes on, if less obviously, in the academy, in the intellectual community, in avant-garde artistic practices and radical theories, even, and indeed especially, in feminism.

(4) Paradoxically, therefore, the construction of gender is also effected by its deconstruction; that is to say, by any discourse, feminist or otherwise, that would discard it as ideological misrepresentation. For gender, like the real, is not only the effect of representation but also its excess, what remains outside discourse as a potential trauma which can rupture or destabilize, if not contained, any representation.[28]

She touches a lot of theoretical bases there, and some may wonder at her political wisdom in touching her fourth assertion on the construction of gender with the chill of the Foucauldian proposition that oppositional discourses (e.g., feminism) are part of the very process they seek to interrogate. Nevertheless, her observations on the all-important subject of representation (there are those two quintessential postmodern words: "subject" and "representation") are extremely insightful. "The representation of gender *is* its construction"—this is well worth remembering throughout the reading of a book (this one) which seeks to examine the cultural work accomplished by texts that are notable for what they say as well as for what they fail to say about gender, and that thereby contribute to its ongoing construction.

The five texts examined critically in *Gender, Theory, and the Canon* provide both kinds of examples. They either present striking representations of femininity or are conspicuously silent on the question of gender at precisely those junctures at which a feminist reading can show that their arguments or stylistic effects depend heavily on unstated gender assumptions and prejudices (some of which, certainly, are imbedded in language). In either case, I seek, as a reader to put into practice the perspective articulated by Peggy Kamuf: a "feminist" reading is one that "points to the masks of truth with which phallocentric thought hides its fictions."[29] In every case—the *Méditations* of René Descartes, the *Economic and Philosophic Manuscripts of 1844* by Karl Marx, Gustave Flaubert's *Madame Bovary,* Sigmund Freud's *Beyond the Pleasure Principle,* and *The Gay Science* by Friedrich Nietzsche—these texts have already been "problematized," as they say, by poststructuralist/postmodernist theorists, including Jacques Derrida, Michel Foucault, Jacques Lacan, Roland Barthes, and Luce Irigaray. But, except for the last named, they have not, in my opinion, sufficiently sought to apply the kind of reading Kamuf calls for. Feminist criticism, encompassing both opposition to the very notion of a canon and formation of new ones, has done the most to ask why such texts as the five to be examined here have been accorded conspicuous cultural status, the operative "hermeneutic suspicion" being that they play important roles in the sex-gender system, reading being an important means of receiving instruction in that system.

Much of feminist criticism shares with Foucault the conviction that one returns to the central texts and attendant cultural apparatuses of the Western tradition today in order to demonstrate their effects but also, in a profound sense, to "unlearn" them in order to get on with the vital task of cultural liberation and political emancipation (I prefer this less pessimistic reading of Foucault). To an extent, that is my feeling about the texts whose guardian I have been trained to be. Trite as it may seem to invoke the phrase "love-hate relationship," I feel when writing about these chefs d'oeuvre much in sympathy with Nietzsche's comment that he writes in order "to get rid of" his thoughts. We find this passage in section 93 of *Die fröhliche Wissenschaft* (*The Gay Science*):

B: Aber warum schreibst du dann? A: Ja, mein Lieber, im Vertrauen gesagt: ich habe bisher noch kein andres Mittel gefunden, meine Gedanken *loszuwerden*.

B: But why, then, do you write?—A: Well, my friend, to be quite frank: so far, I have not discovered any other way of getting rid of my thoughts.[30]

As Bob Dylan put it much more recently: "I need a dump truck, baby, just to unload my head."[31] The logic of the canon is one of hoarded capital, with academic humanists living on the accumulated interest. I am just postmodern enough to be attracted to the political economy of Georges Bataille (who, after all, largely recycled the researches of Marcel Mauss on gift economies), who privileges expenditure (*dépense*), excess, and sacrifice.[32] My own use of these texts assumes that they are not about to be tossed out of their cultural bank vault. In fact, I assume that they will continue to yield something new to us. I also do not assume that one can simply behave as if the canon did not exist. It is just that I do not accept the dubious notion that these texts are inherently more worthy of canonical enshrinement than others that might be located.

All of which leads us to a political question about the kinds of texts being discussed in this book: If feminism, as well as a more heterogeneous canon, is so important to me, why am I spending time on five books by white men? This is no trivial objection. What I believe is this: cultural critics (a designation I have come to prefer to "intellectual historians") must indeed hasten on to reading texts by women and those previously excluded from canons that must be radically revised. But as a modest first step, especially since all kinds of preposterous claims are being made by the likes of William Bennett, Lynne Cheney, and Allan Bloom about the redeeming value of returning to the Western canon of mostly white male texts, cultural critics could demonstrate, by rereading canonical texts through the perspectives of feminist and other postmodern theories, that such a return would accomplish something other than the conservative, civilizing objectives they desire. In the process of exposing the hollowness of claims so often made on behalf of the "great books," we demonstrate as well the link between canonical status and gender politics. Similar points could be made, and are being made, with regard to race and class.

In the concluding chapter, I call for an interdisciplinary cultural criticism informed by feminism and global in its outlook. My work in this book with five texts by great white men is meant politically to be an example of "think globally, act locally." When white people followed the example of African-

Americans and joined the Civil Rights movement, they sometimes went too far in the direction of making pronouncements about what their black comrades ought to be doing, thinking, writing, etc. The response with which this was rightly met was that white people ought to "work on" other white people, i.e., to combat their racism directly. Men sympathetic with feminism have often encountered a similar response, i.e., that they can help the cause most by educating other men, struggling against others' sexism as well as their own (my assumption being that all men, since they have enjoyed patriarchal privileges, are unavoidably sexist. I make a similar analogy with regard to race. The question is always what one tries to do about this). Therefore when I read Marx or Freud as examples of dominant modern figures, one of my chief objectives is to demonstrate some of the subtler ways in which these important texts are skewed and decentered by linguistic, cultural, ideological aspects of gender, for which readers will have to force themselves to remain alert. And there will still be things that we miss. Yet one can attempt to guard against these lapses, and to teach students similar vigilance as readers. As Gayatri Spivak has said, "The politics of the classroom is not to refute and endorse," but to "produce a new politics of reading."[33]

This is certainly what I have tried to work toward in teaching and in writing. The texts by Descartes, Marx, et al. combine theoretical with pedagogical interest for me. If it had not been for the theoretical interventions of the Foucaults and the Derridas I would perhaps not have been drawn to these specific texts, but I have not let them remain ensconced in the airy realm of theory. In each case, I have read them with undergraduate students on more than one occasion, and the seminar settings in which these critical readings took place were decisive for the approach I have taken here. At a key point in my own scholarly activity leading up to *Gender, Theory, and the Canon,* a colleague in intellectual history remarked that these theoretical insights were all very interesting, but how does one convey them to students? Can it be done (assuming that it should be)? At that point midway through the 1980s I had begun to try, and felt that certainly it could and should be done. Nevertheless, his question continued to make me very conscious of the intersection of theory and teaching practice I was experiencing.

The Foucault-Derrida polemic involving the former's *Histoire de la folie à l'âge classique* directed my attention to the *Méditations* of Descartes, and then my immediate point of departure with my students, as I describe in Chapter 2, was the brief characterization given them in an introductory history textook. In the case of Marx's 1844 Manuscripts, my way into them with students was negotiated between Louis Althusser's dismissal of these "non-scientific" marxist texts and the tendency of beginning students to gravitate toward them because they present a Marx less threatening and intimidating ("humanist," as Althusser so scornfully said) than the one they expected. Of the five texts, Flaubert's *Madame Bovary* is probably tied with Marx's *Economic and Philosophic Manuscripts of 1844* as the one I have taught the greatest number of times, always caught between the Scylla of crude historical contextualizing and the Charybdis of arid formalism, while increasingly aware of the centrality of themes of style and representation (Jonathan Culler and Dominick LaCapra, among a number of others, proving helpful here) in the novel to postmodern aesthetic debates. It was Lacan—and then Derrida— who led me to Freud's *Beyond the Pleasure Principle*, although it took the feminist textual critiques of Luce Irigaray, Sarah Kofman, and Jane Gallop (among others) to make me realize one could read it against those Freudian texts more overtly concerned with feminine sexuality. Finally, when we come to Nietzsche's *The Gay Science*, it was specifically Derrida's *Éperons: Les styles de Nietzsche* that attracted my attention, and Luce Irigaray's *Amante marine de Friedrich Nietzsche* that made me realize how hesitantly Derrida had actually approached the question of gender in his reading.[34] Beyond that, Nietzsche's influence and contradictory legacy are felt everywhere in postmodern critical circles.

All five of the texts examined in the chapters that follow play conspicuous roles in the shaping of those cultural tendencies and styles known collectively by the name of "modernity," a term which encompasses both modernism and postmodernism. Descartes's writings are conventionally taken to be part of the theoretical foundation of modern science. Flaubert's *Madame Bovary* has for decades been celebrated as the "first great modern novel," perhaps even the most exemplary modern literary work, with all that "modern" implies. Now, through attention to its intricate, shifting narrative patterns, it is increasingly apt to be celebrated as "postmodern," however incongruous or anachronistic that may sound.[35]

One could not find three more significant intellectual giants of modernity than Marx, Freud, and Nietzsche. To a very great extent, what Jacques Lacan argued about Freud can be applied to all three: that their examples are so daunting and their texts so heedless of our conventional habits of reading that we have shied away from them, and have yet to absorb them. They introduced innovative uses of language in their writings, uses others who came after them have found adaptable to varying purposes. Accordingly, Michel Foucault called them initiators of "discursive practices."[36] Presumably this would place them in a kind of evolving modern theoretical avant-garde. Just as with the aesthetic avant-garde, this apparent progressivism has been a mixed blessing for women and for feminism. The result is, simultaneously, feminist critique of this "radical" triumvirate and feminist uses and adaptations of certain aspects of their theories and writings.

One feature that I hope readers will experience not as a distraction but as a knitting together of the themes of the book is the appearance in a particular chapter of references to one or more of the other major texts. Chapter 2 on Descartes, with its emphasis on representation and subjectivity, sets the stage for each of the others. Postmodernist theory generally has made the category of the subject problematic, and the feminist theories used herein often try to show that the autonomous subject of Western humanism and modern writing is highly gender-specific. The chapter on Marx at several points anticipates the material in the Freud chapter. Much of what Marx had to say about human needs and existence under capitalism had to do with drives and with the "pleasure principle," long before Freud introduced that terminology. Chapter 4 on Flaubert both echoes themes of the reading given Descartes, with its emphasis on representation, and looks ahead, through its consideration of style(s), to Chapter 6 on Nietzsche. Thus the chapters on Descartes ("Writing like a Man(?)") and Nietzsche ("Writing like a Woman(?)") frame the others, and are refracted together through the chapter on Flaubert that arrives midway in the nonlinear sequence of five major chapters. On either side, respectively between Flaubert and Descartes and Flaubert and Nietzsche, lurk the two master narratives of modern (male) theory: marxism and psychoanalysis.

The readings practiced on all five texts draw from a deliberately (unavoidably, joyously) interdisciplinary array of perspectives. This includes more emphasis on and more analogies from the realm of popular culture than the reader might expect. This in turn points to two other features of this book that might seem odd: the present-oriented nature of the readings, and aspects of the style itself that derive from that orientation as well as from the emphasis on popular culture (here taken to include music, film, and the popular press). First to address the question of "presentness": critical studies of major texts of modernity that seek to situate them historically, emphasizing the degree to which they express or intervene in the language and intellectual climate of their day, and what a reader or critic of that time would make of them, occupy an important and necessary place in humanities scholarship. What interests me much more, and therefore accounts for the emphasis on a contemporary context for these readings, is the cultural work the texts can perform in the present. I am much influenced by Foucault's concept of the "history of the present," and I bring similar sympathies to issues of reading, interpretation, and the canon. I am keenly aware of violating the historian's injunction to attempt to filter out all mediating factors that impose themselves between a text that has come down to us and the historian's hermeneutic attempt to grasp its meaning at the time of its composition. I am interested in the temporality of acts of reading that take place belatedly, and wish to maximize the mediations that attend the reading of a canonical text for a postmodern reader living between cultures, both in the territorial global sense and in terms of high culture/mass or popular culture distinctions.

In Allan Bloom's vituperative *The Closing of the American Mind,* he rails against contemporary popular culture, particularly pop music (he doesn't like to see the Sony Walkmans on students' heads as they make their way to and from class),[37] which receives much of the blame for the lack of erudition among the college student population of today. This is arrant nonsense, for anyone who takes the trouble to study the music students listen to will realize that, for many of them, it provides a way into learning about literature and the things Bloom considers culturally superior. I should know: I was one such student. I don't mind saying that I frequently developed a curiosity about poets or philosophers or artists more from references to them in popular songs than from my early educational background. This tendency crystallized for me in the mid-1960s, especially through an interest in the work of Bob Dylan and his contemporaries in what was then called the "folk song movement" on its way to becoming "folk rock." There will be those who will say that nothing in the late-1980s world of popular music approaches the sophistication of a Bob Dylan, but they are almost always the people who stopped listening to pop music after approximately the mid-1970s.

My occasional references to popular songs in response to reading Descartes, Marx, or Nietzsche are "inappropriate" by all conventional standards of scholarship. I insist on committing this transgression for several reasons. First of all, it is a deliberately personal response, and I credit feminist scholars like Jane Gallop with giving me the courage to risk being personal, and to seek to eradicate the boundary between a detached (masculine) academic style and more personal (feminine? feminist?) subjective writing. At precisely the time postmodern theory has offered so many versions of the subject's dissolution, feminists have boldly claimed a subjective status previously denied women. I remain aware of this troubling irony throughout a book in which the subject's status in these texts is interrogated, usually in order to show that it is an inherently (male) gendered subject.

As for the popular references, I must also cite the example of Raymond Williams, not in terms of writing style, for he reserved his more personal tone for his fiction, but because he revised and expanded the notion of "culture" in such a way as to dispense with the dubious distinction between culture as Matthew Arnold had defined it and mass culture. For years I have dabbled in popular culture studies as a sideline to my more "proper" interest in intellectual history, Williams' influence and the influences of those he directly inspired have helped to bring me "out of the closet," so to speak. I will no longer be inclined to hide my popular culture interest from view, as if it diminishes my worth as a student of high culture. Perhaps there is also the negative influence, appropriately, of Theodor W. Adorno, for, while I sympathize with his political views, he brought to cultural criticism a debilitating elite culture snobbism. Approaching canonical texts in the way I advocate becomes an example of what structuralists used to call *bricolage*, i.e., fashioning new devices or strategies out of diverse materials readily available, including materials generated out of past experience. Perhaps it should even be seen as willfully non-Western to honor an alternative cultural economy that cherishes the supplementary, the odd fragment that doesn't fit somehow; that, denying unity and closure, adopts a different temporal logic. Or, as the recent work of James Clifford suggests, we can, applying this logic, discover surprising affinities between so-called "third world" approaches and the modern Western avant-garde.[38] Walter Benjamin's collage-like perspectives meet "primitive" gift economies.

I also believe very strongly that both the tone the reader will discover here and the deliberately acknowledged framework of contemporary popular culture serve to dramatize what can happen when we return to the canon today: actually reading the books to which we encounter so many references, and reading them with students who, like it or not, are situated within a present-oriented media culture whose connections to the past need to be examined critically, and who nearly always derive whatever vague sense they have of a Descartes or a Freud from woefully inadequate textbook references to them. In a real sense, then, I am taking the cultural right up on their challenge to return to a core list of landmark Western texts, but I refuse their dream of a homogeneous white patriarchal culture that generated them and whose values are somehow automatically to be savored and then universalized through new encounters with them. I will have more to say about my sense of the future of "the canon" in this book's conclusion, but the chapters that follow now make clear that I embrace the pluralistic feminist/minority/popular academic culture whose emergence is the real reason for the dyspeptic rumblings of Bloom or Bennett. That their pronouncements have been produced within a right-wing Reaganite political context should be obvious. I want to show what will happen when a more genuinely democratic academic culture, one that will continue to question the canon and to forge new ones, turns its attention to the traditional canon. Against the dream of the apologists for the canon of a tranquil return to enduring truths and a shared culture of the finer things in life, I hope to demonstrate the really volatile experiences that await new generations of readers, and to show that the canon as such can never be the same again.

In an essay published in the *Chronicle of Higher Education* in 1989, W. J. T. Mitchell argues for a more global orientation for new critical theory and criticism, both in order to explore previously unexamined affinities and to defamiliarize us with Western cultural assumptions.[39] As one of the most fundamental examples of the latter, the privileged place accorded reason in Western thought looks odd from a vantage point outside the Occident. As we shall see in the chapter on Descartes that follows, it also may be "defamiliarized" through attention to (Western) feminist theory.

CHAPTER TWO

Writing Like a Man (?): Descartes, Science, and Madness

Your manias become science.
> —Barbara Kruger, *We Won't Play Nature to Your Culture* (1981)

Thinking is a form of human activity which cannot be treated in isolation from other forms of human activity including the forms of human activity which in turn shape the humans who think.
> —Jane Flax, "Political Philosophy and the Patriarchal Unconscious: A Psychoanalytic Perspective on Epistemology and Metaphysics"

Nearly the entire history of writing is confounded with the history of reason, of which it is at once the effect, the support, and one of its privileged alibis. It has been one with the phallocentric tradition. It is indeed that same self-admiring, self-stimulating, self-congratulatory phallocentrism.
> —Hélène Cixous, "The Laugh of the Medusa" (1976)

Unquestioning. I, say I. Unbelieving.
> —Samuel Beckett, *The Unnamable* (1965)

I.   CANON LAWS/LIES

Since this chapter focuses especially on the first of Descartes's *Méditations,* let us begin as he does:

> Il y a déjà quelque temps que je me suis aperçu que, dès mes premières années, j'avais reçu quantité de fausses opinions pour véritables, et que ce que j'ai depuis fondé sur ces principes si mal assurés, ne pouvait être que fort douteux et incertain.

> There is no novelty to me in the reflection that, from my earliest years, I have
> accepted many false opinions as true, and that what I have concluded from such
> badly assured premises could not but be highly doubtful and uncertain.[1]

In addition to its being the starting point for Cartesian systematic doubt,
couldn't this be a realization nearly any educated person would have when
looking back over his or her life? At least it would be if we educated people
to subject their received opinions to rigorous critical examination. Sadly
enough, the educational system contents itself with the primary activity of
relaying information, and it dispenses much misinformation along the way.
One extensively used medium that dispenses concentrated mixtures of misinformation and information is that darling of commercial publishers, the
textbook. Particularly at large state universities like the one at which I teach,
standard textbooks form the bulk of required reading. Students in fact assume that professors will use them. The sight of crowds of students moving
about the campus, each one trudging under the weight of a nylon backpack
crammed with these slabs of concentrated disciplinary lore, is a depressing
one indeed, and suggests that there are reasons beyond cosmetic ones for the
wild popularity among students of "pumping iron."

My denigration of textbooks at the outset of a critical reading of the
Méditations of Descartes can be explained as follows: Like many in my field,
I cringe at the (understandable, if not forgivable) oversimplified, flattened-
out brief notices accorded intellectual or artistic works in survey histories.
Typically, the student is given a few lines about a significant writer whose
ideas, books, etc., are noted and explained within some historically appropriate framework (e.g., "The Age of Reason" or "The Age of Uncertainty"). If,
like Marx or Darwin, the writer in question is a "controversial" figure, the
text is usually carefully worded so as to create the impression that these ideas
have had an important impact on the world but the impact has lessened with
the passage of time. Many people subscribe to these intellectual traditions,
many others emphatically reject them; but in any case, you can make up your
own mind (even if you have a "biased" professor), and by no means do you
need to spend much of your valuable time on these problems. If, like New-
ton or Descartes, the figure in question is not the subject of any readily
apparent ongoing controversy, the textbook will present the ideas or works
as neatly woven into the fabric of the Western tradition, i.e., beyond question. This approach in particular puts the reader's critical guard at rest. In
either case, the implied message is: we have other problems to think about

today, so you will soon (at least by semester's end) be free to forget about this material.

Descartes's *Méditations* (1641) and *Discours de la méthode* (1637) are examples of the latter type, i.e., "beyond controversy," as textbooks present them. Several years ago, as I was simultaneously engaged in absorbing poststructuralist theory *and* in teaching primarily introductory history courses, the by now much discussed conflict of interpretations between Michel Foucault and Jacques Derrida over Descartes's *Première Méditation* held a particular fascination for me. I continue to see in this controversy (which I will discuss at some length below) reminders of the at-times contradictory challenge to historians to situate texts within the "archive" of which Foucault wrote in his later work while at the same time remaining alive to the surprises that a deconstructive reading can always turn up.

If I had not been contemplating this interpretive conundrum, the following sentence about the writings of René Descartes and Francis Bacon from the textbook chapter to which I had referred my students might not have flashed alarmingly across my consciousness:

> Thus a revolution in scientific thinking had been effected, and the foundation of modern science and modern philosophy had been firmly laid.[2]

This was not the first time I had shaken my head in dismay over what the textbook claimed about topics that interested me, and I had been reading Derrida enough to be convinced that texts by themselves do anything but lay firm foundations. The institutional and cultural uses of texts (and here is where Foucault will always be more helpful than Derrida) create the (often illusory) sense of foundations. I decided that the next time I was scheduled to teach the "modern" half of the introductory "World Civilization" course, I would order copies of Descartes's *Méditations on First Philosophy* and put this claim to the test. What I and the students discovered was that if this text was part of that firm foundation of modern science and philosophy upon which their sense of reality would be founded, then they were in real trouble. The students proved that one does not need to be a Jacques Derrida to trace the textual unravelings of Descartes's celebrated demonstration of the steps by which one obtains certain knowledge. They also experienced firsthand what Descartes complained about in his writings: that one absorbs many false opinions even (especially) through one's education, in this case from a history textbook. I also credit this teaching experiment with heightening my awareness of the "false opinions" associated with an educational system that assumes the Western canon as its frame of reference. Increasingly, as this book seeks to demonstrate, I have come to feel that both advocates and opponents of the canon are likely to be mistaken about what is to be found therein.

The authors of the textbook I have been abusing were certainly right about the importance of these writings in the formation of the modern scientific outlook, whatever we may be able to discover about the strangely contradictory character of a text we examine closely. The *Méditations* of Descartes is surely one of the landmark texts of the Western tradition. One of the fundamental assumptions at work throughout this book is that the text's reputation and claims upon our attention cannot be separated from powerful and persuasive (because usually undetected) processes of cultural hegemony that include the exercise of patriarchal bias. The institutional role of college course textbooks is part of this process, bitterly characterized by Michel Foucault, whereby the university provides "the institutional apparatus through which society ensures its uneventful reproduction, at the least cost to itself."[3]

To the extent that canons help to keep this reproduction "uneventful," universities would appear to have a stake in them. Whether students are actually expected to read the canonical works is a separate matter. I am convinced that assent and acquiescence are best guaranteed through the offhand assertion of claims about these texts, claims like "lays a firm foundation." The *Méditations* of Descartes is presumed to be part of this solid foundation of modern learning, and, as a generation of feminist scholars have demonstrated convincingly, the prestige enjoyed by such a "landmark" text can always be found to be closely related to the consequences it has for the patriarchal exclusion or dismissal of women's cultural contributions. Universities have a very long way to go yet in overcoming the results of their long and deep complicity in this cultural process.

Recent feminist critiques of Descartes, several of which figure decisively in my approach to the text, make the assumption that the scientific and cultural prominence accorded Descartes has much to do with his firm establishment of masculinist ways of knowing, especially the cogito—a masculinist epistemological strategy par excellence. I will have more to say about them below, but briefly there are five writers I want to acknowledge: Luce Irigaray does not devote any one of her texts to an interrogation of Descartes, but he lurks here and there as part of the Platonic tradition she takes on, most notably in *Speculum de l'autre femme*. Evelyn Fox Keller consistently exposes the patriarchal foundations undergirding modern science. In

"The Mind's Eye," an essay she wrote with Christine R. Grontkowski, she demonstrates the degree to which rational thought depends on the Cartesian motif of the "mind's eye," exact knowledge thus being associated with an abstracted vision whose distancing from and objectification of what is to be "known" are central to processes of representation that work to the detriment of women. Christine Buci-Glucksmann explores in two book-length studies—*La raison baroque: De Baudelaire à Benjamin* (1984) and *La folie de voir: De l'esthétique baroque* (1986)—a baroque model of "mad" or distorted (as in trompe l'oeil) vision actively repressed by such writers as Descartes. Susan R. Bordo, in *The Flight to Objectivity: Essays on Cartesianism and Culture* (1986), interprets the Cartesian enterprise as a "masculinization of thought" that was part of a general premodern "flight from the feminine." Finally, Dalia Judovitz warns, in *Subjectivty and Representation in Descartes: The Origins of Modernity* (1988), of the mistake common to postmodern writers and critics of equating Descartes's particular kind of subjectivity, as related to representation, with what we have come to expose as "the subject" per se of all humanist thought. She further explores the peculiar ways in which this Cartesian subject inhabits far more disciplines than those found within science.[4]

My intention is to bring together feminist critiques of the patriarchal work being accomplished in this text with the (male) poststructuralist readings that show it to be a troubled text. For too long male theorists influenced by Foucault or Derrida have, like those writers, at best merely paid homage (*homme* age) to feminist theory without developing explicitly feminist positions of their own. As I argued in the introductory chapter of this book, intellectual history continues to show fascination for the currents of theory set in motion by Foucault and Derrida without however demonstrating anywhere near the same degree of attention to feminist theory. In literary fields, feminist uses of male poststructuralist procedures have been far more frequent than the converse.

"Rethinking intellectual history," to borrow Dominick LaCapra's phrase,[5] and other humanities disciplines along feminist lines means an end to business as usual. This includes cherished, time-honored modes of presenting our research. Proceeding from the fundamental insight into the political character of personal experience, feminist scholars have adopted certain gestures and approaches to writing that expose the conventional and, in fact, patriarchal character of standard scholarly peformance. One such gesture is the assertion of the first person, indeed the "foregrounding" of the writer's personal circumstances and situation as the text is being written.

This practice can be unsettling for anyone unaccustomed to the political and theoretical justifications for it. I find it particularly striking and ironic that Descartes's *Méditations,* taken for centuries to be one of the foundations for styles or methods of argument and demonstration that depend upon a downplaying or muting of the personal, embodied source of the ideas being expressed, should itself provide such a vivid dramatization of the personal situation of its author.

This is why I title this chapter "Writing like a Man (?)" The Cartesian cogito may have worked culturally to sanction masculinist cultural practices, but as we will see, at least the first two meditations of Descartes are written in a manner sometimes theorized (even if only strategically and not literally) by contemporary textual criticism as "feminine," if not exactly feminist. Whether feminism would want to embrace the implication that "feminist" style is what undoes rationalism in spite of itself is another highly vexed question. Evelyn Fox Keller, however much she may wish to contemplate alternative "feminist" models of scientific procedure, would certainly not want to accept a crude opposition between (masculine, rational) science and (feminine, irrational) rejection of science. She rightly prefers the establish-ment of a "gender-free" scientific outlook, one that would by definition allow for a variety of approaches.[6] In claiming to discover something tradi-tionally coded as "feminine" in Descartes's text I do not wish to ally myself with the kind of "critical cross-dressing" that finds that feminist thought or feminist style was always already present in male texts. Showalter invokes Dustin Hoffman's award-winning performance in the film *Tootsie* in order to express her suspicion of male critics who appear to use feminist methods in order to go feminists one better; showing them up at their own game.[7] What, in gender terms, interests me here instead is understanding Des-cartes's style as an example of something repressed within seemingly mas-culinist language, something that cultural oppositions between a mono-lithic sense of the "masculine" or the "feminine" obscure from our view. The feminist philosopher Elizabeth Minnich has referred to the way the historic use of the generic *man* as well as feminist opposition to it makes it exceed-ingly difficult to bear in mind the tremendous variety, range, "plurality and difference" locked within the gender out of which patriarchal language at-tempts to universalize man/*l'homme/der Mensch.*[8] Of the several texts with which this book is concerned, Descartes's *Méditations* is the first stylistically and otherwise to contradict whatever assumptions interpretive conventions have generated about what it might have to say about gender. This "herme-neutics of suspicion" includes, even more paradoxically, the expectation that the text will speak most eloquently about gender precisely when it appears to have nothing at all to do with such concerns.

How curious that a text with such a personal tone (perhaps deceptively so, as Judovitz argues) has been pressed into service in order to enshrine would-be "scientific," deliberately impersonal modes of academic discourse. My own first public attempt to acknowledge the transgressively personal style I find so impressive in many feminist writers was rather feeble, but I wish to describe what prompted it, since it came when I presented an earlier version of this chapter at a conference in 1987. The title of my paper was "Gender, Representation, and Textual Politics: Descartes, the Canon, and Cultural Criticism." When I received my copy of the conference program, I was annoyed to see that someone had substituted "canon law" for "the canon." This seemed like a cruel twist of fate, but I came gradually to regard it as fortuitous. Not long after protesting to the conference organizers that "canon law" created a very misleading impression of what my paper would be about, I began to realize that, in terms of rereading the modern European intellectual history canon, I was in fact raising questions about a kind of "canon law," if we understand by "law" what Hélène Cixous characterizes as the phallocentric economy[9] that regulates uses and interpretations of texts in such a way as to prevent women from reading or writing in ways that do not bring about violent forms of self-denial, most notably the denial of the body and of women's desire(s). Thus it was that I came to see the mistake as an opportunity rather than a setback. By referring in my presentation to the misunderstanding that had taken place, I was able as well to provide an illustration of the necessity of self-reference. I hope that, increasingly, scholars will dispense with the pose of impersonality. The idea here is not to steal an enabling gesture away from feminism. If feminist practice, in keeping with the assertion that "the personal is the political," produced this alternative scholarly mode of presentation, our response to this should be not to view it as essentially feminine/ist, but to recognize it as an example of the liberating promise feminism holds for all aspects of our institutional life.

Perhaps the canon does have the force of law (or its proponents would like it to). In any case, I am questioning the laws or conventions that govern our interpretations of Descartes, that guide our steps through the procession of what Edward Said has called "a massive body of self-congratulating ideas"[10] contained in the formative texts of the Western tradition. That deliciously resentful phrase in its hyperbole may have the unfortunate result (unintended by Said) of suggesting a monolithic logic and coherence inhabiting the canon, but he registers it with a painful sense of ways in which

Western culture has been used as a club with which to subdue "Other" cultures and their literatures. Sharing Said's conviction that what should most concern us are the uses to which key Western texts have been put, I hope that my reading of Descartes is deliberately and effectively transgressive, exposing the ways in which "canon law" operates in our cultural placement of Descartes, and then showing that, as with so many other canonical texts, we find, when we return to it, a great deal more confusion and instability than those who urge us back to the canon can possibly have anticipated.

II. DESCARTES, FOUCAULT, DERRIDA

As with many readers, my interest in Descartes's *Méditations,* the first in particular, was sparked primarily by the reading given it in Foucault's *Histoire de la folie à l'âge classique* and by Jacques Derrida's essay "Cogito et histoire de la folie,"[11] an insightful but, as usual, politically more limiting critique of Foucault's use of that text, answered in turn by Foucault in an appendix to the revised 1972 edition of *Histoire de la folie.*[12] As thoughtful essays by Said and others[13] have shown, the significance of their quarrel was in the way it served to demonstrate what was at stake in the distinctive reading strategies associated with Foucault and Derrida.

In his still-influential book on the birth of the asylum, Foucault found it convenient to employ Descartes's text as a representative item within the cultural archive of a classic age no longer, by the time (1641) of the publication of the *Méditations,* able to endure the visible presence of the "insane." For Foucault, *l'âge classique* was defined by the dual maneuver of upholding reason through denial of its opposite, unreason. This negation of reason thus had to be condemned to silence by inaugurating the asylum. As a major intellectual heavyweight who could be cited for helping to carry out this process of exclusion, Foucault selected Descartes, handling his text, characteristically, as one very conspicuous item embedded within a specific cultural "archive" containing all the discourses that operated to produce knowledge in the guise of reason while reducing madness to silence and exile. The majority of Foucault's brief references to Descartes cannot even be found in the abridged edition of *Histoire de la folie* (1963). Perhaps this is why Derrida, known for using a writer's offhand comment or odd textual lapse as the wrench with which to dismantle the textual machine, admits that his isolation of this moment in Foucault's book may indeed seem trivial ("Mon point de départ peut paraître mince et artificiel . . .").[14] Foucault simply touches upon Descartes's First Meditation in order to portray this celebrated philospher who, in the midst of his reverie, approaches the abyss of madness and gazes into its depths only to recoil in horror not unlike that of the female genitals exhibited in differing ways by both Freud (Chapter 5) and Nietzsche (Chapter 6).

Derrida finds this to be an intolerably one-dimensional reading of Descartes, and devotes his own essay to examining the uncertainties and displacements of what he takes to be a highly ambivalent or undecidable treatment of madness. To paraphrase Derrida's argument, it may well have been Descartes's intention to treat the subject of madness in the way Foucault has described, but the text itself—all we as readers of Descartes have—accomplishes a degree of affirmation of madness through the volatile textual alchemy uncovered by a deconstructive reading (what we will also see in Chapter 6, as Nietzsche's text can be shown to affirm what it appears on the surface to condemn). As usual, Derrida is better at demonstrating the multiple textual effects that undo meaning than he is at showing, as Frank Lentricchia claims for the critical method of Kenneth Burke,[15] how meaning is generated within a heterological field of discourse.

Despite Derrida's ability, demonstrated in his more recent work, to refer provocatively to possibilities of feminist interpretation and *écriture*,[16] his reading of Descartes (which took place in 1963), viewed retrospectively through the preoccupations of recent feminist criticism, is seriously lacking in terms of the gender questions he might have raised—the questions those concerned with the critique of the subject and representation find so compelling. For example, why not address the cultural associations, encouraged by the development of modern medicine, among madness, women, and hysteria? Why not, in the same way that Derrida attempts a deconstruction of the binary opposition between reason and madness in Descartes's text, dissolve the boundary separating their supposed sets of implications for masculine and feminine consciousness? In the case of Foucault, why can the discursive privilege accorded reason versus the exile of madness not be reread as an allegory of sexual politics?

The arguments, sketched so briefly above, of Foucault and Derrida have been superseded by recent feminist and gender theory, but this is not to say that these discursive practices do not lend themselves to feminist usages. The same might be said of marxist and psychoanalytic theories. In her movingly poetic essay "Sorties," Cixous writes eloquently of the proliferation of binary oppositions, including the famous Cartesian duality, that have worked throughout Western cultural history to establish what anthropologists call

sexual asymmetry.[17] Irigaray, radically questioning the primacy of the autonomous (masculine) subject and employing the female body with its diverse
"geography of pleasure"[18] as metaphor, strikes at unitary, phallic modes of
knowing as domination (or, as Judovitz argues, at a subjective politics of
representation inaugurated in modern epistemology by Descartes)[19] accompanied by the denial of the polymorphous character of female desire and (as
with Cixous) the multiplicity of feminine modes of knowledge. Keller, as a
leading example of an American feminist who draws upon recent French
feminist thought as well as object-relations theory to formulate a powerful
critique of "normal science" as "male"—a conclusion she qualifies somewhat—historicizes the constructed, masculinist gesture of radical division;
of knowing as distancing, alienation, and objectification (reminiscent of the
language of Marx's *1844 Manuscripts*—see Chapter 3).[20]

III.   I THINK I'M ALONE NOW

In order to bring out additional features of these critiques, I now return
after a long detour to the *Méditations* of Descartes. Readers of Descartes will
recall that the philosopher describes the scene of his first meditation in inti-
mate detail: he is seated in his comfortable dressing gown by a cozy fire,
contemplating the paper he holds in his hands, perhaps the very paper upon
which he is engaged in inscribing his thoughts. Judovitz, among other recent interpreters, warns against confusing this narratological *penseur* with
the biographical Descartes,[21] but nevertheless the lure of the passage is such
as to make the reader long to pull a chair up alongside his warm hearth:

> Mais, encore que les sens nous trompent quelquefois, touchant les choses peu
> sensibles et fort éloignées, il s'en rencontre peut-être beaucoup d'autres, des-
> quelles on ne peut pas raisonnablement douter, quoique nous les connaissions par
> leur moyen: par exemple, que je sois ici, assis auprès du feu, vêtu d'une robe de
> chambre, ayant ce papier entre les mains, et autre choses de cette nature. (MF 268)

> But it is possible that, even though the senses occasionally deceive us about
> things which are barely perceptible and very far away, there are many other things
> which we cannot reasonably doubt, even though we know them through the
> senses—as, for example, that I am here, seated by the fire, wearing a (winter)
> dressing gown, holding this paper in my hands, and other things of this nature.
> (ME 18)

This is actually quite a lot of physical detail for the philosopher who, like Beckett's jar-trapped character "the unnamable" for whom he provided some inspiration, seems to be the epitome of the detached, disembodied consciousness. What attracted Foucault to the passage just described was the memorable moment where Descartes entertains the thought that he, like the types of seriously deluded persons he enumerates, may be hallucinating the entire scene, and then moves abruptly and firmly to disavow such a lapse of sanity:[22]

> Et comment est-ce que je pourrais nier que ces mains et ce corps-ci soient à moi? si ce n'est peut-être que je me compare à ces incensés, de qui le cerveau est tellement troublé et offusqué par les noires vapeurs de la bile, qu'ils assurent constamment qu'ils sont des rois, lorsqu'ils sont très pauvres; qu'ils sont vêtus d'or et de pourpre, lorsqu'ils sont tout nus; ou s'imaginent être des cruches, ou avoir un corps de verre. Mais quoi? ce sont des fous, et je ne serais pas moins extravagant, si je me réglais sur leurs exemples. (MF 268)

> And how could I deny that these hands and body are mine, unless I am to compare myself with certain lunatics whose brain is so troubled and befogged by the black vapors of the bile that they continually affirm that they are kings while they are paupers, that they are clothed in gold and purple while they are naked; or imagine that their head is made of clay, or that they are gourds, or that their body is made of glass? [But this is ridiculous;] such men [sic] are fools, and I would be no less insane than they if I followed their example. (ME 18)

For a reading alive to the nuances of gender, one of the strongest impressions recorded is of the embodied character of thought (more commonly associated with women), rather than the apparent legacy of Cartesian dualism. Considering Foucault's later preoccupation with bodies and their investment by relations of power-knowledge, and given the insistence of Cixous, Irigaray, and other feminist theorists on "writing the body,"[23] we can immediately see missed points of contact between feminist theory and the work of Foucault, despite the latter's notorious lack of concern with feminism and feminine sexuality.[24] There is also the volatile question of madness: for example, as feminist critiques of psychoanalysis have suggested (see Chapter 4), Western thought regularly seems to reproduce a cultural equation associating women with madness. Charcot's mise-en-scène with female hysterics at the Salpêtrière Hospital has been much on the minds of feminists who challenge this equation. Then, of course, there is a variety of feminist argument that asserts "hysteria" or madness as a value, as when Hélène

Cixous invokes Freud's unfortunate "Dora" as a rebel figure. Her co-author, Catherine Clément, challenges that idea, rejecting as hopelessly defeatist a feminist refusal of rational consciousness, and her debate with Cixous on this point provides one of the most compelling sections of *La jeune née* (*The Newly Born Woman*).[25] In spite of such pitfalls, a serious feminist reading of Descartes would want to ask whether the philsopher recoils from the negation of reason as he would from his "feminine" other; as, much later, both Nietzsche and Freud can be seen to do in the texts with which Chapters 5 and 6 are concerned.

Despite the very good reasons we would have not to reproduce the cultural binary opposition between (male) reason and (female) unreason, the formulation of a feminist critique that strategically exploits that motif opens up a larger field of textual debate than the one mapped out through the exchange between Foucault and Derrida. Foucault's reading of Descartes views madness as that which represents for Descartes the impossibility of thought, grouping it along with dreams and waking hallucinations as one of the errors of consciousness.[26] Responding years later to Derrida's essay pointing out all that Foucault's reading neglected, Foucault sharply asserted that one would have to be "deaf"[27] to miss the excluding tone of Descartes's prose in this passage (*Mais quoi? ce sont des fous* . . .). While for Derrideans this is a telltale lapse that places Foucault squarely on the side of logocentrism and univocal meanings in written language, Foucault was interested not in any ability Descartes may have possessed to fix irrevocably the meaning of his text, but in the strategic uses to which the text has been put. Of course this is a vivid example of the more obvious usefulness, for historical study, of Foucault over Derrida. The productive power relations formed of the network of philosophy, politics, and psychiatry are far more the stuff of history than the textual vicissitudes unraveled (too often, with the "Derrideans," merely for the sake of unraveling) through a Derridean reading. By asking in "What Is an Author?" who controls the circulation and proliferation of texts as discourse,[28] rather than who Descartes, e.g., was and whether his text is internally consistent with itself, Foucault also potentially allies his critical approach with feminist ones having to do with the cultural consequences of the text's prestige and influence for women and alternative "feminine" modes of consciousness.

Derrida points to the strangeness of Foucault's carrying out in his *Histoire de la folie* a kind of "archaeology of silence,"[29] as he puts it, since madness is precisely what cannot "speak itself."[30] Roland Barthes, among the first to comment thoughtfully on Foucault's work, had pointed out that

Foucault never defines "madness," except indirectly as that which is condemned to silence by the language of reason.[31] Derrida pointedly charges Foucault with undermining his analysis of reason's repression of madness by his use of the very language of reason itself.[32] Based on his own very different reading of Descartes's text, Derrida does not believe that the Cartesian cogito excludes madness, even if its existence is not explicitly affirmed. Derrida concludes that Foucault ignored this possibility because it did not suit his interpretive purposes, which were to establish the textual meaning firmly in order to conform to the overall scheme of his book.[33] Derrida, of course, is always captivated by the odd or extraneous bit that conventional interpretive wisdom would overlook, and, feisty kitten that he is, he will pull at it until the textual fabric unravels.

Derrida does not counter with a more radical reversal of Foucault's reading, which would be to argue that Descartes's text, in spite of itself, promotes and affirms madness. Instead, Derrida sees Descartes occupying a middle ground, neither affirming nor denying madness. Derrida prefers to focus on passages that come either just before or just after those central to Foucault's argument in order to show the uncertain manner in which Descartes's demonstration of the steps whereby one attains certain knowledge proceeds. Derrida situates madness alongside (*à côté*) dreams and other *erreurs sensibles*,[34] driving home the point that Descartes does not deny the existence of madness any more than he can his dreams. Characteristically, Derrida bears down upon the text at precisely those junctures marked by shifting, sliding, tentative language. However, Derrida does *not* really "deconstruct" the text in the larger sense that he himself calls for in other essays of exposing its fundamental binary oppositions, as well as its figural displacements.

Feminist scholars, from literature to anthropology to philosophy of science, have been quite energetic in interrogating such gender-suspect binary oppositions as mind versus body. Above, we saw that Descartes's passage describing his position sitting by the fire in his comfortable *robe de chambre* certainly retained a vivid sense of the embodied thinker *chez lui*. Taking himself physically as well as mentally apart from other human beings, Descartes significantly revises the Tommy James and the Shondells 1966 hit song "I Think We're Alone Now" so that the lyrics become:

I think I'm alone now,
There doesn't seem to be anyone around.

I think I'm alone now,
the thinking in my head is the only sound.

As Jean-Joseph Goux has shown, the kinds of epistemological demonstra-
tions set forth in this and other writings of Descartes have everything to do
with this unique situation of silence and isolation, one that certainly makes it
easier to assert the prerogatives of the egocentric individual[35]—which brings
us to the timely question of the "subject," so problematic for feminist and
other contemporary theoretical discourses. The doubt dramatized in the
First Meditation concerning the philosopher's waking presence in his study
is thus a momentary threat not only to the cogito but to the physical body as
well.

There is also uncertainty, until recently little discussed in the literature
on Descartes, regarding language. Dalia Judovitz, drawing on Émile Ben-
veniste's description of pronouns as linguistic "shifters," rightfully reminds
us that the first-person pronoun of the *Méditations* is but the *je* (the "I") of
language rather than the (once-) living man René Descartes.[36] Does this *je*
refer only to the supposedly disembodied solitary consciousness, as is
widely assumed, or does it refer to the philosopher's bodily presence? Is
this "I" merely the "mind's eye"? A feminist reading that would "deconstruct" the mind-body opposition basic to patriarchal culture can easily
show how Descartes's text deconstructs itself on this score. Let us remember, however, that an all-out program of feminist/deconstructionist rereadings of canonical texts can never undo the historical fact of the use of
Platonic or Cartesian thought to repress or denigrate the "feminine." This
is why the feminist project of "writing the body," the specific investigations of such topics as rape by feminist scholars like the ones represented in
Foucault and Feminism (1988), and the new "history of the body" being
carried out by scholars whose work shows up in the pages of *Representations* or *Zone* are all of greater consequence than specifically Derridean textual forays.

The First Meditation having established that the solitary thinker need not
doubt the reality of his presence, the second goes on to assert the more
reliable awarenesses of the mind's, rather than the body's, existence—*que
[l'esprit humain] est plus aisé à connaître que le corps* (MF 274). Or does it?
Keep in mind, while examining the following passage, the linguistic view
that "shifters" like *I* can contain an element of ambiguity, in this case continually redirecting the reader's attention to (what?): the textual *I* of narrative;

the still, small "voice" of the conscious mind; the seated, contemplative, actual bodily philosopher?

Puis-je m'assurer d'avoir la moindre de toutes les choses que j'ai attribuées ci-dessus à la nature corporelle? Je m'arrête à y penser avec attention, je passe et repasse toutes ces choses en mon esprit, et je n'en rencontre aucune que je puisse dire être en moi. Il n'est pas besoin que je m'arrête à les dénombrer. Passons donc aux attributs de l'âme, et voyons s'il y en a quelques-uns qui soient à moi. Les premiers sont de me nourrir et de marcher; mais s'il est vrai que je n'aie point de corps, il est vrai aussi que je ne puis marcher ni me nourrir. Un autre est de sentir; *mais on ne peut aussi sentir sans le corps* [emphasis mine]: outre que j'ai pensé sentir autrefois plusieurs choses pendant le sommeil, que j'ai reconnu à mon réveil n'avoir point en effet senties. Un autre est de penser; et je trouve ici que la pensée est un attribut qui m'appartient: elle seule ne peut être détachée de moi. *Je suis, j'existe:* [Descartes's emphasis] cela est certain; mais combien de temps? À savoir, autant de temps que je pense; car peut-être se pourrait-il faire, si je cessais de penser, que je cesserais en même temps d'être ou d'exister. (MF 276–77)

Can I be sure that I possess the smallest fraction of all those characteristics which I have just now said belonged to the nature of the body? I pause to consider this attentively. I pass and repass in review in my mind each one of all these things—it is not necessary to pause to take the time to list all of them—and I do not find any one of them which I can pronounce to be part of me. Is it characteristic of me to consume nourishment and to walk? But if it is true that I do not have a body, these also are nothing but figments of the imagination. To perceive? *But once more, I cannot perceive without the body* [my emphasis], except in the sense that I have thought I perceived various things during sleep, which I recognized upon waking not to have really been perceived. To think? Here I find the answer. Thought is an attribute that belongs to me; it alone is inseparable from my nature.

I am, I exist—that is certain; but for how long do I exist? For as long as I think; for it might perhaps happen, if I totally ceased thinking, that I would at the same time completely cease to be. (ME 25–26)

Assuming the author's intention to establish the priority of abstracted consciousness over corporeal body, how has this passage advanced his argument? Even Beckett's "unnamable" is some kind of withered immobilized body wedged in a jar, i.e., still an embodied consciousness. Descartes's *je* does not appear ready to give up eating in order to test his mind's ability to continue to exist. "He" admits that he needs his body in order to think. What about this relief upon awaking to discover that what was dreamed was not really perceived? Is it relief because the events never happened, or because they were not perceived? Or would such a question return us to pre-Socratic speculations about such situations as trees falling in unpopulated forests? Does the sleeper emerging into wakefulness experience gratitude for rediscovering the regulatory activity of the conscious mind or for finding himself once again in a living, rested body?

The first two meditations are marked vividly by these suspenseful dramas of anxiety over loss of identity and actual existence followed by moments of reassurance—divinely guaranteed by the end of the Third Meditation, *De Dieu; qu'il existe* ("Of God: That He Exists"). If the victory in each case is, respectively, that [Descartes] is not mad and that he is not merely a body, then, giving this passage a critical feminist reading, we could say that Descartes thanks his lucky stars that he is not a (crazy) woman relegated to mere bodily reproductive existence. This is a theme we shall meet with again, as for example in Marx's wish to see workers lifted above the corporeal sphere of existence (Chapter 3).

We could also say that, like Freud's grandson in *Beyond the Pleasure Principle,* Descartes in the *Méditations* and in *Discours de la méthode* (1637) was fond of a repetitive game: pretending to disappear or to be insane only to reassure himself that everything was in fact in good order. Susan Bordo contributed this insightful analogy by way of arguing that, just as Freud's grandson Ernst gained unconscious mastery over his painful separation from his mother in the *fort!/da!* game (see Chapter 5), Descartes, in this recurring drama of systematic doubt, acted out a fantasy of would-be mastery by (masculine) culture over (feminine) nature, "transforming anxiety into confidence,"[37] a powerful fantasy that was to become the founding gesture of modernity.[38] Perhaps similarly, Nietzsche and his friend Paul Rée posed for their famous "comic" photograph pulling a cart driven by Lou Andréas-Salomé (see Chapter 6) in order to play at a game whose outcome was the reestablishment of masculine control.

IV. CLEAR AND DISTINCT

Descartes's *Méditations* are divided into six parts, but in a very real sense they break into two unequal sections, with the first two meditations belonging to a first part, and the last four grouped together. This division can be justified since the tone of fitful uncertainty is absent after the first two meditations. Once the priority of the rational, conscious mind has been established by the end of the Second Meditation, Descartes goes on to erect upon this foundation: the existence of God (Third Meditation), the truth of the ideas that link the human mind with the divine (fourth), the essence of material things, again linked to God's existence (fifth), and (sixth) the existence of all material things, despite the necessity of a distinction between mind and body. Quite a skyscraper! Rather than call attention to long passages from each of the remaining meditations, I prefer to underscore a kind of refrain, indeed almost an incantation, with which Descartes wards off the kinds of (temporarily) paralyzing doubts he entertained during the first two meditations. I do this because of its significance for contemporary feminist discussion of representation and the primacy of (male, voyeuristic) vision in the entire postmodern problematic of representation.

The refrain, so to speak, contains two words: "clear" and "distinct," or, sometimes, "clearly" and "distinctly." What Descartes of course does in all his writings is to express much of what he wants to say about the process of thinking, especially the process of arriving at truth, by using visual metaphors. Keller and Grontkowski have written about this "mind's eye" in *La dioptrique* and other Cartesian texts, and Martin Jay has been engaged in a comprehensive study of the twentieth-century critique of vision in French thought, of which the work of Georges Bataille offers several extreme examples.[39] From feminist film theory to Luce Irigaray's poetics of a female body defined by touch, flow, and the eradication of boundaries, no gender critique can afford to ignore the language of a philosophical founder of modernity who uses visual metaphors for correct thinking. As Alice Jardine argues persuasively, representation is the central problematic for postmodernism (which, *à la mode française,* she prefers to call modernity), yet she also writes it in a way that indicates its complex genealogy as a problematic for Western culture. The following passage captures the rich and highly nuanced treatment Jardine is able to bring to the topic. Consider this in light of Descartes's epistemological agenda, with his game of absence (*fort!*) and presence (*da!*):

> Representation is the condition that confirms the possibility of an imitation (mimesis) based on the dichotomy of presence and absence and, more generally, on the dichotomies of dialectical thinking (negativity). Representation, mimesis, and the dialectic are inseparable; they designate together a way of thinking as old as the West, a way of thinking which French thought, through German philosophy, has been attempting to rethink since the turn of the century.[40]

Now for the Cartesian incantation on clear and distinct ideas, which we find throughout the last four meditations, as the tone becomes increasingly more confident along the royal road (for Goux, resisting conventional wisdom, finds the Cartesian cogito far more conducive to absolute monarchy than to the bourgeois democracy for which it has historically been viewed as a support)[41] to intellectual certainty. At the outset of the Third Meditation, screwing up his courage for his demonstration of the proof of God's existence, Descartes writes:

> Et partant il me semble que déjà je puis établir pour règle générale, que toutes les choses que nous concevons fort clairement et fort distinctement, sont toutes vraies. (MF 284)

> And therefore it seems to me that I can already establish as a general principle that everything which we conceive very clearly and very distinctly is wholly true. (ME 34)

The nightmarish "vapors of black bile" encountered in the First Meditation have been dispelled, and we are now in a world of no-nonsense clear (masculine) levelheaded thinking. The mental fog has lifted, and everything remains firmly anchored—no floating uterus here. Later in the Third Meditation Descartes will bolster his assurances of God's existence by comparing them to his "clear and distinct ideas of corporeal things" (*idées claires et distinctes que j'ai des choses corporelles* [ME 34; MF 293]). While the sticky mortar of Descartes's reasoning in this Third Meditation is still drying, early in the fourth he lays on the next brick:

> Et lorsque je considère que je doute, c'est-à-dire que je suis une chose incomplète et dépendante, l'idée d'un être complet et indépendant, c'est-à-dire de Dieu, se présente à mon esprit *avec tant de distinction et de clarté;* et de cela seul que cette idée se retrouve en moi, ou bien que je suis ou existe, moi qui possède cette idée, je conclus si évidemment l'existence de Dieu, et que la mienne dépend entièrement de lui en tous les moments de ma vie, que je ne pense pas que l'esprit humain puisse rien connaître avec plus d'évidence et de certitude. (MF 301)

> And when I consider that I doubt, that is to say, that I am an incomplete and dependent being, the idea of a complete and independent being, that is, of God occurs to my mind *with very great distinctness and clearness.* And from the very fact that such an idea occurs in me, or that I who possess this idea exist, I so evidently conclude that God exists and that my own existence depends entirely upon him every moment of my life that I am confident that the human mind can know nothing with greater evidence and certainty. (ME 51)

This brick must have partially exploded in the kiln. I have added emphasis on the relevant phrase that contains the refrain of "clear and distinct," but I have quoted the passsage at greater than usual length for these last four meditations because it demonstrates several odd features that cannot escape a textual critique informed by gender. Again there is that shifter, that "I" presented by turns as complete and incomplete, as an agent of active doubt and presence unto itself, yet also as an arena or theater within which an idea "occurs" or presents itself (is not represented, but presents itself). Whatever this "I" is, it seems to be an inside that contains its own outside, or vice versa (in deconstructionist terms, it is "under erasure" because it bears the trace of its other).

The incomplete, dependent "I" of the text relies dialectically on the complete, independent ultimate "I" that is God, and that rescues the lesser "I" from its own limitations. But notice something in the French text: Where Lafleur's translation employs "being" in both instances, we find *une chose* ("a thing") that is dependent and incomplete opposed to *un être* in the (French) original. Only the man can be a complete being (*être*). One result of the project of rereading the canon with gender issues uppermost in mind is the familiar observation that "masculine" aspects of culture will be presented and described as complete, whole, or fully realized, while "the feminine" will be associated with incompleteness (to cite only two other examples: Marx's concern over the reduction of workers to a mere bodily, i.e., feminine, sphere of existence, and Freud's determination to overcome the "mutilated," fragmentary nature of the "Dora" case). Irigaray has shown quite dramatically how "the feminine" designates that which cannot or will not be seen or acknowledged by patriarchal thought, and the convergence of psychoanalysis and feminism in other recent theorists' work teaches us to suspect that the desire to see with total clarity and distinctness is the desire for the assertion and vindication of the phallus.[42] The "I" of the Fourth Meditation thus expresses an emphatic wish not to remain in an incomplete, i.e., "feminine" state. What we have here is a seventeenth-century version of castration anxiety. In fact, time and again, whenever masculine prerogatives are being asserted over the unruly feminine, strong claims are made for the power of masculine surveillance. In popular song, The Who expressed it in "I Can See for Miles" (1968), while The Police (after Foucault, what a perfect name) updated the assertion for the 1980s in "Every Step You Take (I'll Be Watchin' You)."[43]

At each remaining step "Descartes" takes in his epistemological march toward certainty he too boasts of his visual prowess. Since in the Fifth Meditation he must deal with both the essence of material things and (once again) the existence of God, he uses the words *clairement* and *distinctement* on three different occasions (MF 311, 312, 316). Even so, the first sentence of the Sixth Meditation, in which we are returned to the question of material phenomena and the necessary distinction between mind (the French is actually *l'âme,* i.e., the soul, and not *l'esprit,* or the mind) and body, comes as something of a shock: "Il ne me reste plus maintenant qu'à examiner s'il y a des choses matérielles" ("*Nothing more* [my emphasis] is now left for me to do except to examine whether corporeal things exist") (MF 381; ME 68). After all that clear and distinct seeing? The top story of this Cartesian high rise is swaying in the stiff breeze of a metaphysical reluctance to admit the existence of material, bodily (i.e., feminine) reality. This, after all, should be the stage at which all remaining contradictions are resolved and the goal of certainty is reached. Of course, the final meditation ends with the reassurance that material things, *as long as they are capable of being perceived distinctly,* exist. They must be known at a distance, from the vantage point of contemplative solitude that guarantees the supreme status of the egocentric knowing (masculine) subject. As with Freud's troubling lecture "Femininity," whatever is to be observed about the "other" of patriarchal consciousness must be free of fanciful speculation,[44] even if speculation runs rife on topics at least seemingly free of such binary oppositions as masculine/feminine or mind/body. Whether we are talking about Freud (as is the case, in this regard, with Sarah Kofman)[45] or Descartes, the seeming absence of wild speculation on topics either explicitly or implicitly dealing with the feminine is contradicted by complete willingness (e.g., Descartes's first two meditations; Freud's *Beyond the Pleasure Principle*—see Chapter 5) to give free rein to speculation on other occasions.

V. VISION, GENDER, AND KNOWLEDGE

How, apart from its role in silly textbook formulations, has the *Méditations* been deployed in modern Western culture? If Descartes's authoritative text has worked culturally to silence, in patriarchal fashion, alternative discourses waiting to be expressed, then Derrida's demonstration of the textual operations of *différance* that unravel it from within ought to be politically enabling for these discursive forces of counterhegemony, especially feminism. But, where Foucault may be said to err in the direction of hurrying through his reading toward the sociopolitical deployment of a landmark work, Derrida is too caught up in the textual maelstrom ever to reach the shore of "the world," in Edward Said's sense,[46] in which texts produce their effects. It is also worth noting that Derrida's reading leaves untouched—and undeconstructed—binary oppositions other than that of reason versus madness. To move on into the following five meditations in order to subject mind/body or culture/nature to his deconstructionist strategies would have been to move in more obviously feminist directions. Meanwhile, without his specific terminology, and without the paradoxical deference[47] with which the harbinger of "difference" has been received, feminist theorists have undertaken the work of deconstruction on a larger scale, in terms of Cartesianism, than that attempted by Derrida. This passage by Keller may give some indication of this expanded range:

> In sympathy with, and even in response to, the growing division between male and female, public and private, work and home, modern science opted for an even greater polarization of mind and nature, reason and feeling, objective and subjective; in parallel with the gradual desexualization of women, it offered a de-animated, and increasingly mechanized conception of nature. In so doing, science itself became an active agent of change. The ideology of modern science gave (at least some) men a new basis for masculine self-esteem and male prowess.[48]

In the few brief examples that close out this chapter, I want to give some further indication of how feminist theory and criticism have superseded the debate as defined by the two leading (male) lights of poststructuralism, concentrating especially on the alternative epistemological and aesthetic models which feminist cultural criticism and cultural politics, strategically if not "essentially," place in opposition to the Cartesian ones.

Considering Derrida's brilliant dismantling of the opposition of culture to nature in the work of Lévi-Strauss (in the very same volume in which "Cogito et histoire de la folie" was collected),[49] it is at least somewhat surprising that he fails to explore some of the consequences of the more fundamental Cartesian divisions of mind/body and, by implication, of culture/nature. Sherry Ortner's influential essay contains the answer for contemporary feminist thought in the very question posed by its title: "Is Female to Male as Nature Is to Culture?"[50] This conceptual, cultural opposition has had devastating consequences for our world, as artists are often best able to remind us. Barbara Kruger, the postmodern feminist artist known for her arresting combination of photographs and captions that appear resentfully and accusingly to address a male viewer, has produced one particularly disturbing image that suggests the real madness of the Cartesian project of knowing in order to dominate a distant and subjected nature. Appropriately, it appears in her 1981 comprehensive collection *We Won't Play Nature to Your Culture*, and it consists of an image of the atomic mushroom cloud over which has been superimposed the statement "Your Manias Become Science."[51] Kruger's visual statement underscores the fear, inscribed as we have seen in the first two meditations, of the madness implicit in the artificially constructed game of Cartesian intellection.[52]

For Lévi-Strauss, nature is to culture as "raw" (*le cru*) is to "cooked" (*le cuit*),[53] and, from yin/yang to "natural childbirth," we know that what Cixous, mindful of Freud, refers to bitterly as the "dark continent"[54] of women's experience has been the terrain of the raw. Subjecting Descartes's founding text for modern science to the critical insights of recent feminist theory allows us to see what is gender-specific about science and modes of scientific knowledge.

The Cartesian model (not only in *Méditations*, but also in *La Dioptrique* and *Discours de la méthode*)[55] of scientific "knowing" posits a gap or distancing between knower and known, between knowing subject and object of knowledge. We have become so accustomed to this that we take it to be a naturally occurring means of relating subjectivity to representation, and we find it nearly impossible to envision an alternative to our systems of representations. But, as Dalia Judovitz argues, we have come to equate what was a highly specific Cartesian epistemological process with a culturally generalized process of representation as objectification, with all men (particularly men) applying the Cartesian maneuver to an endless range of circumstances.[56]

Feminists have argued convincingly that this objectifying process, so often blatantly disadvantageous to women, is inherently visual, whether pursued through directly voyeuristic acts or through the so-called "mind's eye" of Cartesian rationalism. Cultural critics are busily pointing out that systems of knowledge that create representations are not the only possible ones. Heidegger's groundbreaking essay on the *Weltbild*, or world picture, in which he argued that the Greeks, for example, did not represent the world to themselves in the form of a *Weltbild*,[57] retains its power to challenge our accepted epistemological procedures. As Keller points out, the historical fact that modern science emerged only once, and in a highly specific manner, makes it extremely difficult for us to imagine an alternative science or epistemology that would not have recourse to distinctions like masculine/feminine and reason/feeling. When, in an earlier book, she explored the implications of Nobel laureate Barbara McClintock's phrase "a feeling for the organism," this was not in order to oppose an intuitive, empathetic, essentially feminine science to a cold, aloof masculine one, but to show instead what is forfeited when any one approach holds absolute sway.[58]

Approaching the Cartesian legacy from the direction of aesthetics, Christine Buci-Glucksmann argues moreover that Cartesian vision, both the "mind's eye" that Keller and Grontkowski examine and the assumption that whatever is to be viewed must appear to present itself to one fixed, immobile mastering gaze, was established in opposition to, even usurped the place of, a "mad" baroque vision of anamorphic, willfully distorted trompe l'oeil perspective which for her stands for the repressed and would-be oppositional (including feminist) aesthetics of modernism. Buci-Glucksmann, complementing Jean-Joseph Goux's essay "Descartes et la perspective," also exposes the "illusory" character that Cartesian perspective certainly shared with the formal use of perspective in painting.[59]

Despite a Buci-Glucksmann or a Judovitz, most of the debate about representation continues to identify the Cartesian variety with patriarchal modes of representation *tout court*. Luce Irigaray, taking on patriarchs from Plato to Freud,[60] argues that intellectual activity that works through processes of representation and objectification is inherently patriarchal and excessively visually oriented or, as Martin Jay expresses it, "ocularcentric."[61] From a cursory reading of Irigaray's difficult books, we might conclude that she opposes to masculinist preoccupation with vision a model of "feminine" knowing based on touch, and certainly some feminist critics have accused her of falling back on stereotypical notions of a feminine essence.[62] But a careful reading of Irigaray reveals a more comprehensive, even utopian affirmation of multiple ways of knowing, no one of which may be reified as *the* feminine mode. There is not merely one but many possible epistemological alternatives to the patriarchal model.

Against the Cartesian model of knowledge that apparently depends upon isolated, unitary, full phallic presence and radical, alienating separation and objectification, Irigaray opts for multiplicity and, most radically (in keeping with one of the most persistent tendencies of postmodernism), destroys the link between knowledge and the solitary knowing consciousness. The mother/daughter relation, taken all too literally by Monique Plaza and other critics of Irigaray, serves as metaphor for this epistemological attack on the autonomous subject.[63] For present-day concepts of gender and their discontents, this can signal a rejection of the entire binary logic of masculine/

feminine,[64] and can multiply the ways of knowing available to scientists, feminists, or intellectual historians in the process of becoming cultural critics.

The time is long overdue for gender questions to become the central preoccupation of intellectual history. The many links between gender (in all its cultural aspects) and reputations of texts and authors, between gender and the ability of certain arguments and interpretations to be convincing, need to be anticipated and examined. The implications of such investigations are by no means limited to redefinitions of feminine cultural experience. One of the most radical implications of Irigaray's work, and to some extent the work of Cixous, is that, just as models of feminine knowledge and experience begin to proliferate, we also find it impossible to cling to unitary concepts of masculine knowledge and experience. Escaping the trap of binarism cannot help but be intellectually and politically enabling. I believe Susan Rubin Suleiman has said it best:

> The dream, then, is to get beyond not only the number one—the number that determines unity, of body or of self—but also beyond the number *two,* which determines difference, antagonism, and exchange conceived of as merely the coming together of opposites. That this dream is perhaps impossible is suggested. Its power remains, however, because the desire it embodies is a desire for both endless complication and creative movement.[65]

Descartes may have written six meditations, but, in a very real sense, he failed to get beyond the number two. Whatever was "laid" in that text, or, more important, in its subsequent cultural deployment, it was decidedly something other than a "firm foundation."

The Persistence of the Gendered Subject in Marx's *Economic and Philosophic Manuscripts of 1844*

Marxism is, by all evidence, materialist. To this extent it can be used by feminism.
—Christine Delphy, "A Materialist Feminism Is Possible"

All the same, I am glad to find in Marx—and no longer the "Young Marx"—this re-emergence of subjectivity.
—Félix Guattari, "The Group and the Person"

The Marxist notion of individuals' concrete and specific *needs,* as opposed to their abstract and impersonal *rights,* emphasizes an understanding of the subject as a subject in history, one whose sensual experience is the measure of social liberation. This idea is critical for women because it allows the possibility of articulating subjective needs and desires in terms that are class- and gender-specific.
—Winifred Woodhull, "Sexuality, Power, and the Question of Rape"

The relation of man to woman is *the most natural* relation of human being to human being.
—Karl Marx, *Economic and Philosophic Manuscripts of 1844*

You make me feel like a natural woman.
—Aretha Franklin

I. HUMANISM, HUMAN NATURE, GENDER

Louis Althusser once remarked that the central issues of cultural study and critique in our time would turn out to be questions of reading and interpretation. Those who would argue for reconsideration, from the vantage point of feminism and gender critique, of the whole question of the Western canon would certainly endorse Althusser's assertion. But Althusser's celebrated rereading of Marx, inspired as it may have been by the Lacanian textual *retour à Freud,* was limited largely to *Capital* as the most "mature" and "scientific" member of the marxian corpus. Such texts as *The Economic and Philosophic Manuscripts of 1844* (*EPM*) lay on the other side of that *coupure épistémoloqique* (epistemological break) of 1845 or so that allegedly separated the "young Marx" from the mature architect of the "science" of historical materialism. Anyone interested in them was, for Althusser, seduced by the sly whore of humanism. Yet any serious reconsideration of Marx must ignore Althusser's dubious claim and focus sustained critical attention on texts from every stage of Marx's life. This is true for a number of reasons, including well-deserved feminist suspicion over the claims of "science."

"Humanism," the despised term he opposed to the honorific "science," is the cancer Althusser finds contaminating Marx's 1844 Manuscripts.[1] The leading theoretician of the French Communist Party, Roger Garaudy,[2] was part of the humanist tradition in Western marxism, a tradition that included much of French existentialism and that took inspiration from the post-Lukács rediscovery of Hegel in "the young Marx."[3] Since their belated publication in 1932, *Die ökonomisch-philosophische Manuskripte von 1844* had played a leading role in the formulation of "marxist humanism." Thus, when Althusser crossed swords with Garaudy, not surprisingly he disdained the very concept Garaudy held most dear. For the most part, Althusser was able to formulate a marxist antihumanism that (in theory at least) avoided the Stalinism one might have expected from such a stance. However, as Perry Anderson, among others, has argued, Althusserianism thus oriented was to prove far more congenial to a neo-Nietzschean poststructuralist sensibility than to a Western marxist tradition in profound crisis and badly in need of a theoretically acceptable reaffirmation of individual historically situated human agency.[4]

Humanism is also at the heart of debates over the canon and Marx's place in it. The antihumanism to which Althusser, Lacan, Foucault, and Derrida have so energetically contributed continues to flourish in the poststructuralist theoretical context in which these debates have unfolded. Many teachers have found the *EPM* to be a useful text through which to introduce students to marxism, whether in order to demonstrate the profound philosophical sources of what came to be called marxism, or perhaps to allow the central importance of the marxist concept of alienation to manifest itself.[5] Often in fact, the reason for teaching this text is to disarm students by introducing them to a Marx seemingly less threateningly deterministic and still imbued with more than a vestige of youthful idealism. Students would thus be less likely to be swayed by the familiar reductiveness of such textbook clichés as "dialectical materialism." Whatever the reason for turning to the interpretation of the *EPM*, humanism will certainly be at the center of any critical discussion of the text. One need not subscribe to Althusser's concept (borrowed from Gaston Bachelard, Georges Canguilhem, and Michel Foucault) of an epistemological rupture dividing Marx's thought into distinct biographical phases in order to accept his characterization (whether this means that "humanist" concepts disappear in the later Marx is another story).

This "humanism," which may simultaneously render the *EPM* unacceptable for Althusserian marxists (if any are still left around) and more congenial to otherwise nonmarxist readers, emerges with increasing clarity as a major stumbling block for feminists, including but by no means limited to socialist or marxist feminists. In fact, from the point of view of gender, humanism can be shown to depend upon many of the same assumptions, prejudices, and blind spots that inhabit Western science (see Chapter 2 on Descartes). This is fundamentally because so-called "humanism" has really operated more as a "*man* ism," positing the autonomous subject Althusser finds to be the cornerstone of all ideology,[6] a subject moreover automatically equated with masculine experience. Whatever the real promise of marxism for feminism, this serious limitation can be seen in Marx's *EPM* in passages that discuss human productive activity, "species being," and "nature."

Marxist argument over humanism in the "Young Marx" focuses upon such passages. Norman Geras, a member of the editorial board of *New Left Review,* has demonstrated impressively that such preoccupations are by no means limited to Marx's early writings. His *Marx and Human Nature: Refutation of a Legend* (1986) deals Althusserianism (and many other marxist schools) a further blow by demonstrating amply, through the kind of close reading limited in Althusser's oeuvre to *Capital,* not only that marxism embraces the concept of human nature, but that this nature is individual. The implications of Geras' deliberately shocking *bouleversement* in contemporary marxist theory are significant for the "death of the subject" so widely trumpeted in poststructural critical circles; but, as we will discover, they ought to be even more so for feminist debates over the subjective status of women. Geras' failure to shift marxist theory in this direction is what is *really* surprising about his book. Or, if not exactly surprising, rudely disappointing.

The overwhelming consensus of opinion that no concept of human nature exists (put another way, that marxism is hostile, *tout court,* to any notion of a "human nature") within marxism derives, Geras argues, from miniscule textual evidence. Geras then proceeds to treat those few passages (e.g., in

Theses on Feuerbach and *Grundrisse*), arguing convincingly that his reading is
a more careful, subtly nuanced one than they have customarily received. For
example, examining the famous observation from the *Grundrisse* in which
Marx, echoing Aristotle, asserts that "man" is a gregarious "social" animal,
Geras admits that Marx indeed holds human individuation to be necessarily
social.[7] But this does not mean, Geras shows, that the "individual" thus
dissolves in the "social." Similarly, Geras rereads the sixth of Marx's *Theses on
Feuerbach,* the very one so consistently cited as irrefutable proof that Marx
rejected any theory of human nature. He shows that when Marx locates the
"essence of Man" in the "ensemble of social relations," this does not sanction
the belief that therefore all human essence is denied. Geras demonstrates
repeatedly, and with at times elaborate polemical force, that (1) not only did
Marx retain a concept of human nature but that (2) it was an individualistic
(though not set in opposition to social essence) concept.[8] Finally, through
representative sampling of passages retrieved from throughout the marxian
corpus, Geras lays to rest the cherished Althusserian argument that Marx
outgrew this youthful "humanism."

Elements of our reexamination of *The Economic and Philosophic Manuscripts of 1844* will confirm this thesis, but the contribution of Geras is woefully inadequate, as it stands, for a reading that would bring gender to bear.
Geras has nothing to say about the exclusiveness of Marx's masculinist language, and offers no corrective to it (in fact, he gives no sign that he is aware
of the problem). Moreover, Geras never considers whether the concept of
individuality he recuperates for marxism might be seriously compromised
by an unacknowledged (because unexamined) masculinist bias. One thinks
here of Luce Irigaray's position that any theory of the subject will be a
masculinist one,[9] although other feminist theorists are far less willing to
jettison all subject positions at the very time when actual women are claiming them for the first time.

We don't really need the polemical blitz of a Norman Geras to realize that
marxism has always been inhabited by autonomous subjects—agents of
class struggle and historical forces, but subjects nonetheless. These are the
"men making their own history" Marx writes about in the *Eighteenth Brumaire.* Certainly the existentialist marxism of Jean-Paul Sartre (against
which Althusser and his followers were in full rebellion) was the most notable attempt within Western marxism to reaffirm the individual subject situated within the historical dialectic. This was a significant gain for marxism.
Problems arise, however, when exaggerated claims are made on behalf of the
theory of the subject. Geras assumes categorically that recovery of the "indi-

vidual" basis of the marxist concept of human nature will revive not only marxist theory but praxis. Similarly, Harry van der Linden, in his recent *Kantian Ethics and Socialism,* argues for a renewed (neo-Kantian) ethical basis for contemporary socialism[10] without considering whether, as Sarah Kofman demonstrates forcefully in *Le respect des femmes (Kant et Rousseau),*[11] Kantianism might simply be thoroughly patriarchal in its logic and conceptual categories.

The individual human being Geras extracts from Marx's writings is of course the human being as *producer,* engaged in the act of transforming nature and thus affirming what Marx in the 1844 Manuscripts calls "species being" (*Gattungswesen*). Because in Marx's time "producer" largely (but not exclusively, as Marx almost seems to lament) meant "male," and because feminist theory has so extensively examined the association of "nature" with "the feminine," the contribution of Geras cannot be seen as necessarily an advance. Jean Baudrillard, that most postmarxist of French postmodernists, has furthermore criticized (and broken with) marxism for its assumption which, he argues, it shares with Ricardo and classical political economy, that production is the definitive sphere of human historical and social activity.[12] Thus Baudrillard, by making more specific the standard poststructuralist critique of the subject (the critique of marxism as critique of the subject as producer), offers a counterpoint to Geras. But they are both united by indifference to developing their arguments in a feminist direction.

In a way it is surprising that Baudrillard, whose assessments of postmodern culture as hyperreality and simulation could be read as part of an ongoing critique of representation that has been carried out most energetically by feminists,[13] does not perform this maneuver. If he has theorized his rejection of marxism's productive basis in feminist terms, i.e., that marxism ignores the domestic sphere of unpaid labor to which women in the nineteenth century were increasingly being relegated *and* that, as Alison Jaggar demonstrates, there is no evidence that Marx ever rejected the idea that women should occupy this domestic sphere, even under socialism,[14] then it might be Baudrillard, rather than Foucault, whose theory would seem potentially enabling for feminism.[15]

II. PATRIARCHIAL ASSUMPTIONS

What does it mean for someone who, as I do, admires Marx and finds his writings immensely valuable, to reread a text like the *EPM* in gender terms?

Michèle Le Doeuff, in an essay on the tendency of contemporary French philosophical *maîtres* to ignore feminism or gender issues, expresses it pointedly: "As I said before, when a male philosopher speaks of women, the mode of his discourse deviates from his own standards."[16] This could be said of virtually every writer discussed in this book. In terms of the canon, it means that a supposedly radical text whose inclusion some might think threatening can, when it approaches (or more significantly, fails to approach) the realm of gender, align itself with staunchly reactionary (e.g., Saint Paul or Augustine) views. For, as we will easily see, nineteenth-century patriarchal ideology is inscribed in Marx's text, perhaps most fundamentally by its absence as subject matter. To observe such a thing is to turn one of the most influential contemporary modes of marxist literary criticism back onto the marxian text itself. I refer to Pierre Macherey, another Althusserian, whose *Pour une théorie de la production littéraire* (1966) argued that ideology "decenters" and thus manifests itself in texts as absence, as what cannot be examined (because in linguistic and cultural terms, such things "go without saying"—*Es geht ohne zu sagen,* Marx might have said).[17]

I accept the judgment of Norman Geras that Marx articulates a theory of human nature that assumes the individual, and the Althusserian labeling of early marxism as "humanism." I would amend this in what now seems to me an obvious way, but one not obvious to me before reading feminist theory, to say that, like much of humanism, it defines itself through processes of exclusion and blindness. Attempting to universalize what is particular about its masculinist position, it is constituted by its other. As Biddy Martin has written, "women's silence and exclusion from struggles over representation have been the condition of possibility for humanist thought."[18] Scratch humanism with the sharp nails of gender critique, and you pry loose the "man" in humanism every time. However much we may be able to demonstrate the potential uses of marxism for feminist theory and practice, it must be acknowledged that Marx's humanism is, once again, a "manism." It is difficult to see what is to be gained by, as some recent scholarly works on marxism have done,[19] excusing Marx for his gendered language, explaining that Marx's *Mensch* or translators' "man" really must be read as including women. Such a view might arise from a strong desire to reconcile feminist with marxist theory, but it would depend upon a questionable reading of Marx's texts.

I suggest that we would do well, in reading this text (among others), to try to keep in mind several aspects of gender, including first of all the commonplace but inescapable realization of the author's (and reader's) gender. Second, it will be obvious that searching through Marx's text with a view to the ongoing "unhappy marriage"[20] of marxism and feminism brings a particular kind of reading to the fore. Both in the way that it is written, including its inscription of contemporary patriarchal ideology, and in its dependence upon a sense of the human subject that fails to encompass a broad range of human experience, Marx's text fails to overcome key limitations of patriarchal conceptualizations that weaken marxism's claims on the allegiance of feminists. Every feminist theorist at all inclined to maintain a dialogue with the marxist tradition has faced this problem, whether, like Juliet Mitchell, she patches the cracks in the marxist edifice with psychoanalytic mortar, or, like Christine Delphy, she acknowledges the inadequacies of the marxist approach to gender and sexuality without wishing to join the ranks of "Psych et Po" (the French feminist group "Psychanalyse et Politique"). What Alison Jaggar describes as "socialist feminism" seems best suited to provide an ongoing critical engagement with and revision of marxism thus conceived. By "socialist feminism," to which I also subscribe, Jaggar means a feminism in agreement with the marxist condemnations of capitalism, while at the same time insistent on placing gender, not simply class oppression, at the center of historical materialist concerns.

Much of recent feminist theory, drawing upon marxism itself as well as psychoanalysis, semiotics, and deconstruction, has elaborated an ambitious critique of what are seen as patriarchal or phallocentric tendencies to consider all cultural experience from the perspective, claimed by structuralists to be inherent in language, of binary opposition. In Hélène Cixous's "Sorties," we are confronted with a catalogue of these pairs, including sun/moon, active/passive, culture/nature.[21] In the Derridean terms frequently employed by French feminist theorists, these binary oppositions need to be deconstructed, a process of (among other things) showing how the first term in the pair works to exclude, silence, negate, or deny the second, which is always seen, if at all, as less valuable, desirable, valid, etc.[22] In American (deManian) "literary" deconstruction, the figural rhetoric of tropes in which these acts of exclusionary violence are carried out is relentlessly x-rayed to reveal its fractures and other symptoms. Unfortunately, whatever the as yet unrealized potential of deconstruction for more ambitious projects of cultural criticism (including an interrogation of "literature" as such), this far more deferential procedure has been the one to catch on in our graduate departments of literature.

Recent American feminist social theory, most notably in anthropology, has also subjected certain telltale binary oppositions to a great deal of critical discussion. One of the most fundamental is the opposition between "public" and "private," with patriarchal ideology working in all known cultures to relegate women to the domestic, private sphere—public life, from the Athenian *agora* to the *Öffentlichkeit* in the contemporary marxist theory of Jürgen Habermas, being by definition masculine. Marxist-feminist discussion has centered on the relationship between the capitalist mode of production and the domestic activity, historically assigned to women, of reproducing the means of existence for (male) workers, restoring them to a sufficient level of energy and strength to enable them to return to the workplace. In popular song, Jackson Browne has best captured, if only for the wage laborer, the dreariness of such a routine:

> And when the evening sun goes down
> I'll go home and lay my body down,
> And when the morning light comes streaming in,
> I'll get up and do it again.[23]

Feminists argue convincingly that capitalist profits are greatly enhanced by this system whereby unpaid labor by women in the home serves to maintain workers for capitalist production. Engels, much more than Marx, examined the relationship between class and gender oppression (in *The Origin of the Family, Private Property, and the State*). Despite the inadequacies of his analysis, his work has been much more useful to feminists than have the writings of Marx himself or the collaborative writings of Marx and Engels.[24] But neither Marx nor Engels devotes specific attention to this familiar form of women's oppression, for they simply assume that it is peculiar to the family under capitalism. They certainly give no indication that the kinds of chores culturally assumed to be "women's work" will be shouldered by men as well as women with the advent of socialism. Joan Kelly, in a groundbreaking essay that suggested ways to synthesize feminism and marxism, complained of the tendency in marxist theory to associate men with production, and women with reproduction.[25] This echoes Baudrillard's critique of marxism's production fetish, but adds the issues of gender Baudrillard neglects. In traditional marxist literature, Natalie Sokoloff writes,

> women and their domestic tasks are seen as outside production (that is, surplus value production) and therefore in need of being incorporated on a large scale into social or market production in order to free them for capitalist oppression.

After many examples of modern mid-twentieth century incorporation of women into paid labor, in both capitalist and socialist societies, the sexual division of labor steadfastly persists.[26]

Yet it is also worth noting in Marx's writings that, despite the progressive dialectical tone of advance over the traditional family and, by implication, over the traditional role of women, a certain amount of nostalgia is expressed for the preindustrial working-class home, where women were not subjected to the indignities of factory labor.[27] In part, this must surely be seen as a condemnation of capitalism for taking women out of their rightful, i.e., private (domestic), sphere (another example of the tension in Marx between denouncing the evils of capitalism and viewing them dialectically as historical necessities). It is also a reminder of the persistent tendency within marxism to assign men to production, women to the domestic sphere of reproduction.

In addition to the production/reproduction and public/private dichotomies, feminist anthropologists join with Cixous, Irigaray, and poststructuralist French feminism generally in a critical interrogation of the "culture" versus "nature" opposition—at least as ancient as yin/yang—whereby nature connotes woman's experience (and vice versa) and in which the "natural" role of women is equated with biological reproduction and bodily experience.[28] We have only to think of Plato or Descartes to understand the power for Western culture of the automatic association of masculine existence with the denial of the body, or with transcendence of bodily limits. For women, by contrast, biology, borrowing Freud's most incriminating formulation, "is destiny." Put another way, "culture" has unfairly been a coded reference to masculine experience.[29]

III.   SPECIES AND GENDER

In "Estranged Labor" (*Entfremdete Arbeit und Privateigentum*), the most theoretically significant section of the *EPM*, Marx stumbles into this most pervasive and enduring of patriarchal conceptual frameworks through his introduction of the opposed concepts of species life and species being.[30]

According to Marx, all creatures have species life (*Gattungsleben*), i.e., they must eat, sleep, procreate, etc., in order to survive as a species. But only human beings have "species being" (*Gattungswesen*, i.e., only human beings appropriate all of nature for themselves in order to contemplate their existence independently from fundamentally animal activity. Hence, culture, art, and all truly human expressions of intelligence and creativity follow from *Gattungswesen*. But Marx doesn't actually refer to "human beings" when explaining the concept of species being. He says, "Der Mensch ist ein Gattungswesen," "*Man* is a species being" (*MEGA* 368; *EPM* 112).

In English usage, the generic "man" obviously calls to mind the word for an individual male human being. German appears to allow for a more careful distinction between the latter (*der Mann*) and the word for human being or "person" (*der Mensch*). Some might argue that Marx can be excused somewhat for universalizing from a somewhat gender-specific term because his own German language makes it possible. But, in order to see the clear limits of such a claim, consider for a minute the easy displacement, permitted by German sounds, from *Mensch* to *Männer,* the plural word for male persons. All we have to do is to substitute (somewhat like John Berger's recommended substitution of nude male figures for female ones in classic European paintings in order to realize the conventions whereby females are by definition available for a male gaze)[31] for *der Mensch* as the culturally accepted term for "all human beings" either of the two most common German words for "woman" (*die Frau; das Weib*). We know immediately with what resistance our universalizing claims for such a term would be met. We could not get away with simply using the word generically without explanation or rationale. Marx could get away with using *der Mensch* in this way for the same reasons English-language writers have traditionally been able to use "man" as if it applied to all human beings.

What *man's* species being enables *him* to do, Marx says, is appropriate all nature for himself as "*seinem* unorganischen *Körper*" ("his *inorganic* body") (*MEGA* 368; *EPM* 112), thus realizing the universality of his essence in practice (*praktisch*). Marx further subdivides this category of nature into (1) "his direct means of life" ("unmittelbares Lebensmittel") and (2) "the material, the object, and the instrument of his life activity" ("die Gegenstand/Materie und das Werkzeug seiner Lebensthätigkeit") (*EPM* 112; *MEGA* 368). Capitalism, Marx argues, has estranged *man* from *his* unmediated relationship with nature. But if, as feminist theorists such as Sherry Ortner persuade us to do, we read Marx's "nature" as including "women," then we could point to a fundamentally estranging form of appropriation whereby men in patriarchal societies, including precapitalist ones, have located "woman" within nature, establishing cultural practices in which women serve men as all of nature is made to serve them. If nature is that which provides *man's* "direct means of life," "woman's" inherent role as "man's" *Lebensmittel* or "means of life" is justified.

Forcing such a reading out of Marx's terminology and then carrying this expanded sense over into the remainder of the "Estranged Labor" section then creates continued reverberations as we read and contemplate a socialist feminism that might have been:

> Indem die entfremdete Arbeit dem Menschen (1) die Natur entfremdet, (2) sich selbst, seine eigne thätige Funktion, seine Lebensthätigkeit, so entfremdet sie dem Menschen die *Gattung*. (*MEGA* 369)

> In estranging from man (1) nature, and (2) himself, his own active functions, his life activity, estranged labor estranges the *species* from man. (*EPM* 112)

Likewise, we are alerted to the patriarchal logic unwittingly inscribed in the following, where the word to watch is "animal":

> Das Thier ist unmittelbar eins mit seiner Lebensthätigkeit. Es unterscheidet sich nicht von ihr. Es ist *sie*. Der Mensch macht sein Lebensthätigkeit selbst zum Gegenstand seines Wollens und seines Bewusstseins.(*MEGA* 369)

> The animal is immediately one with its life activity. It does not distinguish itself from it. It is *its life activity*. Man makes his life activity itself the object of his will and of his consciousness.(*EPM* 113)

From yin/yang to the Platonic-Christian tradition through the entire Western metaphysical tradition, woman has been the animal "at one with her life activity." This animal, Marx says, "produces only itself, whilst man reproduces the whole of nature" ("producirt nur sich selbst, während der Mensch die ganze Natur reproducirt") (*EPM* 113; *MEGA* 369–70). Let us read this as a reminder that patriarchal culture also reproduces the habit of locating *woman* in the nature thus reproduced.

According to such logic, *woman,* not *man* is never able to escape her bodily sexed nature; bears permanently the mark of difference; is inescapably *other*. As such, this is a familiar example of the binary opposition(man/woman; culture/nature) deconstruction has taught us to recognize as always already unbalanced by the privilege accorded the prior (man/culture) term. But that more privileged term must always already bear its own mark of "differance;" must always be inhabited by the trace(s) of its supposedly opposite, separate, and wholly *other* term. Derrida's most powerful readings, for example his reading of such a champion of binary opposition as Lévi-Strauss,[32] demonstrate convincingly that the text is under considerable strain from the tension between two separate terms that are not in fact separate at all—strain because the privileged term is given more weight than it can bear, encumbered as it is by the other that clings to it. Nor could it be otherwise, since the very textuality of the text is exemplified by that paradox.

IV. NATURAL DIVISION / UNNATURAL ALIENATION

At key moments, a text will reveal the implausibility of the opposition, and the connecting apparatus will be discovered. Marx's *Gattungswesen* is such a term, groaning under the burden of its would-be opposite, *Gattungs-leben*. We see this in the section of the *EPM* that most notoriously reveals the crudeness of Marx's analysis of human sexual difference. Once more to quote Michèle Le Doeuff, "when a male philosopher speaks of women, the mode of his discourse deviates from his own standards."[33] The section in question is *Privateigentum und Kommunismus* ("Private Property and Communism"), and it begins with Marx attacking the "crude communism" of earlier (utopian) socialist thinkers who postulated a "community of women" (*EPM* 133). As is the case in the *Communist Manifesto*, Marx argues that it is in fact the capitalist bourgeois class that has achieved this. Where the wheels of Marx's critical machine begin to skid out of control is in the long paragraph he devotes to painting a picture of an unalienated state of relations between the sexes. Rejecting "the approach to *woman* as the spoil and handmaid of communal lust," Marx brings to the discourse on human species being a fervently idealized tone. The passage needs to be quoted at length, and even then this is not the entire paragraph:

> In dem Verhältnis zum *Weib,* als dem *Raub* und der Magd der gemein-schäftlichen Wollust, ist die unendliche Degradation ausgesprochen, in welcher der Mensch für sich selbst existiert, denn das Geheimnis dieses Verhältnisses hat seinen *unzweideutigen,* entschiednen, *offenbaren,* enthüllten Ausdruck in dem Verhältnisse des *Mannes* zum *Weibe* und in der Weise, wie das *unmittelbare, natürliche* Gattungsverhältnis gefasst wird. Das unmittelbare, natürliche, notwen-dige Verhältnis des Menschen zum Menschen ist das *Verhältnis* des *Mannes* zum *Weibe.* In diesem *natürlichen* Gattungsverhältnis ist das Verhältnis des Menschen zur Natur unmittelbar sein Verhältnis zum Menschen wie das Verhältnis zum

Menschen unmittelbar sein Verhältnis zur Natur, seine eigne *natürliche* Bestimmung ist. In diesem Verhältnis *erscheint* also *sinnlich,* auf ein anschaubares *Factum* reducirt inwieweit dem Menschen des Menschen geworden ist. Aus diesem Verhältnis kann man also die ganze Bildungsstufe des Menschen beurtheilen. Aus dem Charakter dieses Verhältnisses—folgt, inwieweit der *Mensch* als *Gattungswesen,* als *Mensch* sich geworden ist und erfasst hat; das Verhältnis des Mannes zum Weib ist das *natürlichste* Verhältnis des Menschen zum Menschen. In ihm zeigt sich also inwieweit das *natürliche* Verhalten des Menschen *menschlich* odern inwieweit das *menschliche* Wesen ihm zum *Natürlichen* Wesen, inwieweit seine *menschliche Natur* ihm zur *Natur* geworden ist. (*MEGA* 388).

   In the approach [for reasons which are not entirely clear, Milligan often prefers to translate *Verhältnis* as "approach" rather than "relation"] to *woman* as the spoil and handmaid of communal lust is expressed the infinite degradation in which man exists for himself, for the secret of this approach has its *unambiguous, decisive, plain* and undisguised expression in the relation of *man* to *woman.* In this *natural* species relationship man's relation to nature is immediately his relation to man, just as his relation to man is immediately his relation to nature—his own *natural* destination. In this relationship, therefore, is *sensuously manifested,* reduced to an observable *fact,* the extent to which the human essence has become nature to man, or to which nature to him has become the human essence of man. From this relationship one can therefore judge man's whole level of development. From the character of this relationship follows how much *man* as a *species being,* as *man,* has come to be himself and to comprehend himself; the relation of man to woman is *the most natural* relation of human being to human being. It therefore reveals the extent to which man's *natural* behavior has become *human,* or the extent to which the *human* essence in him has become a *natural* essence—the extent to which his *human nature* has come to be *nature to him. (EPM* 134)

There is much to notice in this long passage. First of all, even by Marx's standards, there are a great number of italicized words. They all but leap from the page. Most of them have to do with nature, men, women, and the assertion of directness (*unmittelbar*) and denial of ambiguity (*unzweideutigen*). Another striking feature is the pendulum-like effect of these long, complex sentences which turn back upon themselves, or even turn themselves inside out (a Möbius strip would probably be a better visualization than a ticking pendulum). The hinge on which they turn is the recurrent *inwieweit* (meaning "how far," "in what way," or, as Milligan translates, "to the extent that"). This is the textual mechanism that allows the series of analogies to flow smoothly along. But, as Derrida and others have certainly shown us, such parts of the textual machine rarely stay well lubricated.

Marx's *inwieweit* would seem to qualify as an example of what Derrida has described as *la brisure* (hinge), a word that performs the mutually contradictory function of "breaking" and "joining."[34] In this case, it either establishes the connections Marx is making between "nature" and human essence, or it breaks those connections. Or, more profoundly, it does both, sublating all seeming oppositions. Derrida's textual strategies have heightened our awareness of the way that the act of reading continually turns up such distractions, like the child in the midst of a carousel ride whose attention wanders to its creaking mechanism.

What Marx's textual language is called upon to do is to establish the appropriateness of a whole series of analogies between "man's" relation to nature and human social relations. At the heart of this argument is the claim that the relationship of a man to a woman is *the most natural (das natürlichste)* one of all, i.e., the one that needs the least explanation. Marx presents it as an unmediated (*unmittelbare*) relationship. But isn't it odd for the marxist language of relations and mediation to insist on lack of complexity and ambiguity here, when elsewhere throughout Marx's writings such terminology as *Verhältnis* and *Vermittlung* has been celebrated for its multivalenced complexity? This, after all, is one of the central points made by Bertell Ollman in his book on the marxist concept of alienation. He explains that Marx had a genius for exploiting the elasticity of German nouns, often compound words such as Marx's own coinages (a similar argument can be made, and, to an extent, is made elsewhere in this book, for both Nietzsche and Freud).[35]

Usually in his writings Marx is at pains to demonstrate the complex mediations that attend social relations. But here, as with so many examples of even the best male writers, he departs from the standards of his own discourse for some "straight talk" ("the relation of man to woman is *the most natural* relation of human being to human being"—Marx as Percy Sledge, "When a man loves a woman . . ."?) about women.

And it is indeed *straight* talk. Jeffrey Weeks, in many books and articles, explores the potential of historical materialism for a theory of alternative human sexualities. While he asserts that marxism is the theoretical tradition most geared toward hope for eventual change in human sexual arrangements, he finds that twentieth-century attempts to synthesize marxism and psychoanalysis have produced little of value from the perspective of gay liberation. Psychoanalysis per se (e.g., Freud's early essays on sexuality and "perversions") might imply such potential for liberation, but the "Freudo-marxist" who devoted more attention than any other to human sexuality, Wilhelm

Reich, settled for a crudely heterosexual orgasm theory.[36] We might agree
that Reich was certainly no match intellectually for Marx, but was he perhaps Marx's equal on the subject of what Marx's *EPM* could not (using
Macherey's sense of ideology in texts) address, i.e., homosexuality? In *The
German Ideology,* Marx and Engels explain division of labor as originating
"in the sexual act."[37] What they were doing, as so often with writers who
assume heterosexuality, was to equate it with what is "natural," what does
not need to be explained. On this point, at least, it is difficult to imagine how
marxism could save psychoanalysis from its more reactionary tendencies.

In Marx's many writings, the *Natur* we find invoked so often in the long
passage quoted above is that which human begins transform, much like the
"raw" material that culture "cooks" according to the theories of Lévi-
Strauss. Marx's uncritical acceptance of but one approach to human sexuality causes him to locate that dimension of human experience in *nature,*
which would also mean that it would be unaffected by the coming of socialism. Similarly, socialism might reverse the relentless drive toward division of
labor in capitalist society, but fundamental human division of labor signified
by heterosexual coitus would presumably survive. Clearly even marxism
must set limits to what in nature can be transformed by human agency in
history, but to set the limits to include sexual preference is to resist the most
radically historicizing tendencies of marxism itself. We will see in Chapter 5
some examples of how Freud built similar kinds of contradictions into the
psychoanalytic tradition.

By making exceptions to his general rule that human beings manifest
Gattungswesen or species being through their appropriation of the whole of
nature, Marx collapses the two categories (*Gattungswesen* and *Gattungs-
leben*) together, subsuming both under "nature," thus providing a stunning
example of the textual deconstruction of a strongly asserted binary opposition. This occurs not purely through the isolated and rarefied procedures of
textuality, but also through the historically specific (to Marx's time) forms of
what Luce Irigaray has called the "blind spot of an old dream of symmetry"[38]
between men and women. This, to adopt Edward Said's sense of "text" and
"world," is how the "world" manifests itself in texts.[39] The text does not
merely reflect its sociotemporal ideology; the text is "decentered," in Ma-
chereyan terms, by what it cannot, by (ideological, specifically patriarchal)
definition, examine.

Throughout his life Marx would continue to return to his themes of the
many forms of division afflicting human beings under capitalism. In the first

volume of *Capital,* he writes of forms of division of labor that arise "naturally" in the (not only bourgeois) family.[40] This is akin to his assertion of the
"natural" human division of labor in (hetero-)sexual intercourse, although it
is clear, since "the family" is not a historical constant, that the coital division
is more fundamental to Marx. By retaining a sense in which at least some
forms of division of labor are fundamental to human experience, or at least
likely to weather a great many historical storms, Marx reduces the force of
what otherwise appears to be a fierce indictment of a mode of production
that fragments human beings through multiple processes of divestiture
(*Entäusserung*) and estrangement (*Entfremdung,* frequently translated as
"alienation"). Like the visionary politics of William Blake, who lamented
the "fall into division" of his contemporaries, Marx's outrage over these processes of fragmentation stems from a romantic idealism that does not, whatever Althusser may have argued, completely disappear in his later writings.

Much of the last few pages has been devoted to showing how Marx's text,
when it approaches the topic of human sexuality, departs from the conventional sense of some of his fundamental terms, and deconstructs some of
"marxism's" most basic opposing categories. The final section of the *EPM*
we want to examine closely is one that contains some of the most memorably
vivid assertions of the kind of life capitalism prevents human beings from
living. It is the section called *Privateigentum und Bedürfnisse* (literally, "Private Property and Needs," translated by Milligan as "The Meaning of Human Requirements" [*MEGA* 418–34; *EPM* 147–64]). It is a rich and richly
contradictory portion of a text famous for its complexities and contradictions. Continuing his twin themes of species life and species being, Marx
deplores the tendency of labor under capitalism to reduce human beings to
the level of mere animal existence (sleeping, eating, copulating, etc.), while
at other points he sees capitalism as having alienated *man* even from these
satisfying animal activities, which now must first be purchased with the
worker's "means of life."

Elements of both senses of Marx's indictment are relevant to the critique
under way here. Geras would find support for his defense of a marxist concept of human nature in Marx's treatment of human *Bedürfnisse* ("needs" or
"requirements"). Here is the particular passage:

> Je weniger du isst, trinkst, Bücher kaufst, in das Theater, auf den Ball, zum
> Wikrtshaus gehst, denkst, liebst, theorisiert, singst, malst, fichtest etc., um so
> [mehr] *sparst* du, um so *grösser* wird dein Schatz, den weder Motten noch Staub

fressen, dein *Capital*. Je weniger du *bist,* je weniger dein Leben äusserst, um so mehr *hast* du, um so *grösser* ist dein entäussertes Leben, um so mehr speicherst du auf von deinem entfremdeten Wesen. (*MEGA* 421)

The less you eat, drink and buy books; the less you go to the theater, the dance hall, the public house; the less you think, love, theorize, sing, paint, fence, etc., the more you *save*—the *greater* becomes your treasure which neither moths nor dust will devour—your *capital*. The less you *are,* the less you express your own life, the greater is your *alienated* life, the more you *have,* the greater is the store of your estranged being. (*EPM* 150)

This is one of the most passionate moments in Marx's writings, suggesting his vision of the good life that capitalism prevents for all but the few, and that presumably will be restored to all with the coming of socialism. It is a passage that ought to give pause to Baudrillard or others who charge Marx with elevating production above all other activities. Marx here seems to be saying that human beings need to do all these kinds of things and more, but that their access to them can come only through alienating labor and the abstraction of money, which he describes later in the *EPM* as "der *Kuppler* zwischen dem Bedürfnis und dem Gegenstand" ("the *pimp* between man's need and the object") (*MEGA* 435; *EPM* 165). Thus, it is in the *nature* of human beings to want to enjoy the "finer things" of life: attending plays and concerts, singing, "theorizing," creating art, and certainly delighting the palate with something better than "scabby" potatoes (*der Lumperkartoffel*) (*MEGA* 420; *EPM* 149). Wage laborers under capitalism are made progressively more oblivious of the wider horizons within which human life may be lived. The climatological changes that determined the cycle of agricultural work matter less and less in the factory age, and even less in the late-twentieth-century civilization Henry Miller called the "air-conditioned nightmare." These lines from "The Man Whose Pharynx Was Bad," by Wallace Stevens, might apply:

Mildew of summer and the deepening snow
Are both alike in the routine I know.
I am too dumbly in my being pent.[41]

Whether or not Marx's emphasis on "needs" implies an idealized or utopian view of human nature, knowledge of history certainly ought to remind us that access to higher cultural pursuits was limited in his day largely to men. After all, in the very Paris in which Marx was writing during the waning years of the July Monarchy (1830–48), George Sand was accustomed to disguising herself as a man in order to attend the opera, where women were excluded from the audience. With that in mind, let us look at the above passage again, this time in relation to the other sections of the *EPM* in which we have experienced the chaos and contradiction of Marx's brief but revealing considerations of gender and sexuality.

Marx here celebrates a rich and vibrant public life of theaters, bookstores, and cafés. But, in mid-nineteenth-century Paris as in so many other locales and historical settings, these public spaces were dominated by men. Sometimes, as in the case of the opera house and certainly in drinking establishments, they were exclusively male preserves. Women were not thought capable of "theorizing," and, if they "painted," they were unlikely to be able to hang their canvases in galleries or exhibition halls (*der Maler,* German for "painter," is, of course, a masculine noun).[42] Marx describes the pleasures of realizing a variety of human capabilities through full participation in a fully developed civilization. But, if elsewhere in the *EPM* and in other texts he has located "woman" in nature, or viewed nature as that which is at the disposal of *der Mensch,* what evidence is there that he envisions equal participation of women and men in the civilizing activities he catalogues? To argue either that Marx's *Mensch* implies more than the masculine gender or that he imagines a socialist future with women participating equally with men in the glories of civilization (and enjoying men's contributions to traditionally feminine household chores)[43] is to read Marx through the lens of the most hopeful marxist feminism. A socialist feminism able to admit the shortcomings of marxism for gender issues while taking historical materialism as its point of departure seems a far more sensible position.

By denying workers access to the higher pleasures of civilization, capitalism reduces them, in a very real sense, to the status of women. Isn't this the unexpressed (all the more conspicious as a result) part of Marx's complaint? Capitalism is a horror for Marx because it robs (male) workers of their manly dignity and self-worth. (As the narrator of John Sayles's 1987 film *Matewan* puts it, "They didn't care no more for a man than they done for a draft mule.")[44] It is a horror furthermore because it makes men *women,* reducing them to the crudest level of bodily experience and relegating potentially more fully realized subjects to the narrowly circumscribed range of experiences assumed to be the destiny of females.

V.   MARXISM, POSTMODERNISM, AND THE SUBJECT

Whether presented as ideal or actual, the human subject that persists in the pages of Marx's writings invariably turns out to be male. Much like the Cartesian cogitating subject on whose behalf inordinate claims are made, the individual masculine subject is universalized in Marx's text. Contemporary uses of Marx (and Freud or Nietzsche) may help to formulate an interrogation of the autonomous subject, but Marx's own texts certainly do not dispense with this subject. Moreover, through what they *fail* to say about gender perhaps even more than through what they *do* say, Marx's texts have little to offer a contemporary socialist feminism, including one concerned with the problematic of the subject.

Perhaps that is why some feminist theorists (and gay theorists like Jeffrey Weeks) have begun to engage the work of Michel Foucault. Prior to the appearance in 1988 of the collection *Foucault & Feminism: Reflections on Resistance,* edited by Irene Diamond and Lee Quinby, there had been several attempts to examine Foucault in light of marxist theory (and vice versa), with attempts even to see Foucault as a kind of Marx for a postmodern "mode of information"[45] or, despite Foucault's own disclaimers, as exhibiting a kind of (Harold) Bloomian "anxiety of influence" where Marx is concerned. As Frank Lentricchia put it, "Marx never existed, and Foucault is his only son."[46] Foucault's concern with the history of the subject—with how we have come to regard ourselves as subjects and have been subjected to discourses of power/knowledge that produce, investigate, and police the subject—and his attendant metaphor of a subject invested with the knowledge/power relations that work on it through a kind of capillary action to produce it as a subject in discourse, constitute a much more radical critique of the autonomous subject than one finds in Marx. Foucault's tradition is, of course, Nietzschean rather than marxist. By contrast, Marx, with his retention of such patriarchal epistemological assumptions as the paired concepts of private/public, feminine/masculine, and nature/culture, is practically a Cartesian idealist. Marx is, nevertheless, sometimes celebrated as a kind of poststructuralist *avant la lettre*[47] for his neo-Hegelian sublations of various paired bourgeois conceptual categories. But Foucault, with his poststructuralist neo-Nietzschean Heideggerianism (!), engages in a more sweepingly radical dismantling of Western epistemology. Biddy Martin, in her influential essay "Feminism, Criticism, and Foucault" does not hesitate to call Foucault's procedures "deconstructive."[48]

Postmodern thought generally—and this is both the threat and the prom-

ise of it for feminism—has produced a thoroughgoing critique of the subject, and postmodern critics often reserve their strongest admiration for art
(paintings of Francis Bacon, fiction of Georges Bataille, William Burroughs, Kathy Acker) and performance (Laurie Anderson, Karen Finley,
Butōh) that seem to enact rites of dismemberment, schizophrenia, fragmentation. Foucault's postmodern politics, shared with Gilles Deleuze, Félix
Guattari, and Jean-François Lyotard, of the subject and its strategies of resistance to the processes that would constitute it as such would appear to have
little in common with Marx's concerns in the *EPM*, among other of his
writings. The very concept of alienation, one supposes, would be an embarrassment to Foucault and those influenced by him. As Terry Eagleton
writes,

> The depthless, styleless, dehistoricized, decathected surfaces of postmodernist
> culture are not meant to signify an alienation, for the very concept of alienation
> must secretly posit a dream of authenticity which postmodernism finds quite
> unintelligible.[49]

Eagleton's prose is characteristically hyperbolic, however much on tar-
get. What happens when, in spite of themselves and whatever the validity of
the contrast (for the sake of argument) between some kind of absolute "modernism" and some kind of absolute "postmodernism," we try to fit Marx and
Foucault together on the theme of the subject? Elsewhere I have written
about the complementarity that can result, as Foucault's perspective of space
(grids, networks, fields) is added to the Hegelian-marxist temporal dimension.[50] Here I wish to carry that speculation further in the direction of feminism, something arguably implied more by Foucault than by Marx, but still
not by very much.

Let us start by returning to that aspect of alienation Marx calls *En-
täussserung,* i.e., "divestiture," by which he suggests fragmentation and a
stripping away from the worker of fundamental human qualities and capabilities, leaving only the portion that can serve as grist for the industrial
mill.[51] What has been stripped away from the worker clothes the commodity
in its aura, for Marx sees the commodity as the place where the worker's
alienated life (*das entäussertes Leben* [*MEGA* 421]) comes to reside. For postmodern capitalist culture, this idea has been superseded by the critique of
spectacular society, and, more convincingly, by feminist analyses of the de-
plorable effects of the proliferation within media culture of objectified images of women, i.e., "woman" as postmodern signifier par excellence. Lu-

kács's great essay on reification[52] is thus revised, in ratios unanticipated by Harold Bloom, by feminist theorists who, especially in France, work within what Martin Jay has described as a critique of ocularcentrism, part of an antivisual discourse taken over from Bataille, Sartre, Merleau-Ponty, Lacan, and Foucault.[53] A familiar illustration of the senses of *Entäusserung* just surveyed can be found in the unwillingness of persons to be photographed by anthropologists for fear that the camera might peel away the outer layers of their essence.

In Foucault's work, particularly after the publication of *Surveiller et punir* (1975), nothing is figuratively peeled away from human exteriors. Instead, discursively circulating *pouvoir-savoir* (power/knowledge) penetrates the interiors of bodies, investing them with complex micropowers that effectively dissolve the human subject within interlocking grids only occasionally interspersed with gaps and potential spaces of resistance.[54] If we attempt to imagine the social field from marxist and Foucauldian perspectives simultaneously, two contradictory (or are they complementary?) social dynamics can be envisioned: in marxist theory the motion is centrifugal, moving away from the human subject as alienated center in a socio-economic landscape, while with Foucault an opposite centripetal motion circulating toward bodies crisscrosses the divested portions fleeing their original sites toward some vanishing point of *Entäusserung*.

Diehard poststructuralists may complain that such theorizing throws a marxist monkey wrench into an already complicated Foucauldian interpretive apparatus that needs no historical materialist assistance. I think instead that the combination of what we usually regard as "modernist" (Marx) with "postmodernist" (Foucault) theory, especially as the latter is pushed in an explicitly feminist direction, helps to correct the tendencies of marxist theory (however persuasive Michael Ryan may be about its latent deconstructive potential) to reintroduce a kind of binary logic or dialectic of individual/society, inside/outside, etc. Think for a minute what this might mean in terms of the inability of marxism to escape the public/private dichotomies that provide the focus of much recent feminist social theory.

If we bring to these perspectives an understanding of the feminist conceptualizations of bodily experience and what Rosalind Coward sees as the social process whereby feminine desires are manufactured,[55] we expand our understanding of the ways in which the ideological effects of emphasis on the subject are deployed, always propelled along by what Jeffrey Weeks, along with such social historians as Edward Shorter and Lawrence Stone, investigates as the relatively recent cultural habit of equating identity, or what Lawrence Stone calls "affective individualism,"[56] with personal sexuality.[57] If we can demonstrate that the subject has been historically constructed in the West as a male bourgeois subject, then marxists and feminists alike stand to gain from its "deconstruction." This cannot simply be a process of containing feminism within a marxism-as-usual that can speak no other language than that of class oppression. As even a feminist strongly sympathetic to marxism has written in language that shows the influence of Gayle Rubin's work,

> Without us [women], and without a frontal attack on the sex-gender systems that "produce" us as women in capitalism, socialist movements to revolutionize the capitalist economy and state really are bound to fail.[58]

To speak of "producing" subjects is to sound a Foucauldian note, for Foucault's late work on the "technologies of the self"[59] extends the industrial metaphor further. Foucault's critique of the subject is more radical and thorough than Marx's, whether or not this makes Foucault a "Marx" for the postmodern age where the subject is proclaimed through spectacular representations even as actual subjects are fragmented into what Gilles Deleuze and Félix Guattari have called "desiring machines."[60] Women have certainly been invaded bodily, and the current hysteria over the legal status of *hysteros*—the womb—which often features a tendency to speak of the uterus as if it is a piece of real estate that just happens to be located in the neighborhood that is the mother's body is an example, as rape most certainly is. But whether feminism should embrace the poststructualist proclamation of the death (or is it only deconstruction?) of the subject, because that subject has been defined as the denial of the feminine other, is quite another matter. At a time when actual women are bravely claiming subjective status for themselves, it is a troubling prospect.

Recent feminist theory has been able to demonstrate contradictory aspects of this concern with women's identity. With very different theoretical agendas, both the object-relations school of feminist psychoanalysis[61] and French feminists such as Julia Kristeva and Luce Irigaray have explored the role played by the mother/daughter relation in the construction of female subjects and feminine desires. The relation to the mother, the cornerstone of the social construction of gender for women, blurs the very boundaries that we imagine for individual identity. The complaint of Luce Irigaray in *Et l'une ne bouge pas sans l'autre,* that she cannot establish herself as daughter as a being truly separate from her mother (*Je suis une autre toi vivante*),[62] is a troubling notion within the broad range of the ongoing feminist discussion of the possibilities open to women.

The much-vaunted demise of the subject is also difficult to reconcile politically with a reclaiming of the status of subject that is in part a rediscovery of the latent possibilities of the marxist concept of alienation and in part, more significantly, a feminist dialectic transformation—what Marx (following Hegel) called *Aufhebung*—of the human subject of the traditional marxist imagination. A contemporary socialist feminist project, synthesizing Foucault, psychoanalysis, or whatever else works, could thus be a way of making Marx live up to some of his own claims for the "partially developed individual" who "must be replaced by the fully developed individual,"[63] ensuring that this full development transcends what is gender-specific.

Earlier, I made the claim that Foucault offers a more truly radical critique of the concept of the subject than does Marx (and we have I hope demonstrated that this was not simply a temporary defect of the philosophy of the "young Marx"). Foucault is but one of many postmodern sages who assail this hallowed humanist category. But *is* the postmodern rejection of the subject as monolithic and uncompromising as is routinely suggested? I think not, and no matter how much I enjoy the wit and intelligence of Terry Eagleton's writing, this is why I find his language, quoted above, about the postmodern erosion of the very grounds of possibility for a concept of alienation unfortunately hyperbolic.

Closer reading of the maverick theoretical explorations of Gilles Deleuze and Félix Guattari (a project far too demanding to permit extensive inclusion here) will reveal other possibilities. Guattari especially, the more politically activist of the two, welcomes a newly conceived theory of subjectivity,[64] and together they offer their at first baffling "body without organs,"[65] not simply as an antipsychiatric (pro-schizophrenic) rejection of ego psychology, but also as a metaphorical newly constituted basis for a postmodern politics of the subject that can uncover strategies of resistance, their *lignes de fuite* (lines of flight),[66] or the *sorties* (ways out) sought by French feminist theory. As I read them, even as they proclaim their break with marxism, their work does not preclude a recuperation of the marxist concept of alienation. I called the "body without organs" "metaphorical," for I view this concept in the same way I view Luce Irigaray's lyrical, seemingly hypostasized female body. These French writers engage, with their writing, in a radical cultural politics in which their oppositional images are assumed by many of their critics to be equally as fetishized as the culturally sanctioned icons they would shatter. Unfortunately, the "body without organs" and the *femme* of

French feminist theory are often read on these shores as new cultural absolutes, rather than as often playfully suggestive alternatives. This point is missed by cultural critics who think they sniff "essentialisms" in the making.

Rereading along gender lines is an activity analogous to the post-Lacanian rereadings of Freud (e.g., Juliet Mitchell, Jacqueline Rose, Jane Gallop) that combine criticism of the patriarchal cast of Freud's thought with reappropriation of elements that can advance feminist theory. I believe that marxist (socialist) feminism or feminist marxism casts a wide enough net to enclose most current critical theory, certainly including Foucault. Feminist theorists such as Joan Kelly, Gayle Rubin, and Heidi Hartmann have vastly improved upon historical materialism's ability to consider what relationships, if any, obtain between processes of class domination and sex/gender oppression. Contemporary socialist feminism is a better historical materialism for postmodern culture (and will I hope produce a careful critique of all marxist texts), for its energies fuel a thoroughgoing critique of the exclusionary violence of binary logic. This is a project that a "purely" marxist theory has been unable to sustain.

Modernism, Postmodernism, and Writing: Style(s) and Sexuality in *Madame Bovary*

Flaubert . . . en maniant une ironie frappée d'incertitude, opère un malaise salutaire de l'écriture: il n'arrête pas le jeu des codes (ou l'arrête mal), en sorte que . . . *on ne sait jamais s'il est responsable de ce qu'il écrit* (S'il y a un sujet *derrière* son langage); car l'être de l'écriture (le sens du travail qui la constitue) est d'empêcher de jamais répondre à cette question: *Qui parle?*

—Roland Barthes, *S/Z* (1970)

The awareness of the problematic nature of representation has been partly inspired by the practice of certain writers, among them Flaubert, but it also generates new readings of those writers, "creates" a new Flaubert. Text and theory are recognized as interchangeable; each can be seen as generating and determining the other.

—Michal Peled Ginsburg, *Flaubert Writing: A Study in Narrative Strategies* (1986)

We can no longer read *Madame Bovary* outside of the "sexual problematic" that Sartre analyzed in its author, but we must no longer separate the sexual problematic from the scriptural problematic, as did Baudelaire, who was the first to qualify Emma Bovary as a "strange androgynous creature."

—Naomi Schor, "For a Restricted Thematics: Writing, Speech, and Difference in *Madame Bovary*" (1985)

And once again Kugelmass entered the cabinet and passed instantly to the Bovary estate at Yonville. "How you doing, cupcake?" he said to Emma.

—Woody Allen, "The Kugelmass Episode" (1980)

Tell me mama, who's that 'while ago?
When I come in, who went out that back do'?

—Little Walter, "Tell Me Mama"

1.   "THE NOVEL OF ALL NOVELS"

Contemporary Flaubert criticism, through which currents of feminist, Lacanian, and deconstructionist theory flow and circulate, demonstrates abundantly the complexities and contradictions of character, narrative, style, and representation in *Madame Bovary*. Theory today teaches us to doubt the seeming unity and stability of the (narrating or represented) subject, to question binary categories like masculine/feminine, and of course to dispense with time-honored notions of the distinctive character of "literature" as a dimension of culture opposed to mass or popular culture (held by traditional criticism to be inherently inferior, "literature" necessarily requiring taste and discriminating judgment).

Even if we could accept Gustave Flaubert's celebrated *Madame Bovary c'est moi* at face value, such a claim would continue to multiply rather than to reduce our interpretive labors. Even if we somehow came to agree that *Madame Bovary* is a book "about" a character named Emma Bovary, we would still be vexed with the questions urgently posed by contemporary feminist theory that would shake our confidence in our ability to define the essence of this character, the degree to which she embodies the "feminine," or even the position she occupies with regard to Flaubertian narrative.

Why have these interpretive difficulties multiplied? I believe that a careful examination of articles and books on *Madame Bovary* or Flaubert's writing in general published within the past ten years or so reveals this to be a case study in postmodern cultural theory, with all that ambiguous label might imply. The fact, for example, that a 1980 conference and a book published as a result of that conference in 1984 could bear the title *Flaubert and Postmodernism*[1] poses a challenge to traditional practitioners of literary history and intellectual history for whom *Madame Bovary* has been a founding text of literary modernism and, in the famous phrase (1921) of Percy Lubbock, "the novel of all novels which the criticism of fiction cannot overlook."[2] In his contribution to the above-mentioned *Flaubert and Postmodernism*, Jonathan Culler demonstrated convincingly[3] that the novel's reputation relies heavily upon the traditional conviction, articulated most memorably by Lubbock, that it is, fundamentally, the story "of a foolish and limited little woman."[4] Culler furthermore shows how the persuasive power of Lubbock's argument depends on widespread unthinking acceptance of sexist stereotypes, i.e., how could Emma be otherwise? With this is mind, I hope to explain how closely considerations of postmodernism and literary style are linked to

questions of gender and sexuality; questions which lead to daring new formulations and political possibilities precluded by a traditional literary history wedded so closely to the canon whose membership, most certainly,
includes *Madame Bovary*. Allan Bloom, whose *The Closing of the American
Mind* includes the critical reputation enjoyed by *Madame Bovary* among the
causes of what he sees as our current educational malaise, bitterly resents the
contemporary pop culture context within which students must carry out
readings of literary masterworks.[5] I want to argue, in strong opposition to
Bloom,[6] that it is precisely this postmodern cultural climate that expands the
range of readings we can give such a text as *Madame Bovary,* taking us beyond the familiar observations: that it is the first "great" modern novel; that
Flaubert realized his objective of writing a book "about nothing," anticipat-
ing Mallarmé, Proust, and other French devotees of the high modern cult of
art; that, along with *Bouvard et Pécuchet* or the *Dictionnaire des idées reçues,
Madame Bovary* ruthlessly dissects bourgeois stupidity and banality (*la
bêtise*); that it introduces the first modern "antihero" in Emma Bovary;[7] that
it achieves true novelistic formal perfection and closure.

First, it will be necessary for me to clarify my use of terms like "modernism" and "postmodernism," keeping in mind that it often makes more sense
to regard postmodernism as an intensification (or something close to Hegelian *Aufhebung* or sublation) of modernism, than as its negation or antithe-
sis. Meanwhile, to supply the other sense of *Aufhebung,* it is possible to
emphasize aspects of postmodernism that seem to negate modernism or to
reinvoke elements of premodern culture. Dominick LaCapra and Arthur
Mitzman are cultural historians who have pursued this idea in relation to the
Bakhtinian "carnivalesque" character of Flaubert's writing.[8] LaCapra has
also demonstrated, through his use of critical strategies derived from Derrida and other postmodern theorists, the complexities of an approach to
Madame Bovary that would situate it historically through reference to its
author and the specific historical period (1852–70) of the French Second
Empire.

Unlike Jonathan Culler, whose *Flaubert: The Uses of Uncertainty* ranges
widely across all of Flaubert's novels, and with whom he shares much in his
critical approach, LaCapra focuses exclusively on *Madame Bovary.* Appropriately for an intellectual historian who has worked assiduously to dismantle
needless distinctions among such objects of critical historical interpretation
as "text," "document," and "souce," the "text" against which LaCapra reads
Madame Bovary is the 1857 trial to which Flaubert and his publisher were subjected. Highlighting the circumstances of the trial itself is not all that remark-

able or unprecedented, yet LaCapra makes the reader realize how seldom
critical pronouncements about literary modernism and Flaubert in particular have included consideration of such events, events which, moreover,
show how what we came to know as "literature" emerges out of a socially
(and in this case, legally) contested concatenation of events and forces. Indeed, critics like LaCapra (who refines his own approach in *History, Politics,
and the Novel*)[9] are helping to write the long-overdue history of literary modernism, a history that does not succumb to the mystification and reification
of a sacrosanct "literature." LaCapra argues his case with obvious relevance
for the efforts to define and redefine modernism and postmodernism:

> Flaubert became a patron saint of "modernists." But the modernist myth of a
> total rupture with tradition finds relatively little in his work to sustain it. The goal
> of a "postmodern" reading of Flaubert may be precisely to undo the deadly dichot-
> omy between tradition and its critique and, in the process, to reopen the question
> of the relation between continuity and discontinuity over time.[10]

However much our definitions of the terms may be in flux, I nevertheless
find convincing Fredric Jameson's distinction between an aesthetic modernism corresponding to the industrial phase of modern capitalism and an aesthetic postmodernism (or a postmodern aesthetic) accompanying the advanced stage of consumer capitalism in the age of the multinationals. Once
again, these correspondences must not be read as marks of rupture between
two historical stages. If it becomes common practice to see "modern" and
"postmodern" as two related phases of "modernity," so much the better.

Some of the observations often made about literary modernism are ech-
oed in much that is noted about the postmodern literary scene, descriptions
of the latter frequently surfacing as exaggeration or intensification of the
former. Flaubert, for example, is one author who has frequently been seen as
a typical modernist figure, one who operated within a distinctive literary
field,[11] with "literature" already existing in his lifetime (1821–80) as a highly
codified set of cultural practices. Especially with regard to literature, "modernism," then, would convey some of the following tendencies: a highly
specialized sense of authorship and a strict compartmentalization, even
reification, of "Literature"; in fiction, psychologically and sociologically detailed depiction of principal characters seen usually in sharp relief against so-
called "society"; a very strong emphasis on the labors of literary creation
(Flaubert providing an extreme example), and an increasing tendency down
through the modern era for literature to be "about" its own possibility or

impossibility, so that modern authors tend to be those who foreground the "literariness" of their writing, the formal challenges they face, and their attempts to surmount them.

Briefly to demonstrate how literary postmodernism might constitute an intensification of these characteristics, let us take the example of Samuel Beckett, whose name regularly appears in provisionally canonical lists of postmodern authors. As long as he remains pigeonholed in our minds with, say, William Burroughs, Thomas Pynchon, or Jorge Luis Borges, it might be possible to lose sight of what he as an author shares with such modernist precursors as Flaubert or Proust (both of whom he certainly acknowledged, and he was not a writer given to name-dropping). True, his characters would not appear to be as vivid as an Emma Bovary, but, as I hope to show, her clarity and autonomy have been greatly exaggerated (and, of course, one of the wonders of Beckett's work is that his characters are all the more compelling as they are more grotesquely reduced in circumstances). Beckett certainly typifies the other tendencies I've cited, particularly in the way his fiction is so preoccupied with its own formal possibilities and seeming impasses. Thus, if Beckett is postmodern and Flaubert is modern, then the postmodern is but a stepped-up phase of the modern, or, put another way, Flaubert was "already" postmodern by the criteria we've chosen to apply. Following this logic, some theorists opt for the term "modernity" to encompass both phases, if that is what they are. Better perhaps to call them sets of characteristics, or even "symptoms."

Flaubert's writerly perfectionism, as his correspondence attests, is the stuff of legend in the annals of modernity. The postmodern experience of writing, so closely wedded to word processing and the visual display of texts on computer monitors, along with similar kinds of video and audio technologies that permit information storage, playback, editing, and erasure, offers us unprecedented and perhaps unavoidable perspectives for reading Flaubert's texts. Like a director repeatedly setting up a shot until satisfied with the take, Flaubert is often described as reworking the same sentence again and again,[12] so that one can easily imagine how convenient he would have found electronic word processing. Artists who work with audio or videotape enjoy a wealth of creative possibilities afforded by strategies of rewinding, fast forwarding, tape delay, tape editing, etc. Beckett's character Krapp, if not Richard Nixon with his "Watergate" tapes, easily comes to mind as an embodiment of this brave new electronic world.[13]

Elizabeth Wilson has suggested that "rewinding the video" is the quintessential postmodern procedure, and her essay with that title darkly implies the as yet unpredictable ways that technological capability will haunt our aesthetic or creative imaginations.[14] Postmodern art of all kinds features abundant use of video. The avant-garde "sculptor" Nam June Paik inserts video screens into a wide range of works, or to use the increasingly common terms for art that blurs distinctions between sculpture and painting (among many other distinctions), "installations." "Performance" has become a shorthand term for postmodern manifestations that may include elements of drama, music, dance, recitation, and much more, so that the term implies a kind of "dynamic" installation in which people participate, and thus in which "something happens." Just as postmodern art has introduced the concept of a performance "space," so has postmodern critical theory encouraged the notion of a text like *Madame Bovary* as a "space" in which somewhat unpredictable acts of reading transpire.

One of the best-known "performance" ensembles, The Wooster Group (founded by Elizabeth LeCompte and Spalding Gray), recently invoked Flaubert in a work very loosely based on his *Temptation of Saint Anthony.* In September and October of 1989, The Wooster Group, under Elizabeth LeCompte's direction, performed "The Road to Immortality: Part Three of Frank Dell's 'The Temptation of Saint Anthony' at The Performing Garage on Wooster Street in Soho, New York City. The piece was notable, among other things, for its use of actors on videotape interspersed with and interacting with live actors on stage. In most cases these were the same actors, and on videotape they were nude, suggesting the hallucinations that tempted the desert hermit Saint Anthony. Most important (for the "postmodern" aesthetics of Flaubert), scene after scene was replayed, with the lead actor directing that videotapes be rewound. As the repetitions accumulated, the live actors delivered their lines at an increasing pitch of intensity. And, as the pace became almost unbearable, from the audience it looked as though subtle but important modifications occurred in the videotaped scenes, but this was difficult to determine. As a result, one was both annoyed by the abundant repetition and curious to study the tape once again, like the character in Julio Cortázar's (and Michelangelo Antonioni's) "Blow-Up," who is sure that further clues will emerge with the reproduction of the next print.[15]

The Wooster Group's performance, then, moved far afield from Flaubert's text. And yet they were in many ways closest to Flaubert's aesthetic at the very point at which they seemed most ensnared in the complexities of postmodern technology. With his many "takes" and "retakes" of scenes in his novels (the correspondence, as many critics have noted, showing us alternative scenes, eventually scrapped, in *Madame Bovary* and other novels), and with his indeterminate "free indirect style" that multiplies perspectives and points of view, Flaubert's always seems to be on the verge of reediting. Whose point of view are we getting in this scene? That of Emma, Charles, Rodolphe, the Yonvilleans? Why is our attention directed to this or that physical detail (e.g., the dead flies in the dregs of a glass of cider)? Who sees it? Who is meant to see it? "Rewinding the video," indeed.

The point of encouraging a videomatic or cinematic sense of Flaubert's writing, and thus to invoke the central aspects of postmodern visual culture, is that we are thereby brought into contact with the debate concerning representations of the feminine. This is the heart of postmodern cultural theory, and we here confront its greatest area of political urgency. The aspects of postmodernism we have been exploring allow significant themes of style and sexuality to emerge from a critical examination of *Madame Bovary*, and, precisely because so many critics have wanted to see it as a novel that coldly dissects its "limited" and "foolish" central character, a reading that draws on recent feminist theory and criticism cannot help but assume a "postmodern" framework.

First, however, I feel a need to confess my own anxiety over my handling of this text. Intellectual historians are, typically, adept at explaining historical context and development, at tracing influences, and at historicizing the interpretive systems we bring to our reading practices. When it comes to matching wits with the literati, they (I) experience a marked sense of inferiority. However much we may believe in the interdisciplinary character of reading and of cultural study, it is damned hard to shake off the feeling that literary texts somehow "belong" to literary critics who today, of course, almost exclusively carry out their professional transactions within the academy.

In 1987 I participated in a session of the Midwest Modern Langauage Association sponsored by the Society for Critical Exchange. After I sent a preliminary draft of my paper to the panel organizer, she called to offer compliments and to say, "I'm really looking forward to the *close* (her emphasis) reading." My heart sank as I thought, "But that *was* the close reading!" Also during 1987 I sent a similar paper to a fellow historian (well-known feminist historian) whose response was that there was probably too much textual emphasis and not enough historical context. Damned if you do, damned if you don't?

Certainly those trained (I wish to invoke the full range of implications of that awful word, one certainly also used in the field of history) in literature grow tired of being lectured about historical context by intellectual historians, and intellectual historians, especially if they prefer to be "cultural critics," do not want to be told, "Read these same texts, but read them according to our procedures." Plenty of literary critics demonstrate impressive historical knowledge and insights, and many of their counterparts from intellectual history have been attracted to the interpretation of literary texts precisely by the new critical practices still unfortunately monopolized by literary academics. Boundaries between literary criticism and intellectual history (and, more broadly, between "Literature" and "History") that may once have seemed to serve some useful purpose now seem increasingly pointless. In any case, the reader of this essay will not find biographical information about Flaubert or material about the French Second Empire. Excellent studies that combine literary with historical analysis already exist. One fine example, already mentioned above, is Dominick LaCapra's *"Madame Bovary" on Trial* (1982). Whatever its merits, my strategy, as with other texts discussed in this book, will be to emphasize the situation of reading *Madame Bovary* today, to see what difference that makes and to explore added possibilities our postmodern cultural context, the very one Allan Bloom would wish away, affords in our reading.

II. PICTURES OF EMMA

We live in an overwhelmingly visual postmodern culture of spectacle and simulacra offering a specular order of representation that operates individually and culturally to create strong libidinal investments in images of women, men, and commodities, or, if you prefer, women and men *as* commodities. Working especially within a poststructuralist framework that first emerged in France (especially after 1968), contemporary feminists have extensively examined the ways in which images of women are central to this powerful and mystifying media culture. Poststructuralist fascination with textual surfaces and writing (including, in the work of Roland Barthes, a tendency to see gesture, dress, or any surface inscription as "writing"), and theorization of postmodern cultural life as an order of simulacra, come together in the writings of Jean Baudrillard. One of the many disturbing aspects of Baudrillard's work, as Jane Gallop has pointed out,[16] is his tendency to equate deceptive, artificial surfaces with woman or the feminine. Not that this is anything new in Western culture, for something very similar can also be found in Nietzsche's *The Gay Science* (see Chapter 6). The fact that French feminist theorists like Hélène Cixous, adopting many of Jacques Derrida's insights concerning logocentrism and patriarchy, appear to associate women with writing makes Baudrillard's misogyny all the more disturb-ing (and this also serves to remind us how unresolved questions of postmod-ernism's political direction are).

Despite this conundrum, some of feminism's most powerful critiques continue to be those involving the representation of women within and by a patriarchal culture. These perspectives certainly lend themselves to a study of Emma Bovary. To return briefly to Percy Lubbock's argument, if *Madame Bovary* enjoys high critical esteem in part because of its convincing portrayal of a "foolish woman," this in turn has much to do with men's willingness to accept such a stereotype. Of course, the lure of verisimilitude and the habit of accepting the central position in our culture of the autonomous subject and its representations also account for this acceptance. Flaubert's free indi-rect discourse (*le style indirect libre*) and shifting narrative perspectives make it difficult and unwise to generalize concerning the representation of Emma Bovary in the novel. Nevertheless, it is striking how many passages there are in which she is described as being viewed by principal male characters (Charles, Léon, Rodolphe), and that, while her thoughts and feelings are so often described in indirect passages that may or may not emanate from a stable aloof narrator, she is alotted many fewer passages of quoted conversa-tion than such a character as Homais, who never seems to shut up. Of course, instances of Emma's speech and interior monologue (if one can call it that) serve to undermine somewhat the uniformity of her represented image.

Using selected key passages from the novel, I would like to examine the "cinematic" effects a postmodernist sensibility helps us to locate in *Madame Bovary*. From its earliest days, cinema made use of narrative techniques de-rived from prose fiction. Recent film theory, increasingly preoccupied with fundamentally postmodern questions of representation and subjectivity, in-vites us to return to prose fiction by way of these critical questions. By "cinematic," I mean the moments in the text in which representations of Emma and other characters take place, with emphasis on light or shadow and with often multiple shifts of perspective. Such shifts suggest a crisis in representation, as the framing of shots, as it were, or the mise-en-scène jumps from Flaubert himself to the occasionally evident fictionalized narra-tor to one or another of the characters. Thus it is no accident that film theory, especially feminist film theory (in either case developed in close dia-logue with psychoanalysis), has provided the most powerful and disturbing critiques of representation.[17] Its relevance for a consideration of the problem of representation in *Madame Bovary* is inescapable. I also wish to introduce the theme of the construction of feminine desire(s) evidenced by the text, and to relate this theme to questions of representation. Gérard Genette,[18] Pierre Danger,[19] and Mieke Bal[20] have each briefly described some of the cinematic touches Flaubert's text achieves. In Bal's essay, the representation of Emma can be seen also in terms of free indirect discourse. She comments on the use of the nonspecific pronoun *on* in the ball scene at La Vaubyessard, where Emma, clad in a gown with bare shoulders, is described in a way that emphasizes, as does the scene at Les Bertaux when Charles enters the kitchen in which dead flies can be seen in the dregs of cider, the drops of sweat on her bare shoulder: "On voyait sur ses épaules nues des gouttes de sueur."[21]

Who saw? The sense of the French *on*, which, like Flaubert's ubiquitous imperfect tense, enhances the narrative indeterminacy of the novel, is that anyone who happened to be present at the scene being described could have seen this. Despite scenes in which specific masculine characters (Léon, Rodolphe, Charles, Justin) regard Emma, the ever-shifting Flaubertian point of view so complicates the reading of even so seemingly simple a passage that we begin to ask: Everyone could see (and interpret as nervousness, excessively heavy dress, etc.) Emma's sweaty shoulders? If they had looked, this is what they would have seen? People (given the imperfect tense) spent the entire evening staring at these shoulders? Flaubert/the narrator sees? The narrator wants us to see? Emma saw, or knew, without anyone else's being the wiser? Readers steeped in contemporary American media culture might well react to the description (if that is what it is) in terms of the widespread contemporary rallying cry: "Never let 'em see you sweat." But, even if the sentence could be imagined as a stage or screenplay directive, this anachronistically cinematic novel features a mise-en-scène that can only multiply and render undecidable the directionality of the gaze accompanying the representations of Emma.

Two of the novel's most memorable scenes, the *comices agricoles* and the cathedral tour and *fiacre* scene in Rouen, combine and deconstruct public and private spheres[22] in a sonic atmosphere of cacophony worthy of the films of Robert Altman. In the former scene, the dialogue between Emma and Rodolphe spirals around loud public exclamations and exhortations so that we have difficulty determining whether the lovers in fact hear this "background" commentary and whether they escape being overheard. Someone (narrator? reader?) "overhears" everything, of course, and whoever possesses that ear has the last laugh, of course: as when the salacious Rodolphe's seductive conversation is interrupted by shouts announcing the prize hogs[23] or when Léon, in lust with Emma, bolts with her from the Rouen cathedral tour with the verger's cries about the steeple ("Eh! monsieur. La flèche! la flèche!") resounding in his (our?) ears (MBF 547). Perhaps the most cinematic scene in the novel follows when the hastily hired *fiacre* takes its helter-skelter course through the streets of Rouen. The scene, in which private intimacies take place in public (or one could say that the opposition between public and private is deconstructed)[24] while remaining nevertheless concealed, unfolds for the reader courtesy of a disembodied narrative agency that could appear to occupy a position like that of a camera hovering over Rouen in a blimp. The angels in Wim Wenders' 1987 film *Wings of Desire* hover over Berlin like that, but perhaps the moment in film that best captures the ludicrousness of the scene occurs in Man Ray and René Clair's 1924 surrealist film *Entr'acte* (score by Erik Satie) in which a camel pulls a hearse around and around the Eiffel Tower (Eh! monsieur. La flèche! La flèche!).

In scenes like these, those available to look, whether characters or readers, both see and do not see Emma. The hideous figure of the blind man (*l'aveugle*) mocks the reader almost as surely as he mocks the Yonvilleans. But what about the scenes in which Emma is specifically on display to another character? There are instances of the objectifying gaze, and most of them involve the isolation if not, indeed, fetishization of parts of Emma's body. Mary Ann Caws has shown, with regard to surrealism, how central figurative dismemberment of women's bodies has been to modernist strategies of representation,[25] and the Garnier edition of *Madame Bovary* contains as frontispiece the famous Lemot caricature (*Flaubert disséquant Emma Bovary*) that depicts Flaubert as a surgeon triumphantly plucking the bleeding heart from Emma's prostrate, cadaverous body.[26] Yet these passages are isolated, have an almost hallucinatory quality, and are nearly lost in the shuffle of passages in which Emma is dissolved into both the text that Flaubert is writing and the texts of the romantic fictions that propel her through life in a world they have failed to construct.

Charles is the character whose love for Emma seems most complete and enduring. Yet he (and we) never sees her whole. Upon their first meeting, "his" gaze isolates her fingernails, fingers, hands, eyes, neck, and hair (MBF 338–39). On the first page on which Emma makes her appearance, we read:

> Charles fut surpris de la blancheur de ses ongles. Ils étaient brillants, fins du bout, plus nettoyés que les ivoires de Dieppe, et taillés en amande. Sa main pourtant n'était pas belle, point assez pâle, peut-être, et un peu sèche aux phalanges; elle était trop longue aussi et sans molles inflexions de lignes sur les con-

tours. Ce qu'elle avait de beau, c'étaient les yeux: quoiqu'ils fussent bruns, ils semblaient noirs à cause des cils, et son regard arrivait franchement à vous avec une hardiesse candide. (MBF 338–39)

Charles was surprised at the whiteness of her nails. They were shiny, delicate at the tips, more polished than the ivory of Dieppe, and almond-shaped. Yet her hand was not beautiful, perhaps not white enough, and a little hard at the knuckles; besides, it was too long, with no soft inflections at the outlines. Her real beauty was in her eyes. Although brown, they seemed black because of the lashes, and her look came at you frankly, with a candid boldness.[27]

At first glance, we appear to have a familiar example of the objectifying, fetishizing male gaze. We are reminded of Mallarmé's sonnet "Ses purs ongles très haut dédiant leur onyx"[28] (Mallarmé being a great modernist poet whose poems often feature fetishistic uses of hair, eyes, and finger-nails). But it is more than just another example of obsessional fixation on isolated parts. For, unlike the averted gaze of conventional female figures in paintings, this woman gazes back, and does so powerfully. In terms of the theory of visual experience, this is less a case of John Berger's "Men look at women . . ."[29] than it is an illustration of Sartre's observations on the aggres-sive aspects of the gaze.[30] Emma's gaze is not that of a victim *tout court*, no matter what fate Flaubert will arrange for her. She looks at Charles with *une hardiesse candide*.

Let us examine other scenes in which Emma is the object of a masculine gaze.

Upon her arrival in Yonville, the fascinated Léon, dining at the inn where her coach has stopped, feasts his eyes upon her as she warms herself in front of the fireplace:

Le feu l'éclairait en entier, pénétrant d'une lumière crue la trame de sa robe, les pores égaux de sa peau blanche et même les paupières de ses yeux qu'elle clignait de temps à autre. Une grande couleur rouge passait sur elle selon le souffle du vent qui venait par la porte entr'ouverte. (MBF 397)

The flame lit up the whole of her, casting its harsh light over the pattern of her gown, the fine pores of her fair skin, and even her eyelids, when she blinked from time to time. A great red glow passed over her with the wind, blowing through the half-open door. (MBE 56).

Where for a premodern reader this scene, in which the figure of Emma is bathed in the fire's light, might evoke the paintings of Georges de La Tour, for us this has a keenly cinematic quality (and, indeed, the thought of a director and his/her crew spending hours setting up such a shot, since interior lighting effects frequently pose major technical challenges to filmmakers, calls to mind the well-documented labors of Flaubert). The effect of Flaubert's free indirect discourse is such that we cannot be certain whether this is what Léon exclusively sees as he studies his future lover or whether this is what occurs to the *metteur en scène*, and therefore what "we" are supposed to see. Certainly Léon's Emma is at this point more specular than real. Soon after this first meeting, for example, Léon stands "kibbitzing" behind Emma's chair while she plays cards at the home of Monsieur Homais. The passages that describe what, presumably, Léon sees isolate primarily the rise and fall of the folds of Emma's dress as she plays her cards, and her dark hair flowing down behind. When Léon accidentally treads upon her skirts, he is described as recoiling as if he had stepped on "something alive"—"il s'écartait comme s'il eut marché sur quelqu'un" (MBF 414–15; MBE 70).

Rodolphe regards Emma with a far less idealized vision, yet the "cinematic" play of light persists. Flaubert describes his first glimpse of her, bending down to place a basin under the table, using similar details about her dress flowing around her, but Rodolphe, already beginning to assess her potential as another of his conquests, takes note of the tightness of the dress about her heaving bosom (MBF 442; MBE 92). But the first truly dramatic objectification of Emma for the Rodolphe episode takes place at the *comices agricoles* (agricultural fair) at which Rodolphe expertly seduces her with his conversation.

In the midst of the hubbub at the fair, Rodolphe takes a long look at Emma in profile:

> Son profil était si calme, que l'on ne devinait rien. Il se détachait en pleine lumière, dans, l'ovale de sa capote qui avait des rubans pâles ressemblant à des feuilles de roseau. Ses yeux aux longs cils courbés regardaient devant elle, et, quoique bien ouverts, ils semblaient un peu bridés par les pommettes, à cause du sang qui battait doucement sous sa peau fine. Une couleur rose traversait la cloison de son nez. Elle inclinait la tête sur l'épaule, et l'on voyait entre ses lèvres le bout nacré de ses dents blanches. (MBF 449)

> Her profile was so calm that it revealed nothing. It stood out in the light from the oval of her hat that was tied with pale ribbons like waving rushes. Her eyes with their long curved lashes looked straight before her, and though wide open, they seemed slanted at the cheek-bones, because of the blood pulsing gently un-

der the delicate skin. A rosy light shone through the partition between her nostrils. Her head was bent upon her shoulder, and the tips of her teeth shone through her lips like pearls. (MBE 97).

What (male) director could resist filming that scene? A surprisingly beatific vision for a Rodolphe, it nevertheless contains elements of a latent eroticism. (What a perfect combination for advertising! This one brief passage suggests increased sales for makers of cosmetics, mascara, and toothpaste.)

Compare this vignette with one of the strongest passages in which Emma, at the height of her affair with Rodolphe, seems to emerge bodily from the text:

> Jamais madame Bovary ne fut aussi belle qu'à cette époque . . . Ses paupières semblaient taillés tout exprès pour ses longs regards amoureux où la prunelle se perdait, tandis qu'un souffle fort écartait ses narines minces et relevait le coin charnu de ses lèvres, qu'ombrageait à la lumière un peu de duvet noir. On eut dit qu'un artiste habile en corruptions avait disposé sur sa nuque la torsade de ses cheveux: ils s'enroulaient en une masse lourde négligemment, et selon les hasards de l'adultère, qui les dénouait tous les jours. Sa voix, maintenant, prenait des inflexions plus molles, se taille aussi; quelque chose de subtil qui vous pénétrait se dégageait même des draperies de sa robe et de la cambrure de son pied. Charles, comme aux premiers temps de son mariage, la trouvait déliceuse et irrésistible. (MBF 503)

> Never had Madame Bovary been so beautiful as at this period . . . Her half-closed eyelids seemed perfectly shaped for the long languid glances that escaped from them; her breathing dilated the fine nostrils and raised the fleshy corners of her mouth, shaded in the light by a slight black down. Some artist skilled in corruption seemed to have devised the shape of her hair as it fell on her neck, coiled in a heavy mass, casually reassembled after being loosened daily in adultery. Her voice now took more mellow inflections, her figure also; something subtle and penetrating escaped even from the folds of her gown and from the line of her foot. Charles thought her exquisite and altogether irresistible, as when they were first married. (MBE 140)

Flaubert's free indirect discourse prevents the portion of the novel that treats Emma's first affair from being merely a series of objectifying portraits of a woman at the height of her sexual desirability or fulfillment. It is significant that, at the moment of her first tumble with Rodolphe (one can imagine how the scene would be filmed, with the horses' hoofbeats replaced on the soundtrack by the lovers' heartbeats), what for Rodolphe is just another sexual conquest is *not* presented from his point of view:

> Le drap de sa robe s'accrochait au velours de l'habit, elle renversa son cou blanc, qui se gonflait d'un soupir, et, défaillante, tout en pleurs, avec un long frémissement et se cachant la figure, elle s'abandonna.
>
> Les ombres du soir descendaient; le soleil horizontal, passant entre les branches, lui éblouissait les yeux. Ça et là, tout autour d'elle, dans les feuilles ou par terre, des taches lumineuses tremblaient, comme si des colibris, en volant, eussent éparpillé leurs plumes. Le silence était partout; quelque chose de doux semblait sortir des arbres; elle sentait son coeur, dont les battements recommençaient, et le sang circuler dans sa chair comme un fleuve de lait. Alors, elle entendit tout au loin, au delà du bois, sur les autres collines, un cri vague et prolongé, une voix qui se traînait, et elle l'écoutait silencieusement, se mêlant comme une musique aux dernières vibrations de ses nerfs émus. Rodolphe, le cigare aux dents, raccomodait avec son canif une des deux brides cassée. (MBF 472)

> The cloth of her dress clung to the velvet of his coat. She threw back her white neck which swelled in a sigh, and, faltering, weeping, and hiding her face in her hands, with one shoulder, she abandoned herself to him.
>
> The shades of night were falling; the horizontal sun passing between the branches dazzled the eyes. Here and there around her, in the eaves or on the ground, trembled luminous patches, as if humming-birds flying about had scattered their feathers. Silence was everywhere; something sweet seemed to come forth from the trees. She felt her heartbeat return, and the blood coursing through her flesh like a river of milk. Then far away, beyond the wood, on the other hills, she heard a vague prolonged cry, a voice which lingered, and in silence she heard it mingling like music with the last pulsations of her throbbing nerves. Rodolphe, a cigar between his lips, was mending with his penknife one of the two broken bridles. (MBE 116)

In the masculine imaginary, the scene is one in which a woman has been brought to sexual fulfillment by a lover much more capable than her own husband. But a more careful reading of the passage reveals that Emma is in charge, that she determines the outcome (*elle s'abandonna*), not unlike Joyce's Molly Bloom ("as well him as another").[31] Unlike Molly Bloom, however, Emma launches into no soliloquy. Her obsessive reading fails her, and in a long-awaited moment of supreme bliss, there are only, in the somber phrase of Wallace Stevens, "flawed words and stubborn sounds."[32] After the interlude of passion, "Prince Charming" turns out to be only an ordinary man chewing on a cigar, and the latent ennui and banality of the entire scene are underscored by Flaubert's languid imperfect tense.[33]

One of the most fascinating aspects of the representations of the novel's central character is that, the more any one feature of her appearance is examined, the more its contradictory effects are multiplied. Her abundant hair is by turns carefully, meticulously arranged, and then carelessly unattended. Alone for the first time with Léon in Rouen, Emma's chignon is viewed in profile as she leans back in a chair, and simply becomes one item among others in the room's furnishings (MBF 538; MBE 168). Yet when the adoring Justin, whom she ignores, enters her room as she is brushing her long hair, and

quand il aperçut la première fois cette chevelure entière qui descendait jusqu'aux jarrets en déroulant ses anneaux noirs, ce fut pour lui, le pauvre enfant, comme l'entrée subite dans quelque chose d'extraordinaire et de nouveau dont la splendeur l'effraya. (MBF 523)

when for the first time the poor boy saw this mass of hair fall in ringlets to her knees, it was as if he entered suddenly into a new and strange world, whose splendour terified him.(MBE 156)

III. REPRESENTATION: SUBJECTS, OBJECTS, COMMODITIES

Each of Flaubert's works, Michal Peled Ginsburg has argued, can be understood as a separate, distinct attempt to overcome the problem of representation.[34] In *Madame Bovary,* the author's relationship to his central character, a relationship that runs the gamut from the famous pronouncement *Emma Bovary, c'est moi* to the remotely dispassionate treatment often accorded the "protagonist," is at the heart of this problem. Teresa de Lauretis, in an essay on the "postmodern" fiction of Italo Calvino, locates fictional representation of women in the masculine "imaginary" of psychoanalytic and film theory. Interpreting this operation as the deployment of the "Other" which serves to validate the position of the male author, she also plays on Flaubert's celebrated remark:

Woman is still the ground of representation, even [why does she say "even" and not "especially"?] in postmodern times. Paradoxically, for all the efforts spent to re-contain real women in the social, whether by economic or ideological means, by threats or by seduction, it is the absent Woman, the one pursued in dreams and found only in memory or in fiction, that serves as the guarantee of masculinity, anchoring male identity and supporting man's creativity and self-representation. Just as it was with Flaubert, Madame Bovary *c'est lui*.[35]

What can be said about the instances of representation we have cited from *Madame Bovary*? That they tell us more about the fantasies of male characters than they can convey about the physical reality of Emma? That they are intended for the reader's visualization of Emma? That, with their use of light and their "freeze-frame" immobilization of Emma, they prefigure the penultimate deathbed scene? There is some truth in each of these points, but this far from exhausts the possibilities of these novelistic effects of representation. Unlike more obviously realistic novelists, Flaubert does not appear, in these passages, to be stepping forward, briefly interrupting the action of the story, to fill us in with significant details about the character. Flaubert's *style indirect libre* or free indirect discourse, often avoiding direct pronouns, deliberately minimizing action and heightening a sense of ennui through heavy reliance on the imperfect tense, inconsistently employing reported speech,[36] and keeping the reader guessing as to whether observations are being made by the characters or by "the" narrator, works cumulatively to compound the uncertainty about how Flaubert, the novel's characters, and we could/should/can feel about Emma, and ends up apparently justifying Flaubert's famous claim (in his letter to Louise Colet of January 16, 1852) to have intended a novel "about nothing."[37]

In a certain sense, to persist in viewing *Madame Bovary* as the story of its eponymous character is to resist the most radically austere claims of aesthetic modernism. In another letter complaining to Ernest Feydeau of his prodigious labors of composition, Flaubert compared his book-in-progress to a pyramid: "ça ne sert à rien! et ça reste dans le désert! mais en le dominant prodigeusement" ("that serves no purpose! and remains in the desert! but dominating it prodigiously").[38] Here Flaubert prefigures the austere modernist sense of the literary oeuvre that later finds expression in Wallace Stevens' "Anecdote of the Jar," in which the jar intervenes in the "slovenly wilderness," compelling it to surround what "did not give of bird or bush, like nothing else in Tennessee."[39]

Much has been written concerning the depiction of objects in Flaubert's fiction,[40] and certainly any feminist critique of representation must grapple with apparent objectification of principal female characters. Yet in one sense, Flaubert's embrace of the literary work as enduring object is in conflict with what his free indirect narrational style achieves. In Jean-Paul Sartre's *Qu'est-ce que la littérature,* which in many ways prefigures the three thousand-odd pages of *L'idiot de la famille,* one passage which rings with particular eloquence (and has, as a result, been widely quoted) is this observation about Flaubert's style:

> Flaubert écrit pour se débarrasser des hommes et des choses. Sa phrase cerne l'objet, l'attrape, l'immobilise et lui casse les reins, se referme sur lui, se change en pierre et le pétrifie avec elle. Elle est aveugle et sourde, sans artères; pas un souffle de vie, un silence profond la sépare de la phrase qui suit; elle tombe dans le vide, éternellement, et entraîne sa proie dans cette chute infinie.

> Flaubert writes in order to get rid of people and things. His sentence moves in on the object, seizes it, immobilizes it and breaks it back, envelops it, turns into stone and petrifies the object as well. It is blind and deaf, bloodless—not a breath of life; a deep silence separates it from the sentence that follows; it falls into the void, eternally, and drags its prey along in that infinite fall.[41]

The first sentence of that breathtaking passage recalls Nietzsche's claim that his reason for writing was simply that he could find no better way of "getting rid of my thoughts."[42] Sartre's insight suggests that Flaubert wrote in order to dispense with the very objects Sartre's own politics would suspect Flaubert, as a "bourgeois," of reifying. Sartre's love-hate relationship with Flaubert, whom, in part he tackles in order to get at the bourgeois ideology of which his art is presumably an expression, is well known.[43] But once the Flaubertian textual machine gets going, as Sartre and others after him have suggested, objects and persons are devoured and obliterated. The demands of style win out over other agendas, and, in a sense, this gets Flaubert "off the hook," just as at least one recent critic has argued that Flaubert's indeterminate style aided his defense against charges of "obscenity."[44]

Whether as juror or critic, the longer one puzzles over Flaubert's text, the more difficult it becomes to locate the narrator's vantage point, and other textual indeterminacies multiply accordingly. The more attention is focused on Emma, the more relentlessly her "reality" seems to be pursued, the more rapidly she recedes into the distance (or is it, as with Walter Benjamin's aphorism concerning Paul Klee's *Angelus Novus,* the future?—the future of reading, including so-called "postmodern" readings?).[45] Emma's hair, her eyelids, even her hands seem to take on a life of their own from passage to passage, never remaining the same. Her hair appears bound up in a chignon, then flows free; her eyes stare piercingly, then emit languid glances; her flesh appears *sans molles inflexions* and, later in the story, with *des inflexions plus molles*. Much like the postmodern photography of Cindy Sherman, in which she poses herself in a variety of "feminine" caricatures, with eyes that express a wide range of possibilities, the representations of Emma multiply until the very possibility of representation is in serious doubt.[46]

If, as Dalia Judovitz's work on the subject and representation suggests,[47] the epistemological status of the subject is inseparable from the project of representation, then it would make sense to use these uncertainities of representation to destabilize the position of the subject. In the remainder of this chapter, I would like to relate this problematic of representation to that of the construction of feminine desire and the dubious status of the subject.

In order to accelerate this process, let us examine the one scene in *Madame Bovary* in which Emma looks at herself (but is it "herself" she sees?). The moment occurs after her first tryst with Rodolphe:

> Mais, en s'apercevant dans la glace, elle s'étonna de son visage. Jamais elle n'avait eu les yeux si grands, si noirs, ni d'une telle profondeur. Quelque chose de subtil épandu sur sa personne la transfigurait.
>
> Elle se répétait: "J'ai un amant! un amant!" se délectant à cette idée comme à celle d'une autre puberté qui lui serait survenue. Elle allait donc posséder enfin ces joies de l'amour, cette fièvre de bonheur dont elle avait désespéré. (MBF 473)

> But when she saw herself in the mirror she wondered at her face. Never had her eyes been so large, so black, nor so deep. Something subtle about her being transfigured her. She repeated: "I have a lover! a lover!" delighting at the idea as if a second puberty had come to her. So at last she was to know those joys of love, that fever of happiness of which she had despaired! (MBE 117)

Most significant here is that Emma sees herself in relation to another,[48] much as women in our culture have been encouraged and coerced in myriad ways to view and define themselves and their aspirations in relation to men ("I wanna be Bobby's girl!").[49] In this scene of misrecognition which shares some of the characteristics of the Lacanian version of the mirror scene, Emma, in the words of Rainer Warning, is "caught in the idea of representation and thus supposes that she sees the image of her own essence."[50] The phrase "second puberty" reminds us as well that Emma's desires and romantic longings were forged in adolescence through reading novels. These helped to form her "someday my prince will come" attitude. As Rosalind Coward has demonstrated for our age, it is through such experiences as

Emma's reading that women's desires are socially constructed.[51] Certainly in Emma's case, these desires are passive in the extreme and are, in Lacanian terms, the "desire of the other." Of Emma's passivity, Michal Ginsburg writes:

> In terms of the novel, Emma does not exist as a desiring subject before she is made such, first by literature, then by the men who chose her. Rather than being an autonomous subject whose desire originates within herself and whose consciousness of herself is independent of other people, Emma exists only as an object of desire created by the others (men and literature).[52]

The onset of Emma's affair with Rodolphe seems to her like the fulfillment of her longstanding wish to something extraordinary to happen *to* her: "Au fond de son âme, cependant, elle attendait un événement ("All the while, however, she was waiting in her heart for something to happen") (MBF 382; MBE 44). She was "waiting for someone to come out of somewhere,"[53] like the earlier invitation to the ball at La Vaubyessard (*quelque chose extraordinaire tomba dans sa vie* [MBF 366]). Michael Danahy sees this passivity as central to the genre of the novel, the novel being, like women in traditional society, relegated to spheres of intimacy and passivity.[54] He furthermore likens the novel to women in that it has been common to assume that, in both cases, there is something to hide, some secret to be guarded,[55] as in the case of Freud's strong conviction that his patient Dora concealed something terribly personal and precious from him, a dark secret he would have to penetrate and expose.

Emma's extreme passivity is akin to the passivity of a consumer society, and her relation to certain objects in the novel serves to illustrate something of what Marx (in volume 1 of *Capital*) meant by "commodity fetishism," i.e., the tendency in capitalism for commodities to be invested mystically and arbitrarily with properties and qualities that have little to do with their use value but everything to do with their exchange value, a tendency that therefore, especially through advertising, guarantees tremendous profits for the capitalist. The best example of this in *Madame Bovary* is Emma's fetishizing of the cigar case, which she uses to reinvoke the experience at La Vaubyessard and, by extension, to bring herself into contact with a more romantic, genteel, privileged milieu. Ralph Lauren ads, for example in the *New York Times Magazine,* pander to this fantasy today, as they evoke an ambience of the studied casualness of the privileged class off in the country for the weekend (leaving the grimy urban landscape to its burgeoning homeless

population). If "late capitalism" is another way of referring to the postmodern era (or vice versa) and if, as Fredric Jameson has argued, this is the stage
of capitalist development in which commodity fetishism reaches unprecedented extremes and exchange value (signifier) is magnified out of all pro-
portion to use value (signified),[56] then this supplies another justification for
claiming Flaubert as a "postmodern" writer. And yet, as Sartre's compelling
insight into Flaubert's style reminds us, the text itself threatens the very
stability of the objects it elevates to prominence, providing an excellent
example, we would say, of the Hegelian *Aufhebung*—at once affirming and
negating.

IV.   COVER VERSIONS

If we agree that stylistic, subjective, and representational indeterminacy
are postmodern, then so is this novel. If, upon further reflection, those turn
out to have been "modern" traits, then the term "postmodern" will have
been a means of examining aspects of modernism that much more intently.
No matter how much space we might devote to demonstrating the connections among these aspects in *Madame Bovary*, however, we would still find it
difficult to avoid the mistake of Woody Allen's Kugelmass,[57] i.e., believing in
the reality of Emma. The packaging of the book as literary product complements this tendency. In the edition prior to the one now available of the
Lowell Bair translation of *Madame Bovary* published in paperback by Bantam Books (with critical material included from such "new new critics" as
Gérard Genette and Leo Bersani), a vivid artist's conception of a dark-eyed
Emma stares out at us from the cover. She is dressed in white, with her
beautiful black hair tied back in a chignon. Cows graze in the rustic background of the illustration, and one notices that Emma's eyes have been ren-
dered to resemble the large, doleful eyes of those beasts. Perhaps the artist's
intention was merely to situate the fictional protagonist in the rural French
setting she reviled, and not necessarily to identify women with domesticated
animals. Still, wittingly or unwittingly, the paperback cover's graphic design
thus accomplishes the familiar and persistent identification of "woman"
with all that is passive and "natural."

Nevertheless, we ought always to remember the advice of Bo Diddley:
"You can't judge a book by looking at the cover."[58] The textual examples
explored above ought, at the very least, to offer some challenge to the acceptance, epitomized by Percy Lubbock, of the plausibility of the existence of

such a character as Emma Bovary. In fact, as Tony Tanner, for one, has pointed out, the novel (which furthermore begins and ends with Charles in the spotlight) is not "about" Emma at all, but about "Madame" Bovary.[59] She is not even permitted her own name as supposed protagonist. Defined in relation to men—first to Monsieur Rouault, her father, then to Charles, then to her lovers—she exemplifies what contemporary theorists mean by "the traffic in women."[60] To the extent that she is a subject she is "sub-ject," i.e., she is placed or thrown under (as the word's Latin derivation suggests) men. In terms of the history of women's oppression, this is plausible, yet as a social "subject" Emma, as I hope has been demonstrated, is fictive/decentered/incomplete as a result of narrative indeterminacy and contradictory modes of representation. *Emma Bovary, c'est moi,* Flaubert is reputed to have said, and because, to sensible people, the subjective status of that author is beyond question, so, by implication, should be that of his creation. Yet Eugenio Donato has suggested that the very authorial signature "Flaubert" stood for something significantly different at the time of publication of each of his novels.[61] What Michel Foucault described as the "author-function"[62] would account for our stubborn insistence on identifying a unitary, stable figure called "Flaubert" with an unproblematic literary corpus marked with this name.

Complicating or undermining the autonomous subjective status of an Emma Bovary *or* an author named Flaubert would certainly be a predictably postmodernist move. Feminist theory and practice continually remind us that the stakes for men and women who would occupy such a critical position are vastly different. But, as a comment on the politics of representation and the reputation of the novel as a founding modernist text, and on the narrative and stylistic complexities of this text in particular, Roland Barthes's remark quoted at the beginning of this essay bears repeating. *Qui parle?* Who is "speaking" in *Madame Bovary?* Who speaks for Emma? Who speaks when Emma speaks? Who speaks for women? Who speaks for the reputation of this novel and its place in the canon? Who speaks for its readers?

CHAPTER FIVE

Gender and Temporality in
Beyond the Pleasure Principle

It is not a matter of naively accusing Freud, as if he were a "bastard." Freud's discourse represents the symptom of a particular social and cultural economy, which has been maintained in the West at least since the Greeks . . . Whatever may be the inequalities between women, they all suffer, even unconsciously, the same oppression, the same exploitation of their body, the same denial of their desire.

—Luce Irigaray

Psychoanalysis is what makes Marxism in the Western world today different from Marxism in the rest of the world.

—Fredric Jameson

There is no single concept of the unconscious in Freud, as any responsible reading of his work shows. This is because there are two Freudian topographies or maps of the mind, earlier and later (after 1920), and also because the unconscious is a dynamic concept. Freud distinguished his concept of the unconscious from that of his closest psychological precursor, Pierre Janet, by emphasizing his own vision of a civil war in the psyche, a dynamic conflict of opposing mental forces, conscious against unconscious. Not only the conflict was seen thus as being dynamic, but the unconscious peculiarly was characterized as dynamic in itself, requiring always a contending force to keep it from breaking through into consciousness.

—Harold Bloom, "Freud and the Poetic Sublime: A Catastrophe Theory of Creativity" (1978)

I started a landslide in my ego.

—U2, "A Day without Me," 1980

PROLOGUE: SEX AND DEATH

Freud, as is well known, appreciated a good joke, but humor does not surface in most of his books. He seems to have relegated all of it to his study

94

Jokes and Their Relation to the Unconscious. For many years, coinciding with the period during which I had first begun seriously to study Freud's writings, I would have a recurring dream about visiting Freud's office, which, as everyone knows, was located in his home at 19 Berggasse in Vienna. But in my dream, which in my memory is only a fragment of a dream, like one of the ancient fragments Freud might have used as a paperweight for one of his works in progress, Freud's house is actually one in the neighborhood in which I grew up. The houses in this neighborhood date from the early years of the twentieth century, a time that marked the height of Freud's career in many ways. Significantly, the people I knew who lived in this house were high-spirited people who knew how to laugh. In my dream, the atmosphere of this familiar place has been transformed into a somber and funereal one.

After all, psychoanalysis is serious business, isn't it? Still, it is easy to imagine Freud in occasional moments of relaxation, leaning back in his chair, surrounded by the elegant clutter of his impressive collection of antiquities, cigar in hand, chuckling over an ironic observation, if not exactly doubled over with laughter, tears streaming into his neatly trimmed beard. In his many books and professional papers, Freud nevertheless put on the serious face of science. *Beyond the Pleasure Principle* is a grim book in the extreme, and it defies a humorous response. Yet much of modern Western humor, so often fueled by rich ethnic varieties (such as Jewish or Irish humor), has been precisely a kind of "gallows humor," where, the bleaker the situation, the more determined the hilarity. Freud's dark little meditation on death and desire might best be associated in this way with the comedy of Woody Allen, in whose films psychoanalysis has so often been a humorous motif. Probably the most "appropriate" comic scene to bear in mind while contemplating *Beyond the Pleasure Principle* is one that occurs at the end of Allen's *Sleeper* (1973), when "Miles," the Woody Allen character, underscores the paramount importance of "sex and death: the two things that come once in a lifetime—but at least after death, you're not nauseous."[1]

I.   NO TIME FOR PSYCHOLOGY

Where do you go, in a well-stocked bookstore, to find paperback copies of Freud's writings? To the psychology section, of course. There, along with titles by Jung, Fromm, Erikson, Klein, Bettelheim, Horney, maybe even Lacan, and among the endless volumes of "self-improvement" pop psychology ("psychobabble"), you will probably locate many of the various Norton

or Collier paperback titles from James Strachey's Standard Edition translations. Despite all that recent theoretical inquiry and activity have done to
demonstrate the interdisciplinary range of psychoanalysis, including its significance for historical thinking, and indeed despite the "literary" narrative
quality of Freud's writings, these books will no doubt continue to be located
in that section of shelves designated "Psychology." Introductory psychology
textbooks certainly do their share to prevent generations of students from
being surprised by this standard classificatory practice of the retail book
business.

Examining what a colleague in psychology assures me is a representative
introductory textbook currently in use, I am struck by two things, apart
from the usual observations one makes about the "dumbing-down" language in which textbooks are written these days: First of all, there is the
presentation of Freud as a founding figure of psychology, with psychoanalysis as his contribution to that discipline. Second, the unconscious is represented as the territory explored and surveyed, if not originally discovered, by
Freud. As a historian, I find an analogy with American history textbooks'
discussion of the first European explorers who voyaged to the new world.

The aura of "science" is guaranteed by the way Freud is introduced to the
reader, in the very first chapter, as the ambitious medical student who pains-
takingly "dissected 400 male eels to prove for the first time that they had
testes." This sets the beginning student of psychology up for an encounter,
several chapters later, with Freud as the anatomist of the psyche. Not only
does this occur, but the section in which it occurs bears the title "Structure of
the Personality." Here the unconscious is treated as a static, structured reality, something very much at odds with the temporal, dialectic reading of the
Freudian unconscious at work in this chapter. The author of the textbook
even provides an illustration, what I would call a map or blueprint, of
"Freud's model of personality structure." In fact, since it appears in chapter
12, it is labeled "Figure 12.1."[2]

The illustration apparently is meant to suggest a largely submerged ice-
berg, with the "conscious" portion located just above the water, so to speak,
and the "preconscious" submerged but still just visible below the surface.
Lurking in the shadowy depths, of course, is the "unconscious." Overlap-
ping these vertical divisions are the three zones of "ego," "superego," and
"id." "Id," naturally, is miles below the surface. The entire picture looks
more to me like a diagram of the cooling tower of a nuclear power plant,
with a meltdown under way deep within the id. In any case, not only does
the diagram reinforce the notion of the unconscious as a structure naturally

occurring but hidden from view in remote regions until Freud's psychoanalytic expedition claimed it for the Royal House of Psychology; its appearance in the introductory psychology textbook also drives home the impression that "Psychology" is the rightful scientific owner of Freud's legacy. Freud thus appears as psychology's equivalent of Dalton in modern chemistry or Darwin in biology.

But psychoanalysis (and, for that matter, the avowed object of study in the "field" of psychology) is thoroughly interdisciplinary, regardless of the territorial imperatives of either psychology or psychiatry, which latter institution has kept psychoanalysis well domesticated in the United States. The so-called "metapsychological" texts of Freud, of which *Beyond the Pleasure Principle* (1920) is one of the earliest examples (*Totem and Taboo* was published in 1913), illustrate abundantly the folly of attempting to contain psychoanalysis within any one disciplinary domain. *Beyond the Pleasure Principle* also resists that mystique of an atemporal "science of human behavior" fostered by psychology, and this becomes crucial for the feminist project of demonstrating the cultural constructedness of "femininity," as opposed to a feminine "essence" that psychology, among other disciplines, is all too willing to dissect.

Beyond the Pleasure Principle (*Jenseits des Lustprinzips*) remains one of Sigmund Freud's most baffling, difficult, and contradictory texts, one in which he seems to alternate between confident scientific pronouncements and apologies for farfetched speculation. In this short study that, by introducing a more dynamic conceptualization of the unconscious, signals a threshold in the history of psychoanalysis, Freud's investigations of the drives and their relation to the various agencies within what initially appears to be his topographic model of the unconscious carry him into the metapsychological dimension. Of course, the text is most notorious for introducing the concept of the death drive (*Todestrieb*), borrowed, as Freud admits in a footnote, from Sabina Spielrein, an all-but-forgotten member of the early psychoanalytic movement.[3] This dark theme imparts to *Jenseits des Lustprinzips* a morbid tone, one Freud's biographers have conventionally attributed to the disillusioned immediate postwar climate in which Freud wrote it.

The "beyond" (*jenseits*) of the title implies not so much a repudiation of the pleasure principle as an entering into the territory of the psyche left unexplored by that concept; beyond in the sense of "in addition to," or "supplementary to," or "not previously accounted for." This is how Harold Bloom treats the title, and he also offers his explanation for the centrality of this Freudian text to the Lacanian tradition in psychoanalysis: that the text retains a profound ability to shock through its theorization of the *Todestrieb* and its demonstration of the priority of psychological over biological determinants (a dichotomy dismissed by Frank Sulloway in his notable study of Freud).[4] *Beyond the Pleasure Principle* thus offers dramatic confirmation of the Lacanan claim that the very writings of Freud have had to be repressed because they pose a volatile threat to the institutional agendas of psychoanalysis.[5]

Beyond the Pleasure Principle has been only marginal to the ongoing feminist critical engagement with Lacanian psychoanalysis, with discussion focusing more on such notoriously problematic texts as the *Three Essays on the Theory of Sexuality* (1905), *Fragment of an Analysis of a Case of Hysteria* (better known simply as the "Dora Case") (1905), the short article "The Uncanny" (1919), and "Femininity," from the *New Introductory Lectures on Psychoanalysis* (1933). But when *Beyond the Pleasure Principle* is examined in light of these texts where Freud directly takes up the topics of gender and sexuality, it becomes possible to locate a more oblique but still significant textual code of gender, as well as to demonstrate the persistence in the text of generally masculine concepts of sexual desire.

Jacques Lacan initiated the recent wave of reconsiderations of this text. Lacan inaugurated a return to Freud informed by a radical rereading of the master's work, a rereading that would unmask the acts of repression carried out by the psychoanalytic movement against the more uncomfortable or disturbing conclusions toward which many Freudian arguments advance. Lacan suspected that claims made for Freud or for psychoanalysis could not survive the acid test of close rereading of the Freudian texts. Whatever the limitations of Lacanian psychoanalysis, this suspicion about the institutional uses of founding texts certainly inhabits the present book, concerned as it is with issues of the canon and its strategic deployment. *Beyond the Pleasure Principle* was, for Lacan, a strategic text in his campaign against psychoanalytic orthodoxy. The Lacanian school is now in disarray, while Lacanian reading practices abound in contemporary criticism. In fact, "Lacanian psychoanalysis" exists largely as a terrain on which debates over interpretive strategies are enacted, particularly with regard to film theory and feminist criticism, across a spectrum that ranges from Juliet Mitchell, who sees psychoanalysis as an indispensable theoretical framework for contemporary feminism, to Luce Irigaray, for whom Freud provides merely a modern version of the "blind spots of an old dream of symmetry" that (Western) patriarchal culture has been living out ever since Plato.[6]

One of the most persistent claims, thoroughly well supported through research in a number of disciplines, of contemporary feminist theory is that categories of gender and sexuality are social constructs with histories that can be traced. This conviction drives the many exciting new historical studies of sexuality, and the newly discovered "history of the body" that has developed in response to Michel Foucault and other postmodern theorists. A characteristic expression of this political position is found in Sarah Kofman's *The Enigma of Woman: Woman in Freud's Writings:*

> One is not a woman, one is not born a woman, one becomes a woman. Which also implies that one may never complete the process, that it can be carried out to varying extents, that in those we call "women," because they possess "feminine" genital organs, there is thus always a greater or lesser degree of "masculinity . . ."[7]

The result of this emphasis is that alternative histories can be imagined, and, building on this foundation, significant future transformations can be plotted and anticipated. Gender and sexuality are thus rescued from the category of human "essence." Freud's writings, however they may come down unfortunately on the side of essence, e.g., echoing the Napoleonic adage that "anatomy is destiny," also contain a number of admissions of the fluid or culturally malleable character of human sexuality. For example, to the very essay ("The Transformations of Puberty") in which he presented an uncompromisingly ironclad formula whereby girls attain womanhood by, so to speak, giving up the clitoris for the vagina (a turning inward, a bodily metaphor for acceptance of a passive cultural role), Freud added a lengthy footnote ten years later (1915) that quite literally deconstructs the text above it, arguing in opposition to the 1905 text that masculinity (*Männlichkeit*) and femininity (*Weiblichkeit*) simply do not exist in any absolute sense, but must be understood rather as existing along a continuum, whereby any individual may contain greater or lesser degrees of those personality traits conventionally regarded as either "masculine" or "feminine."[8] This remarkable addition is one of the reasons Steven Marcus calls Freud's text a "palimpsest,"[9] i.e., a text that retains glimpses of previous layers only partially and imperfectly erased (making it difficult to determine what the parch-meant).

Freud's better-late-than-never footnote accords well with the dynamic, temporal cast of his approach to the unconscious in *Beyond the Pleasure Principle.* I take to heart Lacan's formulation that Freud "temporalizes" the unconscious in this text, i.e., brings it into history in a manner that accords well with the tentative, fluid sense given *Männlichkeit* and *Weiblichkeit* in the former text.[10] Bloom also underscores this reading of the text by referring to the dynamic model of the unconscious that is introduced, even if it cannot be said to displace the more topographic view of the unconscious found in such a text as *The Ego and the Id*. Another way to maximize the temporal dimension of Freudian psychoanalysis is through attention to the narrative style of Freud's texts, which he on occasion (especially with his case studies) worried were too much like literary texts, "lacking the serious stamp of science."[11] The theorist who has done the most to associate narrative with historicism is Fredric Jameson, for whom narrative functions as a "political unconscious" of utopian yearnings that resist the radically atemporal "presentness" of contemporary ideology.[12] This emphasis on temporality is crucial for a reading that seeks to combat the reification and static treatment often accorded Freudian studies of the unconscious, including those by Freud himself. A temporalized, dynamic sense of the unconscious is also virtually unrecognizable to readers whose introduction to Freud has been mediated through introductory psychology textbooks. It is to be hoped that such a historicist (in Jameson's sense) reading of Freud would also do more to encourage a "utopian" feminist politics of fundamental change in what Gayle Rubin, who now shies away from the phrase, once designated as the "sex-gender system."[13]

Beyond the Pleasure Principle may also be read within the continuing problematic for contemporary theory of the autonomous subject, central to traditional Western humanism, including mainstream psychoanalysis, and crucial to feminist theory.[14] Many of the texts, including those with which this book is concerned, whose critical interrogations have constituted some of the most conspicuous activities of poststructuralism, seem to lend themselves to what it has been fashionable, if ungainly, to call the "problematization" of the subject. Lacan shares with Foucault and Derrida a rejection of the automatic assumption of the conscious, fully present subject, and upholds Freud as one whose most radical (and, therefore, most repressed) discovery was the fragmentation ("deconstruction") of this subject. The Freudian *Ichspaltung*, or "splitting of the ego" (*clivage du moi*, Lacan called it), was one of the most significant supports for the radical Lacanian rejection of the Ego Psychology school, and receives serious attention in the Lacan-inspired *Vocabulaire de la psychanalyse* of Laplanche and Pontalis.[15] Michel de Certeau referred to this psychoanalytic insight as the "insurmountable division" of the subject caught between the two conflicting drives discussed in *Beyond the Pleasure Principle*.[16] Some versions of this Lacanian emphasis risk simply reworking Aristophanes' famous opinion expressed in Plato's *Symposium* that every sexed creature has in fact been split off from the "missing half" with which it longs to reunite,[17] but the concept of the *Ichspaltung* can be pushed in a more radically fragmented direction, i.e., beyond binary categories. Lacan's own theories at least triangulate, so to speak, the division through the concepts of the imaginary, the symbolic, and the real. Despite Lacan's influential, and characteristically postmodern, critique of the subject, this problematic category remains relevant for a re-reading that emphasizes gender and temporality. If *Beyond the Pleasure Principle* can be shown to provide the framework for a historical, rather than a static (read here "essential"), account of human psychosexuality, then it becomes available as a theoretical source for the ongoing feminist effort to trace the social construction of gender.[18]

The perception that his writings offer only a static, temporal mapping of the unconscious and a fixed, rigid sense of human sexuality lies behind many feminist rejections of Freud or of psychoanalytic theory. This is the case, for example, with Elizabeth Wilson, the British feminist writer who movingly describes her rapt attention to Freud's "narratives," which seem to her always to be approaching an exciting new insight (and this provides the reading pleasure that precedes disappointment) only to conclude with "the dusty old machinery of the castration complex or some other familiar and overworked formulation, which creaks onto the stage with as much conviction as a pantomime horse."[19] It is very much as if she is attuned to the narrative in the political sense theorized by Jameson, only to be brought crashing to an abrupt halt by Freud's overworked concept. In a move far more typical of British than of French or American feminists, Wilson prefers marxism to psychoanalysis when it comes to the hope for change in the sex-gender system, though this is likewise the position of the American philosopher Alison Jaggar, who, proclaiming her own socialist feminism, seizes upon aspects of the historical materialist dialectic to provide a way out of the overwhelming cumulative oppressive effects of patriarchal culture on women. For her, human nature is historicized by marxism in ways that promise to overcome oppressive aspects of what is assumed to be "feminine" nature; this despite her impatience with marxism's relative lack of attention to women's oppression.[20]

But one need not take up the extreme advocacy of psychoanalysis of a Juliet Mitchell to retain a sense of its potential benefits for feminism. If, through close attention to some of the overlooked aspects of Freud's texts, psychoanalysis can be shown to escape the atemporal, doctrinaire picture fostered by its institutional guardians, then it retains its theoretical usefulness for a feminist cultural criticism and cultural politics. This is certainly not to say that feminism then surrenders somehow to psychoanalysis, admitting that all the theoretical weapons needed for the struggle were already there. Feminist theory and practice, already unfolding on a multitude of cultural and political fronts, cannot limit itself to merely one useful modern(ist) theoretical tradition. As Linda Alcoff, writing of the political necessity of a feminist critique of the subject, puts it in a careful, useful recent essay:

> Yet while a theorizing of the unconscious is used as a primary means of theorizing the subject, certainly psychoanalysis alone cannot provide all of the answers we need for a theory of the gendered subject.[21]

If temporality, or the historical awareness that no cultural category is fixed or inevitable, provides one of the "ways out" (*sorties*) for women that Cixous discusses in her influential essay,[22] then another way out is Freudian psychoanalysis, if it can be shown to have established—however paradoxically—a profoundly temporal dimension of the unconscious.

With these interpretive issues in mind, let us get on with Freud's dark, dense little essay.

II.   FREUD'S TERMINOLOGY

The words "economic," "dynamic," and "topographic" catch our attention in the very first paragraph of Freud's text:

> Wenn wir die von uns studierten seelischen Prozesse mit Rücksicht auf diesen Ablauf betrachten, führen wir den ökonomischen Gesichtspunkt in unsere Arbeit ein. Wir meinen, eine Darstellung, die neben dem topischen und dem dynamischen Moment noch dies ökonomische zu würdigen versuche, sei die vollständigste, die wir uns derzeit vorstellen können, und verdiene es, durch den Namen einer metapsychologischen hervorgehoben zu werden. (*JLP* 3)

> In taking that course into account in our consideration of the mental processes which are the subject of our study, we are introducing an 'economic' point of view into our work; and if, in describing those processes, we try to estimate this 'economic' factor in addition to the 'topographical' and 'dynamic' ones, we shall, I think, be giving the most complete description of them of which we can at present conceive, and one which deserves to be distinguished by the term 'metapsychological.' (*BPP* 1)

In order to establish a metapsychological dimension for his work, Freud must introduce an "economic point of view" to supplement the "dynamic" and "topographic." Already we are introduced to the multiple possibilities for reading *Beyond the Pleasure Principle:* from the static to the temporal, one not necessarily to the exclusion of the other. By analogy, the marxist project sought both a structural and a dialectical understanding of capitalist society. Before contemplating a historical materialist reading of *Beyond the Pleasure Principle,* it might be useful first to remark upon the somber scientific tone with which Freud launches his speculative voyage.

From the first sentence, Freud adopts the full phallic presence of a spokesman for "the theory of psychoanalysis ("In der psychoanalytischen Theorie . . . wir"), implying that the hard-won scientific status of psychoanalysis must now be shored up and defended, especially when the theory is poised to negotiate unfamiliar territory. This prepares the reader for Freud's liberal use of scientific terms borrowed from nineteenth-century physics (Helmholtz, e.g.) and biology (Weissmann, e.g.) in order to lend added weight to his argument.[23] The scientific aura is essential for such a speculative exercise, yet in other contexts (and in gender terms, we do mean "other" for Freud), Freud scorned speculation. Sarah Kofman points out the irony of Freud's indulging in speculation here when elsewhere, particularly when addressing questions of feminine sexuality, he had warned against any departure from clinical observation.[24]

Any historical materialist (as well as feminist) reading would seem to be imperiled by the apparent biologism of *Beyond the Pleasure Principle,* particularly once Freud begins to employ biologistic explanations for the nature of unconscious drives, as opposed to the argument of Nancy Chodorow that all unconscious characteristics have social origins.[25] Elsewhere, in *The Ego and the Id* Freud wrote that "the character of the ego is a precipitate of abandoned object-cathexes and . . . it contains the history of those object-cathexes."[26] Does this present us with a contradiction between biology and history? If so, it is one of many contradictions that guarantee the future of Freud's text as the site of conflicting interpretations. In any case, Frank Sulloway and, with a decidedly different agenda, Harold Bloom argue that there is not necessarily a contradiction in the way Freud develops these dimensions of his text. It is also well to remember, as Michel Foucault's *Les Mots et les choses: L'archéologie des sciences humaines* (1966; in English translation as *The Order of Things: An Archaeology of the Human Sciences*) demonstrates,[27] that modern biological science and history developed within the

same nineteenth-century intellectual climate, with similar kinds of conceptualizations about development and change. Our own culture's tendency to
pit biology, or science generally, against history, politics, or culture generally
is by no means an inevitable pattern of human consciousness, though it is
certainly crucial for a feminist critique of biological determinism. We, therefore, tend to view history and biology through the distorted lens of our own
cultural habit of placing in opposition categories that are not necessarily or
inherently arrayed against each other.

Freud is not long in providing us with examples of language that lend
support to those who would oppose biologism. On page 7 of the German
text, in a paragraph devoted to discussion of unconscious forces (*Kräfte*)
that oppose the tendency toward the pleasure principle, we encounter the
word *Verhältnisse* (relations). For some reason, translator James Strachey
chose to render this rather blandly as "circumstances." (We saw in Chapter 3
a similar lessening of the force of the word in Marx's text, once translated.)
No doubt it is due in part to the influence of such mistranslations that so
many should assume the inherent antagonism of marxism and psychoanalysis. The point I am making here is the opposite of Bruno Bettelheim's argument concerning the Standard Edition translation. Whereas he argued that
Freud's essential humanism was obscured by difficult, forbidding jargon, I,
persuaded more by a postmodern "antihumanist" reading of Freud, find
here an instance of the substitution of the lackluster, unthreatening "circumstances" for the complex dynamism of the German word, a word whose
import for marxist theory Bertell Ollman explains admirably well in his
Alienation: Marx's Conception of Man in Capitalist Society.[28] "Relations" is
thus a more thoroughly materialist term than the matter-of-fact "circumstances," and this example at least casts doubt on Bettelheim's lament for a
neglected or repressed humanism throbbing at the heart of Freud's writings.
I make this point about "relations" because I wish to replace the static (reified), topographical reading of the Freudian unconscious by one that hon-
ors process and shifting, fluctuating states of relatedness. Put another way:
the dialectic.

This Hegelian-marxist sense of *Verhältnisse* can converge with the Freudian usage of the term. Some currents of recent French thought feature, in
spite of the much-publicized French disenchantment with marxist thought,
a fascination with a "libidinal economy" of the psyche that can almost seem
like a latter-day Freudo-marxism. Georges Bataille, with his iconoclastic notions of *dépense* ("expenditure") and the heretical political economy, derived
from Marcel Mauss and other French ethnographers, he theorized in *La*

Part maudite (1949), inaugurated the tradition more recently modified by
Jean-François Lyotard (*Économie libidinale*)[29] and Jean-Joseph Goux, but
Freud himself begins it with his use of terms like *Besetzung* ("investment,"
though Strachey translates it as "cathexis").

When it was still possible for French poststructuralist theoreticians to
consider Marx as seriously as they have Nietzsche or the psychoanalytic
tradition, Jean-Joseph Goux published a fascinating study called *Économie et
symbolique: Freud, Marx* (1973). In it he likened the "neurotic subject's" formation by the relations of the unconscious realm to the ideological subject's
determination by the economic relations of the mode of production:

> Si le sujet de l'idéologie est déterminé par sa place dans les rapports d'échange
> économiques, juridiques, politiques, institutionnels, le sujet de la nèvrose sera
> déterminé et constitué par sa place dans les rapports d'échange signifiants, in-
> tersubjectifs, sexuels . . .[30]

> If the subject of ideology is determined by its place in relations of economic,
> juridical, political, and institutional exchange, the subject of neurosis will be deter-
> mined and constituted by its place in relations of signifying, intersubjective, sex-
> ual exchange. (My translation)

This view of the ideological subject (a pleonasm for much of contemporary
theory) as being "constituted" and produced through language and therefore through the formation of the unconscious, as well as through myriad
social and institutional practices, was advanced further in the remarkable
Althusserian-Lacanian-Barthesian synthesis achieved by Rosalind Coward
and John Ellis in *Language and Materialism: Developments in Semiology and
the Theory of the Subject* (1977).[31] The idea of a "dialectic" of the unconscious
as revealed, even if not named, by *Beyond the Pleasure Principle* is one which
we will bear in mind throughout this critical reading.

Recent critical theory thus provides a number of positions from which to
interrogate the seemingly stable unities of Freud's conceptual system.
Jacques Lacan made it his reading practice to take very seriously those points
in the Freudian text in which the splitting (*Spaltung*) of the unconscious ego
is suggested. Such splits oppose the supposed unity of the ego (in the sense
in which that term—*das Ich*—has come to be employed by the very psychoanalytic establishment with which Lacan fought). I want to suggest that the
first appearance of this *Spaltung* in *Beyond the Pleasure Principle* not only
supports a Lacanian reading, but also suggests a relationship with the critique by Marx (see Chapter 3) of the fragmentation of the subject in capital-

ist society.[32] There, Marx sees the human subject as divested (*entäussert*) of essential human qualities by alienated conditions of capitalist labor. It becomes possible to hear echoes of Marx's complaint in this passage from Freud's text:

> Unterwegs geschiet es immer wieder, dass einzelne Triebe oder Triebanteile sich in ihren Zielen oder Anspruchen als unverträglich mit den übrigen erweissen, die sich zu der umfassenden Einheit des Ichs zusammenschliessen können. Sie werden dann von dieser Einheit durch den Prozess der Verdrängung abgespalten, auf niedrigeren Stufen der psychischen Entwicklung zurückgehalten und zunächst von der Möglichkeit einer Befriedigung abgeschnitten. (*JLP* 7)

> In the course of things it happens again and again that individual instincts or parts of instincts turn out to be incompatible in their aims or demands with the remaining ones, which are able to combine into *the inclusive unity of the ego* [italics mine]. The former are then split off (*abgespalten*) from this unity by the process of repression, held back at lower levels of psychical development and cut off, to begin with, from the possibility of satisfaction. (*BPP* 5)

III.   "FORT!/DA!" AND FEMINISM

After some brief comments concerning the "traumatic neuroses" ("shell-shock," e.g.) suffered by World War I veterans and "anxiety," to which he promises to return later, Freud moves on to a concept that accelerates the process of questioning and qualifying the role of the pleasure principle in unconscious mental activity. This is the "repetition compulsion" (*Wiederholungszwang*), which Freud announces as the result of his brooding upon the odd *fort/da* game repeated constantly by his infant grandson Ernst. The death of his mother, Freud's daughter Sophie, would plunge Freud into profound grief only a few months later.[33] Freud writes that this child of one and a half years was as a rule quite well behaved, never disturbing his parents during the night and able to amuse himself contentedly with the little toys he scattered throughout the room and under the furniture—his one annoying habit. He also basked in the constant attention of his mother, so that her infrequent absences were surely to be reckoned as significant events in his life. Absorbed in his play, the little boy would carry out the following ritual, which Freud came to associate with the mother's absences:

> Dieses brave Kind zeigte nun die gelegentlich störende Gewohnheit, alle kleinen Gegenstände, deren es habhaft wurde, weit weg von sich in eine Zimmerecke,

unter ein Bett usw. zu schleudern, so dass das Zusammensuchen seines Spiel-
zeuges oft keine leichte Arbeit war. Dabei brachte es mit dem Ausdruck von
Interesse und Befriedigung ein lautes, langgezogenes *o - o - o - o* hervor, das nach
dem übereinstimmenden Urteil der Mutter und des Beobachters keine Inter-
jektion war, sondern "Fort" bedeutete. Ich merkte endlich, dass das ein Spiel sei,
und dass das kind alle seine Spielsachen nur dazu benütze, mit ihren "fortsein" zu
spielen. Eines Tages machte ich dann die Beobachtung, die meine Auffassung
bestätige. Das Kind hätte eine Holzspule, die mit einem Bindfanden unwickelt
war. Es fiel ihm nie ein, sie zum Beispiel am Boden hinter sich herzuziehen, also
Wagen mit ihr zu spielen, sondern es warf die am Faden gehaltene Spule mit
grossem Geschick über den Rand seines verhängten Bettchens, so dass sie darin
verschwand, sagte dazu sein bedeutungsvolles *o - o - o - o* und zog dann die Spule
am Faden wieder aus dem Bett heraus, begrüsste aber deren Erscheinen jetzt mit
einem freudigen "Da." Das war also das komplette Spiel, Verschwinden und
Wiederkommen, wovon man zumeist nur den ersten Akt zu sehen bekam, und
dieser wurde für sich allein unermüdlich als Spiel wiederholt, obwohl die grös-
sere Lust unzweifelhaft dem zweiten Akt anhing. (*JLP* 12–13)

This good little boy, however, had an occasional disturbing habit of taking any
small objects he could get hold of and throwing them away from him into a
corner, under the bed, and so on, so that hunting for his toys and picking them up
was often quite a business. As he did this he gave vent to a loud, long-drawn-out
"o-o-o-o," accompanied by an expression of interest and satisfaction. His mother
and the writer of the present account were agreed in thinking that this was not a
mere interjection but represented the German word "*fort*" [gone]. I eventually
realized that it was a game and that the only use he made of any of his toys was to
play "gone" with them. One day I made an observation which confirmed my
view. The child had a wooden reel with a piece of string tied round it. It never occurred to him to pull it along the floor behind him, for instance, and play at its being a carriage. What he did was to hold the reel by the string and very skillfully
throw it over the edge of his curtained cot, so that it disappeared into it, at the
same time uttering his expressive "o-o-o-o." He then pulled the reel out of the cot
again by the string and hailed its reappearance with a joyful "*da*" [there]. This,
then, was the complete game—disappearance and return. As a rule one only witnessed its first act, which was repeated untiringly as a game in itself, though there
is no doubt that the greater pleasure was attached to the second act. (*BPP* 8–9)

While certainly no match as an observer of children for Melanie Klein,
Freud was nonetheless a keen observer of this repeated episode, and his
"reading" of it went a long way toward shaping the direction of *Beyond the
Pleasure Principle*. The game, Freud concluded, celebrated the child's significant achievement of surviving the trauma of his mother's absences by re-

enacting the drama of her departure (*fort*) followed by her welcome return (*da!*). Freud asserts that the child cannot possibly have experienced these absences as pleasurable, so why would he want to relive them or reenact them? The answer he provides is one that uncovers the pleasure hidden within what would appear to be a painful experience:

> Man sieht, dass die Kinder alles im Spiele wiederholen, was ihnen im Leben grossen Eindruck gemacht hat, dass sie dabei die Stärke des Eindruckes abreagieren und sich sozusagen zu Herren der Situation machen. (*JLP* 14–15)

> It is clear that in their play children repeat everything that has made a great impression on them in real life, and that in doing so they abreact the strength of the impression and, as one might put it, make themselves master of the situation. (*BPP* 10–11)

I cannot resist pointing out that Jacques Derrida, of all people, lavishes attention on the biographical and historical setting for this experience, even making the commonplace observation that the Great War may be responsible in part for the dark tone of *Beyond the Pleasure Principle*. To be sure, Derrida also busies himself with demonstrating and describing the textual quirks that shape as well as distort Freud's argument.[34] Derrida's essay "Spéculer—sur Freud" remains one of the most significant close readings of this text.

What, in temporal terms, is the *Wiederholungszwang*? A Nietzschean eternal recurrence? A repeating of history that denies active human agency? Or is it something more akin to what Marx, in *The Eighteenth Brumaire,* saw as "men making their own history," though not completely through free choice? Later in *Beyond the Pleasure Principle,* this concept is illuminated somewhat by what Freud will say about the conservative character of the drives as well as the grim *Todestrieb*—the death instinct. According to Derrida, Ernst was driven in the *fort/da* game not just, as Freud argues, by his need to "abreact" or repeat the trauma of his mother's abandonment, but by what Serge Leclaire, a Lacanian psychoanalyst, has described as the "primary narcissism"[35] that must be related to the death drive.[36] In any case, as has frequently been pointed out, the very young child experiences the mother's departure as if it meant the child's own extinction.

As Jane Gallop points out, Freud doesn't so much explain the repetition compulsion as act it out.[37] He treats the spectacle of the game as one in which the child, through abreaction, repeats the primal trauma, but, through the agency of the game, exercises a measure of control over the situation that lessens its pain with each repetition, as the child's passivity in the face of his mother's departure becomes less total. In addition, Freud attributes a kind of satisfaction to the child, resulting from its partial sense of mastery,[38] that is similar to the jubilation Lacan assigns to the child in the mirror-stage recognition scene. From a feminist psychoanalytic standpoint, both Freud and Lacan in these respective interpretations exhibit signs of countertransference, Freud in particular failing to entertain the alternative explanation: that the scene of *fort/da* reenacts the subject's *Spaltung*/fragmentation. Freud is blind to his countertransference just as he was in his bungling of the "Dora" case, failing to see the reality of the fragmentation before him because it threatened his own anxieties and sexual uncertainties.[39] In a similar manner, Lacan was unable to see how his *trotte-bébé* was, in his blissful hallucination of his erect posture and bodily wholeness, a generalized male, one flattering Lacan's own unconscious denial of castration.[40] Above I asserted that Freud was less observant of children than Melanie Klein, but he still appears more attentive than Lacan. And somehow, when one rereads the *fort/da* section of *Beyond the Pleasure Principle*, it's easier to imagine him helping to pick up the toys.

But Lacan's specific handling of the *fort/da* scenario contrasts fundamentally with Freud's, for Lacan reads the ritual as the exact opposite of a celebration of mastery, however slight. Applying the eccentric ideas of Georges Bataille, who David Macey has recently argued was, in opposition to the structuralist tradition, the really decisive "surrealist" influence on Lacan,[41] it is possible, in opposition to dominant cultural values, to experience fragmentation (Bataille is more extreme: dismemberment, mutilation, sacrifice) as something celebratory.[42] Lacan argues that the *fort/da* episode has been grossly misinterpreted as evidence of the unconscious strategies of the unifying ego, for the endless repetition in his view refers to and intensifies the subject's alienation[43] and splitting into something that is both "gone" and "there," *fort* because *da* and *da* because *fort*.[44] The Lacanian school of psychoanalysis came to see this primordial division in terms of "the subject in quest of its lost identity."[45] If the game is at all celebratory, it celebrates language, and this accounts for the repetition of the two words, which mark the entry into language prior to Lacan's oedipal-stage surrender to *le nom du père*. The language signifies the subject's radical vacillation, but that stark reality cannot be grasped directly or consciously. What speaks in the *fort/da* game is the unconscious, or in Lacan's phrase, *le discours de l'autre*.[46]

We may say here in the spirit of Lacan that, if this is an example of Freud's temporalizing of the unconscious, of its entry into history, it is a "history" understood as metonymy and displacement. The child experiences pleasure not simply from the motions of the game, but, more significantly, from the decisive uttering of the words (*fort! da!*). The scattering or deferral of meaning experienced unconsciously by the subject through its entering into language, into chains of trace structures where *fort* is always already marked by a *da,* was a realization too terrible (on a conscious level) for a Freud but not for a Heidegger or a Derrida. But it takes on additional life in an *other* register, i.e., that of gender. The patriarchal Freud of the Dora case, the lecture on femininity, or the essay on the "uncanny" ("Das Unheimliche")[47] distrusts the *différance,* dissemination, and implicit castration of meaning as full phallic mastery and presence that contemporary feminist criticism has taught us to associate with women's writing and desire. And the metonymic flux and process of displacement operating in the unconscious for a Lacanian reading of Freud will be, for all Lacan's failures with gender questions, friendlier to feminism than the Freud of the Dora case or the lecture on femininity.

Both Freud and Lacan, however, fail to anticipate a radically different feminist reading of the *fort/da* scenario. Eugénie Lemoine-Luccioni, a feminist and neo-Lacanian psychoanalyst, asks us to imagine the same scene with an infant girl, instead of a boy. Lemoine-Luccioni argues that, because of her gender identification with her mother, the girl would be as likely to associate the spool tossed away and retrieved each time with *herself,* her own body whose disappearance and erasure she thus mimes.[48] While equally as disturbing as the exclusively male Freudian scenario wherein the castration complex always lies ready for its hermeneutic deployment, Lemoine-Luccioni's approach to the text and to the scene suggests the need to rethink commonly held assumptions about child development, anxiety, mastery, and loss. Her work also serves as a reminder that masculinist assumptions inhabit the psychoanalytic language of drives; that, as Jane Flax reminds us in a recent essay, we have to be alert to all that the Freudian language descriptive of the so-called drives conceals or excludes.[49]

All of which brings us to an appropriate point at which to consider this very reasonable objection to all the above theoretical wrangling: if Freud and Lacan are both so thoroughly compromised by sexist assumptions, intentionally or not, why should anyone concerned with rethinking human gender relations and sexuality waste time on them? Long before the Lacanian wave began to pound against so many foreign shores, Kate Millett emphatically and passionately stated the feminist case for rejecting psychoanalysis, and did so much more definitively than Luce Irigaray or Catherine

Clément,⁵⁰ both of whom (whether *Psych et po* becomes *po et psych* or not) appear to want to keep their hand in when it comes to psychoanalysis as an activity beneficial to feminism. David Macey, whose *Lacan in Contexts* (1988) is the most recent comprehensive (in English) attempt to reevaluate Lacan, also views Lacan as hopelessly sexist, and faults Lacan's call for a return to Freud's text as the kind of servile, icon-worshiping behavior antithetical to psychoanalysis at its best.⁵¹ Against this last view could be cited the dialectically arresting assertion of Shoshana Felman that

> Lacan can be said to be the first disciple in the whole history of pedagogy and of culture who *does indeed believe in the ignorance of his teacher—of his master.* Paradoxically enough, this is why he can be said to be, precisely, Freud's best student . . .⁵²

The example of Lemoine-Luccioni, like that of Jane Gallop, similarly shows a pupil convinced of her teacher's ignorance, who goes beyond him in ways far more helpful for feminism.

IV.   SPECULATION, DEATH, AND TEMPORALITY

In the section of *Beyond the Pleasure Principle* that follows the material on *fort/da,* one senses that Freud continues to be haunted by the game precisely in terms of its temporal dimension of repetition and reenactment. This, perhaps, is what leads him to posit, against his emphasis on unconscious mental processes (*die unbewussten Seelenvorgänge* [JLP 28]), the "timeless" (*zeitlos* [*JLP* 28]) character of much of unconscious life. It is as if Freud, in the Lacanian sense, approached a deeper understanding of unconscious time but withdrew, content to deny that "time" was anything more than an abstraction. In fact, until the reader is confronted with the statements on death in section 5, Freud's tone is soberly cautious, as he explains the conservative nature of the drives and describes the reaction of the psyche to external excitation as if in reference to the twitchings of a Galvanic frog, though in his unique blend of language consisting of "cathexis," "binding," etc.

The tone of exaggerated caution most marks the beginning of section 4, after Freud's exhaustive treatment of the implications of the abreactive character of children's play, and on the threshold of his foray into biological theories about germ plasm and the *Bläschen* or "vesicles" whose behavior demonstrates a longing for stasis and thus exemplifies the *Todestrieb*. Again Kofman's question confronts us: why does Freud permit himself speculation here when he so notably shies away from it when explicitly examining questions of femininity and female sexuality? Why is he afraid of speculation in the latter case, when, after all, it is easy to demonstrate how many of his unabashedly sexist statements belong to the realm of patriarchal mythmaking about women? With this in mind, let us examine the brief passage more closely:

> Was nun folgt, ist Spekulation, oft weitausholende Spekulation, die ein jeder nach seiner besonderen Einstellung würdigen oder vernachlässigen wird. Im weiteren ein Versuch zur konsequenten Ausbeutung einer Idee, aus Neugirde, wohn dies führen wird. (*JLP*, p. 23)

> What follows is speculation, often far-fetched speculation, which the reader will consider or dismiss according to his individual predilection. It is further an attempt to follow out an idea consistently, out of curiosity to see where it will lead. (*BPP* 18)

In the German text, the phrase *ist Spekulation* is set off in commas, as if Freud were holding a horribly contaminated laboratory specimen away from himself, using special tongs or tweezers. Is this Freud the would-be scientist distancing himself from the flight of fancy he is about to launch? In place of that metaphor of a diseased bit of organic matter, let us substitute one of a glowing hot coal Freud dares not touch. For this reason: I am arrested by the *holende* in the compound word *weitausholende,* correctly translated by Strachey as "far-fetched." For me Derrida's textual principle of *différance* comes into play here, explaining why my reading of *holen* produces an "inappropriate" mental association with *Hölle* (hell). On other occasions, Freud recoils from the gaping jaws of the "hell" of speculation about the feminine (and *Hölle* is a feminine noun in German).

Quite possibly, no German "ear" would pick up the trace that for me marks *holen,* so I'll return for a minute to "fetch," the literal meaning of that verb. "Fetching" is an adjective commonly used in English for an attractive woman. With emphasis now on Strachey's English translation, speculation becomes "far-fetched," fraught with dangers, taking us far from home into something "uncanny" (*unheimlich*). Jane Marie Todd has demonstrated that, for Freud, the female genitals are *unheimlich,* and women's sexuality a "dark continent."[53] Speculation is still dangerous, still *unheimlich* and far-fetch(ing)ed, but not as dangerous as when it consciously engages topics of women and feminine sexuality. Logically, the preceding bit of textual play is far from appropriate, and would seem to have little to do with Freud's willingness to speculate in *Beyond the Pleasure Principle* when he sought to avoid it elsewhere. However, psychoanalysis, especially after Lacan, locates the unconscious in language, and vice versa. Turning the psychoanalytic attention to even minor quirks and details of language back upon itself becomes here a strategy for demonstrating the persistently sexualized character of a Freudian text supposedly unconnected to questions of gender. One last observation on this score: Freud's text announces the attempt to follow the thread of a speculative idea consistently, "to see where it will lead." When Freud adopts a guarded, reticent tone in such texts as the lecture on femininity, isn't this a sign of lack of interest in consistency and intellectual rigor when the topic is "merely" femininity?

But once Freud begins to develop his discussion of the death drive, he reopens what for us become questions concerning dialectical processes, desire, and gender. How is the death drive experienced? Freud of course warns us that he has embarked upon another round of speculation, and, as with the *fort/da* game, he proceeds obliquely. From Freud's own text, as well as from the suggestions of such interpreters as Serge Leclaire[54] and Samuel Weber,[55] we can begin to approach this hypothetical realm through the more commonplace experience of anxiety.

Much of what Freud says about the *Todestrieb* suggests that the organism experiences it as a "desire" to avoid stimulus and to adhere to or return to stasis. The "vesicle" is like a sound sleeper hoping that the alarm clock will break down so that it will not have to stir. Freud emphasizes the conservative nature of the drive, something that would almost seem to be a contradiction in terms ("conserve" versus "drive"):

> Ein Trieb wäre also ein dem belebten Organischen innewohnender Drang zur Wiederherstellung eines früheren Zuständes, welchen dies Belebte unter dem Einflüsse äusserer Störungskräfte aufgeben musste, eine Art von organischer Elastizität, oder wenn man will, die Äusserung der Trähigkeit im organischen Leben. (*JLP* 38)

> *It seems, then, that an instinct is an urge inherent in organic life to restore an earlier state of things* [Strachey's italics] which the living entity has been obliged to abandon under the pressure of external disturbing forces; that is, it is a kind of organic elasticity, or, to put it another way, the expression of the inertia inherent in organic life. (*BPP* 30.)

Life = "an external disturbing force"?

Not long thereafter, Freud states the case in the starkest possible terms:

Wenn wir es als ausnahmlose Erfahrung annehmen dürfen, dass alles Lebende aus inneren Grunden stirbt, ins Anorganische zurückkehrt, so können wir nur sagen: Das Ziel alles Lebens ist der Tod, und zurückgreifend: Das Leblose war früher da als das Lebende. (*JLP* 40)

If we are to take it as truth that knows no exception that everything living dies for *internal* reasons—becomes inorganic once again—then we shall be compelled to say that "*the aim of all life is death*" and, looking backwards, that "*inanimate things existed before living ones.*" (*BPP* 32; Strachey's italics)

The assertion of the priority of inorganic over organic matter calls to mind Freud's enigmatic formulation (discussed below) "Wo es war, soll Ich werden."

One of the most striking illustrations Freud employs, despite the disclaimers that soon follow, of the alternation within the organism of the death drive with life-preserving instincts, appears to be the very image of a dialectical process, and thus returns us to the temporal dimension. Freud writes,

Es its wie ein Zauderrhythmus im Leben der Organismen; die eine Triebgruppe stürmt nach vorwärts, um das Endziel des Lebens möglichst bald zu erreichen, die andere schnellt an einer gewissen Stelle dieses Weges zurück, um ihn von einem bestimmten Punkt an nochmals zu machen und so die Dauer des Weges zu verlängern. (*JLP* 43)

It is as though the life of the organism moved with a vacillating rhythm. One group of instincts rushes forward so as to reach the final aim of life as swiftly as possible; but when a particular stage in the advance has been reached, the other group jerks back to a certain point to make a fresh start and so prolong the journey. (*BPP* 34–35)

Though Freud appears here to be describing a physiological process as if he were thinking of meshing gears, it might be best to consider it all as a dramatization of the agencies operating within the unconscious, with the unconscious understood here as the sum total of the *Strukturverhältnisse* (accent on the second half of that compound noun) in their shifting realignments and temporal displacements. The passage provides an image of an erratic mechanism, like the "marvelous toy" that "went 'zip' when it moved and 'bop' when it stopped, and 'whirrr' when it stood still,"[56] perhaps an appropriate way to envision the dynamism of the unconscious. Or, in modernist fiction, think of Beckett's Watt, with his hopelessly energy-wasting but carefully routinized (as with Murphy's "biscuits" or Molloy's "sucking stones") method of walking.[57] Whatever the value of such visualizations, if we see Freud's vacillating rhythms in dialectical terms, and force a dialectical reading of the passage, we may very nearly approximate the efforts of the Frankfurt School theorists to complicate the dialectic in order to allow for the fits and starts—the retrograde motion—of history.[58] One of the results of their studies has been to suggest that the dialectic operates not smoothly or predictably, but in multiple, shifting, complex patterns.

In attempting to apply this idea to a temporal reading of the unconscious, we must keep in mind alternate models of temporality. The Hegelian-marxist dialectic, however complicated or refined by Horkheimer, Adorno, or Fredric Jameson, still would not exhaust the possibilities for determining the temporal modalities of the unconscious, something I hinted at by suggesting (above) that the *Wiederholungszwang* could be viewed as an example of Nietzschean eternal recurrence. Michel de Certeau refers to conflicting "strategies of time" at work in *Beyond the Pleasure Principle*,[59] something that contemporary physical theory tells us to anticipate in nature. Stephen Hawking, the leader of the quest for "Grand Unified Theory" in physics and astronomy, writes of multiple aspects of time unleashed by the Big Bang and still operating within the expanding universe. He calls them "arrows of time," launched by this primordial event but now following different, seemingly contradictory trajectories (all of which would comfort science fiction writers wishing to describe time travel).[60]

One of the most gifted and original writers in the modern historical materialist tradition, Walter Benjamin, included in his "Theses on the Philosophy of History" a brief reverie inspired by Paul Klee's painting *Angelus Novus*. Benjamin describes historical time as a "storm blowing from paradise" that propels the angel, who longs to stay and assist those who suffer the outrages of history, violently forward into the future.[61] This is actually an appropriately poetic image for Hawking's "arrows of time" (and perhaps also for the "time" of unconscious drives), time advancing, however uncertainly or erratically, ever since that first "event" in Einsteinian space-time. Hawking may not be aware of Walter Benjamin, but physicists have increasingly shown themselves to be quite receptive to metaphysical and aesthetic concepts in constructing their often highly poetic theories. It is high time those of us in the humanities began to take seriously the implications for our own theories of such fundamental concepts as the relativity of time. I am acutely aware that I am raising far more questions about temporality than I am willing or able to begin to try to address here, but I do so in order to indicate how far we still have to go in rethinking psychoanalysis through the kind of dynamic temporal dimension congenial to, but seldom theorized by, history. The political conviction that drives me in these speculations is always that the more "temporalities" of unconscious desire that can be suggested, the more feminist "ways out" (*sorties*) of patriarchal discourse can be multiplied.

Having begun section 5 with discussion of the death drive, Freud closes affirmatively with "Eros," whose efforts "to combine organic substances into ever larger unities" ("immer grösseren Einheiten") (*JLP* 45; *BPP* 37) are noted. Whatever Freud is contemplating here, we are reminded of his own hysterical fear of fragmentation/division/castration acted out in other texts (Toril Moi shows how this is at work in the "Dora" case)[62] as well as in *Beyond the Pleasure Principle*. Or Freud is some kind of theoretical Pan*dora* who, having let loose terrifying concepts, frantically tries to get them all back in the box.

V.   WHERE IT WAS

To open the next, and final, long section, Freud poses the question of the role of "ego-instincts" (*Ichtrieben*) (*JLP* 46; *BPP* 38) in exerting pressure toward death:

> Unser bisheriges Ergebnis, welches einen scharfen Gegensatz zwischen den "Ichtrieben" und den Sexualtrieben aufstellt, die ersteren zum Tode und die letzteren zur Lebensforsetzung drängen lässt, wird uns gewiss nach vielen Richtungen selbst nicht befriedigen. (*JLP* 46)

> The upshot of our inquiry so far has been the drawing of a sharp distinction between the "ego-instincts" and the sexual instincts, and the view that the former exercise pressure towards death and the latter towards a prolongation of life. But this conclusion is bound to be unsatisfactory in many respects even to ourselves. (*BPP* 40)

"Amen" to that last sentence. Even though Freud appears to back down from this opposition between ego and sexual drives, interesting questions are nevertheless raised: that "ego" is a fragile unity, in fact seeking obliteration, and that desire affirms life. Such a view throws into sharp relief the celebrated, enigmatic remark we find at the end of Freud's thirty-first "New Introductory Lecture," "The Dissection of the Psychical Personality": "Wo es war, soll Ich werden," translated by Strachey as "Where id was, there ego shall be,"[63] despite the fact that Freud's German omits the definite articles. Thus, as many readers of his text have pointed out, a better translation would most likely be: "Where it was, there I shall come to be." Catherine Clément, in her unrelievedly sarcastic *Les fils de Freud sont fatigués (The Weary Sons of Freud)*, pokes fun at Marie Bonaparte, "the psychoanalytic princess," for having translated the passage "Le Moi doit déloger le Ça (Ego must dislodge id.).[64] Clément, in adopting the reading favored by Lacanian critics of the ego psychology school, vindicates Lacan in a way surprising for *Les fils de Freud,* but not out of keeping with her more sympathetic, though not unmixed, treatment in *Les vies et les légendes de Jacques Lacan.*[65]

Above, the statement "Wo es war, soll Ich werden" was connected to that section of *Beyond the Pleasure Principle* in which the priority of inorganic matter is being asserted. One of the things I mean to suggest is the possibility of a thoroughgoing materialist (antihumanist) reading of Freud, one certainly in keeping with the Lacanian agenda. However, the red warning flag of gender should go up when we suggest that *es* means inorganic matter, so that "Wo es war . . ." becomes merely a formula for the death drive. The problem, we will see, is in Freud's language describing the drives. Freud's treatment of these questions of desire, life, and death at the opening of this section of *Beyond the Pleasure Principe* has the disadvantage of appearing to limit the range of sexual expression and drives Freud has indicated elsewhere, and it also serves to foster a crude topographical dualistic distinction between what are then seen exclusively as two types of drives. Freud attempts just that near the end of *Beyond the Pleasure Principle (JLP* 56; *BPP* 46). In the face of this reductionism, it becomes difficult to retain the subtler concept of "ego" as "agency" within a complicated unconscious world in process.

We have not said all there is to be said concerning the implications of the concept of the death drive for larger questions of desire and gender. The problem, simply, is the tendency of *Beyond the Pleasure Principle,* for all its subtleties, to reduce discussion of libidinal drives to a crude dualism that too easily gets reworked into "masculine" and "feminine" categories (*"einen scharfen Gegensatz"*). As usual, the latter is treated with denial, scorn, overgeneralization, or a combination of all three. At first, it is difficult to see how the discussion of the drives in *Beyond the Pleasure Principle* is compromised by gender bias. But then we are forced to recognize a recurring motif borrowed from the much earlier text *Three Essays on the Theory of Sexuality* (1905): the dialectic of excitation and release. Freud uses this in relation to the death drive and to the supposed need for "the organism" to regain an earlier state devoid of excitation and external stimulus. But this is a pattern developed by Freud in his third Essay on Sexuality, notorious to feminist critics of Freud for its discussion of the clitoris as a little penis, inferior to though resembling the male organ in terms of sexual arousal.[66]

Thus the theory of the drives is tied to an exclusively masculine model of pleasure (as is argued eloquently by Michèle Montrelay)[67] into whose Procrustean bed feminine desire must be made to fit, just as the generalized subject is somehow always masculine despite its universal claims. The desire for wholeness, for integration, for resolution of all contradictions—all these we have remarked upon in Freud's text. For a text that promises to comment on "life" and "life forces," *Beyond the Pleasure Principle* far from exhausts the realm of possibilities for human experience of pleasure or gratification of desire. Feminist critique proceeds by combating the essentialism of such limiting definitions and characterizations, as do the best of Freud's writings, even occasionally just pages away from the most unacceptable pronouncements. *Beyond the Pleasure Principle,* for one, abounds in Freud's own apologies and disclaimers, including this one:

> Only believers, who demand that science shall be a substitute for the catechism they have given up, will blame an investigator for developing or even transforming his views. (*BPP* 58)

For some feminists, as well as for lesbians and gay men, alternative modes of desire can be theorized and affirmed within a corrected psychoanalytic tradition. For others, such as Luce Irigaray, Freud's text is far too compromised by the patriarchal logic, traceable at least to Plato, of which it partakes.[68] Her project calls for the construction of a new logic and language of desire. As Hélène Cixous puts it:

> All the great theorists of human history have reproduced the most commonplace logic of desire, the one that keeps the movement toward the other staged in a patriarchal production, under Man's law.[69]

Luce Irigaray, exploiting the possibilities for puns afforded by the French word *homme* (man), calls attention to the *hommo* logic of Freud's theorizations of desire, and also to the *hommo-* sexuality within the male-bonded philosophical tradition from Plato to Freud that has been capable of regarding feminine sexuality only, if at all, from within a framework of masculinist assumptions about desire and the status of the desiring subject.[70] Along with

Cixous, Kristeva, and other French feminist theorists, Irigaray has argued persuasively that woman's desire must be understood not in relation to its object, but in terms of her relatedness to her own mother.[71] But, for some other feminists, Irigaray's willingness to characterize woman's desire, indeed to dare to speak of something as general as "woman," condemns her as a kind of essentialist—patriarchal in spite of herself.[72] Whether or not this is true, those of us who wish to plead for multiplicity and difference within a newly emerging concept of gender as socially constructed would do well to maintain the delicate balance between articulating a feminist position too long excluded and silenced by our culture's master interpretive systems and guarding against a new kind of theoretical reification in the name of gender.

One argument perhaps worth considering is that advanced both by Jane Gallop and Shoshana Felman (albeit from different positions within a feminist spectrum), namely this: what makes Lacanian psychoanalysis enabling for critical theory is its fundamental refusal of mastery and its resistance to being enshrined as the new orthodoxy. For Gallop in particular, this translates as the basis for a new feminist style of argument that, taking its cues from Lacan, reveals that no one, not even men, "possesses the phallus" when it comes to knowledge and authority.[73]

Regardless of how one defines oneself in relation to psychoanalysis, the project, in the wake of new feminist practices of reading and interpretation, of critically rereading such a canonical text as Freud's *Beyond the Pleasure Principle* must remain one of exposing the less apparent ways that gender assumptions and *hommo* logic are at work in it. Simultaneously, the activity that must proceed is one of exploiting such interpretive possibilities as the text's implied temporalizing of the unconscious, in order to maximize its theoretical resources for a feminism that would wrest control of the psychoanalytic tradition away from its patriarchal guardians. Perhaps we can now understand how Freud's text, like so many texts in our "humanistic" tradition, is thoroughly fissured, riven with and undermined by contradictions from within, and thus all the more pregnant with possibilities, unanticipated by the canon's guardians, for feminist and other emancipatory agendas. Nietzsche's *The Gay Science,* the subject of the next chapter and the last of the five texts we are considering, provides vivid examples of such possibilities.

CHAPTER SIX

Writing Like a Woman (?): Nietzsche's *The Gay Science*

Drop down, mama let your papa see,
You got somethin' babe that keeps worryin' me.
> —Sleepy John Estes, "Drop Down Mama"

[La femme] n'oppose pas, à la vérité masculine, une vérité féminine.
> —Luce Irigaray, *Amante marine de Friedrich Nietzsche* (1980)

When [Nietzsche, Paul Rée, and Lou Andréas-Salomé] met again in Lucerne on 13 May 1882, she [Lou] wanted to reject Nietzsche's proposal of marriage, while he wanted to explain that he had not made one. But the embarrassment did not last long enough to prevent the three of them from posing for a photograph: the two writers pretended to be hauling a cart with her perching on it, a whip in her hand.
> —Ronald Hayman, *Nietzsche: A Critical Life* (1982)

Another image also comes to mind: Nietzsche leaving his hotel in Turin. Seeing a horse and a coachman beating it with a whip, Nietzsche went up to the horse and, before the coachman's very eyes, put his arms around the horse's neck and burst into tears.

That took place in 1889, when Nietzsche, too, had removed himself from the world of people. In other words, it was at the time that his mental illness had just erupted. But for that very reason I feel his gesture has broad implications: Nietzsche was trying to apologize to the horse for Descartes.
> —Milan Kundera, *The Unbearable Lightness of Being*

I. NIETZSCHE, FEMINISM, ROCK 'N' ROLL

Feminist critics, particularly those inspired by recent French theory, have devoted a great deal of attention to the question of what it means to write "like a woman,"[1] drawing from the work of theorists of *l'écriture féminine* in order to contemplate relationships among women, writing, and the body. When, in my title, I raise the question of whether Nietzsche's writing in *Die fröhliche Wissenschaft* (*The Gay Science*)[2] is perhaps "feminine" in character, I bring to the discussion, carried out by Jacques Derrida, Sarah Kofman, and others, of Nietzsche's style(s) the speculative and strategic explorations by Luce Irigaray, Hélène Cixous, and less well known French feminist theorists of *l'écriture féminine*.

To do this by way of a consideration of a text in which Nietzsche appears to equate woman with style, artifice, deception, and skepticism is to foreground the "scandalous" implications of the claims made for women's writing by these complex theorists and to join the ongoing debate begun by Christine Delphy and Monique Plaza in reaction to Annie Leclerc and Irigaray over so-called "essentialism" in feminist thought.[3] As readers of *Critical Inquiry* know only too well, a newer, somewhat different version of this debate has emerged from Toril Moi's writings[4] and has found its way into the pages of that journal, where a complicated and impassioned polemic was joined by Frank Lentricchia, Sandra Gilbert, and Susan Gubar.[5]

In a recent essay, William Gass complained that the poststructuralist French Heideggerian interpreters of Nietzsche (i.e., Deleuze, Derrida, Foucault) had been no more convincing or successful than an earlier generation of right-wing exegetes in getting Nietzsche "right." Actually, what he says is that Deleuze et al. "depart from the spirit of Nietzsche."[6] So what else is new? Is Gass unaware that poststructuralism has not exactly been a quest for spirit? With Derrida's *Éperons: Les styles de Nietzsche*[7] providing the leading example, the point has been more to use Nietzsche's text as a discursive strategy to explore a radically deffered, indeterminate style of writing in order to avoid all essentialisms and stable categories.

This is precisely what that best-selling proponent of joyless wisdom and anti-gay science Allan Bloom warns us about in *The Closing of the American Mind*. This very Nietzschean quote from Michel Foucault, that most learned advocate of unlearning, provides a powerful example of the perspectivism, or relativism (to use a word from Bloom's danger list), he attributes to Nietzsche's pernicious influence:

> However, if the genealogist refuses to extend his faith in metaphysics, if he listens to history, he finds that there is "something altogether different" behind things: not a timeless and essential secret, but the secret that they have no essence or that their essence was fabricated in a piecemeal fashion from alien forms.[8]

Given as he is to ungainly titles (try the full subtitle of *The Closing of the American Mind* on for size), he even devotes a chapter to "The Nietz-scheanization of the Left or Vice Versa,"[9] and what he calls the left would include most of the membership of the Modern Language Association. Such a use of "left" could gain legitimacy only in a political culture in which that label is thought to apply to Michael Dukakis or Dan Rather. Bloom's pejorative "Nietzschean" strikes different chords. For Bloom, Nietzsche is one of the most virulent strains of the pestilence of modernity (here I am using "modernity" in the manner of Alice Jardine, who shares more with Jürgen Habermas than she cares to realize)—one his University of Chicago-based Center for the Control of Antihumanistic Diseases is monitoring along with feminism and rock 'n' roll. Modernity began when Flaubert failed to denounce Emma Bovary's adultery clearly and forcefully, and it has been going downhill ever since. As with Jesse Helms's campaign against what he considers "immoral" art, Bloom again and again provides clear examples of the time-honored conservative (to give it an undeservedly nice name) practice of blaming societal ills on so-called culture (and others would be equally offended by the opposing historical materialist explanations with which I am obviously in greater sympathy).

Presumably, Nietzsche's *Gay Science,* which appeared at a time (1882) when its author was buoyantly confident and exuberant,[10] is a text from which Bloom would particularly recoil, for this *fröhliche Wissenschaft* is a lilting, dancing approach to culture. We might say, just to annoy Bloom (whom I see as the "square" high school principal grimacing and holding his hands over his ears at the sock hop in vintage 1950s movies), that it has a good beat and we can dance to it. But, even if Bloom wanted to dance to it (whether or not women would want to dance with him, not to mention with Nietzsche), he would still want to be able to tell the dancer from the dance. I plan most deliberately in this chapter to bring together all the things Bloom hates most: Nietzsche, feminism, and rock 'n' roll. And, since *The Gay Science* is a text in which Nietzsche sings about how low-down and no-good women are, I'll throw in some blues while I'm at it. This is an essay with a soundtrack.

Are we having too much fun at Bloom's expense? Probably not. Think of this more as a response in kind to the joyous ("gay") spirit of affirmation (always bearing traces of negation)[11] in Nietzsche's text. This joyousness is in the dance—the Mediterranean gaiety Nietzsche preferred over somber Nordic *Kultur* of the eternal return of the coming into being of "what one is." Much of feminist writing, from Emma Goldman on, calls for "dance," and in "Choreographies," Christie V. McDonald, who begins the interview with Goldman's famous "If I can't dance, I don't want to be part of your revolution," hauls a somewhat reluctant Derrida out onto the dance floor to attempt steps he was too shy to take in *Spurs*.[12] It seems clear to me that feminist responses to ideas only briefly sketched out or suggested in that text have forced Derrida to engage new feminist arguments, though he has yet to demonstrate serious consideration of Irigaray, Cixous, or other theorists of *l'écriture féminine*.[13] I wish to move from Nietzsche into an examination of some of their texts, hoping to step a little more lively. Indeed, the Nietzschean hope for writing may well be that it avoid failing us in the way that human speech, in Flaubert's gloomy formulation, is reduced to "a cracked cauldron on which we beat out rhythms to make bears dance."[14]

II. STYLE(S) I: NIETZSCHE AND DERRIDA

Nietzsche did not hesitate to make pronouncements about women and, in the words of Walter Kaufmann, they did him "little credit."[15] Kaufmann did much in his translations and in his writings on Nietzsche to show how difficult it is at any given point to affix one overriding meaning to Nietzsche's stylistically varied writings. But he still believed that Nietzsche stood for something that could be distilled as the essence of his thought, and he appears to have wished that these misogynist statements would just go away. However, Derrida's deconstructive reading in particular almost presents Nietzsche's text as feminist *malgré lui*. He shows, for example, how, in spite of or in addition to Nietzsche's more virulently misogynist statements, women's characteristics are described in ways similar to what Nietzsche has to say about art and writing. (In fact, in many ways in Nietzsche's text, woman = writing; more about this below.)

This has a familiar ring, this need to explain away what one acknowledges as unattractive or offensive in an otherwise exemplary thinker. Derrida's detractors, especially in the wake of the revelations concerning Paul de Man's wartime writings in a Belgian collaborationist newspaper and Derrida's excessively long-winded responses to the controversy in *Critical Inquiry* (as if he were conducting a deconstructionist version of the Watergate hearings: "What did de Man know and when did he know it?"),[16] would, fairly or not, say that "deconstruction" is politically suspect because any prejudice a writer appears to exhibit in a text may be excused or explained away as always already under textual erasure. Still, one need not subscribe to such a caricatured view of deconstruction in order to be attentive to the textual means by which even the most stridently ideological convictions of an author suffer myriad textual reversals and displacements. Which brings us back to the thought expressed a few lines above, that Kaufmann appears to wish that Nietzsche's authorial sins would just go away. Despite all their fancy footwork, it seems clear that Paul de Man's apologists really wish his *Le Soir* columns would "just go away."

A feminist reading (distinct from, even if influenced by, a deconstructive reading) of Nietzsche's text, thus an approach that has already made the step of deciding that *The Gay Science* is worth reading because its critique can be of use to feminism, can proceed in one of two ways: The critic/reader could assume that Nietzsche was a determined misogynist who would, were he around today to read over the feminist reader's shoulder, be extremely pissed off to discover the textual deferrals and unravelings undeciding his authorial intentions, unfolding as they do in individual acts of reading situated much later in time. Or the critic/reader could proceed on the assumption that it matters little whether Nietzsche intended to proclaim or obscure his actual position on the woman question, since the rhetorical density of Nietzsche's text invites a wealth of interpretations and uses. Since Walter Kaufmann's translations of Nietzsche began to appear, the weight of critical opinion has shifted heavily in the direction of the latter part of that formulation, i.e., that Nietzsche wished to obscure his own meanings, surrendering to literary style itself with the same delicious abandon with which Flaubert took up the writing of *Madame Bovary* (see Chapter 4). Alexander Nehamas asserts, for example, that Nietzsche's chief distinction as a philosopher is his abandonment of the metaphysical assumption that careful ordering of the sage's thought should precede the (as Derrida has amply illustrated, abased and undervalued) act of writing.[17]

Before going any further, the reader needs to gain a sense of the places in *The Gay Science* in which the most distasteful apparently misogynist statements appear. The lion's share of them are to be found in numbered sections 59–75. There is no way around quoting at length from these passages, although I will abridge frequently. I will follow the sequence of statements in order, allowing the contradictions as well as their cumulative force to emerge.

In the original German, each numbered section of *Die fröhliche Wissenschaft* comprises a single paragraph, though often Kaufmann chooses to break them up in his English translation. It is common to refer to these nuggets of writing as aphorisms, and one could profitably trace the development of this arrangement of texts through figures of modernity that include Benjamin, Adorno, and Barthes. For her *Amante marine de Friedrich Nietzsche* (1980), in which she addresses the Nietzsche of *The Gay Science* and other texts in which he treats of women, Luce Irigaray puts her own stamp on the literary genre of aphorism. In the case of Nietzsche, I will refer to each "section," as I will call it, by its number.

Section 59 of *Die fröhliche Wissenschaft*, titled *Wir Kunstler!* (*We artists*), begins on a dismal note:

> Wenn wir ein Weib lieben, so haben wir leicht einen Hass auf die Natur, aller der Natürlichkeiten gedenkend, denen jedes Weib ausgesetzt ist . . . (*FW* 78)

> When we love a woman, we easily conceive a hatred for nature on account of all the repulsive natural functions to which every woman is subject. (*GS* 122)

Here woman, as has so often been the case in Western thought, is assigned to the sphere of nature, the very realm that artists, as Nietzsche defines them, disdain. Nature is that which is base, even "repulsive," and, as we shall soon see, Nietzsche feels this way about the female genitals, above whose questionable condition woman, unlike *Wir Kunstler,* can never rise. Remember that one of the familiar German terms for genitals is *Geschlechtsteile: Geschlecht*, meaning "sex," containing "schlecht," which, of course, means "bad." *Geschlechtsteile* = "bad parts," or "naughty bits," as they used to say in the Monty Python skits.

An equally familiar placement of woman in patriarchal texts, especially for feminist film theorists of today, is in terms of distance, and in section 60 Nietzsche, in a passage evocative of Homer's description of Odysseus lashed to the mast of his ship during the Sirens' serenade, relegates women to a distant point from where they can "work their magic." *Die Frauen und ihre Wirkung in die Ferne* (*Women and their action at a distance*) begins:

> Habe ich noch Ohren? Bin ich nur noch Ohr und nichts weiter mehr? Hier stehe ich inmitten des Brändes der Brandung, deren weisse Flammen bis zu meinem Füsse heraufzüngeln . . . (*FW* 79)

> Do I still have ears? Am I all ears and nothing else? here I stand in the flaming surf whose white tongues are licking at my feet. (*GS* 123)

As with the odd remark about the umbrella that *spurs* Jacques Derrida's reading of *The Gay Science,* it is almost impossible to say what this passage

means or why it occurs in this place. Ears and feet. In his reading of Nietzsche's "autobiographical" *Ecce Homo,* Derrida has a great deal to say about
Nietzsche and "ears,"[18] while Luce Irigaray (see section III of this chapter)
has commented memorably on this image of the feet awash in the "flaming
surf." Standing there, "Nietzsche," if that is who this fragment is about,
hears howls and screams coming toward him, and then glimpses a ghostly
sailboat coming his way. Commenting on these hallucinations, he builds
toward his climactic view of "women and their action at a distance":

> Es scheint, der Lärm hier hat mich zum Phantasten gemacht? Aller grosse
> Lärm macht, dass wir das Glück in die Stille und Ferne setzen. Wenn ein Mann
> inmitten *seines* Lärms steht, inmitten seiner Brandung von Würfen und Entwür-
> fen: da sieht er auch wohl stille zauberhafte Wesen an sich vorübergleiten, nach
> deren Glück und Zurückgezogenheit er sich sehnt—*es sind die Frauen.* Fast meint
> er, dort bei den Frauen wohne sein besseres Selbst: an diesen stillen Plätzen werde
> auch die lauteste Brandung zur Totenstille und das Leben selber zum Träume
> über das Leben. Jedoch! Jedoch! Mein edler Schwärmer, es gibt auch auf dem
> schönsten Segelschiffe so viel Gerausch und Lärm, und leider so viel kleinen
> erbärmlichen Lärm! Der Zauber und die mächtigste Wirkung der Frauen ist, um
> die Sprache der Philosophen zu reden, eine Wirkung in die Ferne, eine *actio in
> distans:* dazu gehört aber, zuerst und vor allem—*Distanz!* (*FW* 80)

> It seems as if the noise here had led me into fantasies. All great noise leads us to
> move happiness into some quiet distance. When a man stands in the midst of his
> own noise, in the midst of his own surf of plans and projects, then he is apt also to
> see quiet, magical beings gliding past him and to long for their happiness and
> seclusion: *women.* He almost thinks that his better self dwells there among the
> women, and that in these quiet regions even the loudest surf turns into deathly
> quiet, and life itself into a dream about life. Yet! Yet! Noble enthusiast, even on
> the most beautiful sailboat there is a lot of noise, and unfortunately much small
> and petty noise. The magic and the most powerful effect of women is, in the
> philosophical language, action at a distance, *actio in distans:* but this requires first
> of all and above all—*distance.* (*GS* 123–24)

"Quiet, magical," but above all quiet, for this sirens' song is a song of silence,
and it is up to men to make the noise in this world. Vision, the sense which is
wedded to distance, must place the women "over there," where they can enact their quiet magic, which is to say become screens for men's fantasies. Barbara Kruger's art captures this best, when over a photo of a man whose face
is shaded by the brim of his hat and who holds the warning finger of silence
to his lips, she superimposes the legend "Your comfort is our silence."[19]

Nietzsche's passage locates woman in a hallucinatory, superficial reality that cannot help but be deceptive. Metaphorically, however, woman stands for the coldest Nietzschean "truth," that behind the veil of truth there is no truth, only a debased coinage of counterfeit value masquerading as that which should be held sacred. And somehow, for Nietzsche women are threatening because they see through the game in which they are made to participate. In section 64, *Skeptiker* (*Skeptics*), we have a chilling passage that puts this theme into play along with the image of "veils" that will become a major motif for Irigaray's symptomatic reading:

> Ich fürchte, dass altgewordene Frauen im geheimsten Versteck ihres Herzens skeptischer sind als alle Männer: sie glauben an die Oberflächlichkeit des Daseins als an sein Wesen, und alle Tugend und Tiefe ist ihnen nur Verhüllung dieser "Wahrheit," die sehr wünschenswerte Verhüllung eines *pudendum*—also eine Sache des Anständes und der Scham, und nicht mehr! (*FW* 81)

> I am afraid that old women are more skeptical in their most secret hearts than any man: they consider the superficiality of existence its essence, and all virtue and profundity is to them merely a veil over this "truth," a very welcome veil over a pudendum—in other words, a matter of decency and shame, and no more than that. (*GS* 125)

No sooner has Nietzsche presented this image of women wiser than men in the sense of seeing through male fantasies and ideals, then (after very brief unreflective asides in sections 65 and 66 on, respectively, women's relationship to virtue and "shame" and women's "survival skill," so to speak, of exaggerating their weaknesses to win men's sympathies) he confronts us with woman as a docile, domestic animal. In *Zarathustra*, Nietzsche would write, in a passage on women's inability to experience true friendship, of women as cows "at best."[20] Here, in section 67, *Sich selber beucheln* (*Simulating—oneself*), woman is also cowlike:

> Sie liebt ihn nun und blickt seitdem mit so ruhigem Vertrauen vor sich hin wie eine Kuh: aber wehe! gerade dies war seine Bezauberung, dass sie durchaus veränderlich und unfassbar schien! (*FW* 81–82)

> Now she loves him and looks ahead with quiet confidence—like a cow. Alas, what bewitched him was precisely that she seemed utterly changeable and unfathomable. (*GS* 125)

All of which suggests the disillusionment of man's discovering that what he took for profound mystery in woman was stultifyingly uncomplicated animal ignorance, like that of the simpleton Chance in Jerzy Kosinski's *Being There*, who, in that disturbingly prophetic parable of the Reagan age, is perceived as refreshingly, disarmingly candid and intelligent.[21] Notice how Nietzsche leads the reader from one seemingly firm assertion to another, while, through their contradictory aspects, they dissolve away one after another. Still, there is a persistent undercurrent of hysterical dread concerning women.

In the very next section, number 68, *Wille und Willigkeit* (*Will and willingness*), a sympathetic, even though condescending and patronizing, view of woman's lot is expressed and considered in a dialogue between a young man and an elderly sage:

> Man brachte einen Jüngling zu einem weisen Mann und sagte: "Siehe, das ist einer, der durch die Weiber verdorben wird!" Der Weise Mann schüttelte den Kopf und lächelte. "Die Männer sind es," rief er, "welche die Weiber verderben: und alles, was die Weiber fehlen, soll an den Männern gebusst und gebessert werden,—denn der Mann macht sich das Bild des Weibes, und das Weib bildet sich nach diesem Bilde." "Du bist zu mildherzig gegen die Weiber," sagte einer der Umstehenden, "du kennst sie nicht!" Der weise Mann antwortete: "Des Männes Art ist Wille, des Weibes Art Willigkeit—so ist es das Gesetz der Geschlechter, währlich! ein hartes Gesetz für das Weib! Alle Menschen sind unschuldig für ihr Dasein, die Weiber aber sind unschuldig in zweiten Grade: wer könnte für sie des Öls und der Milde genug haben." (*FW* 82)

> Someone took a youth to a sage and said: "Look, he is being corrupted by women." The sage shook his head and smiled, "It is men," said he, "that corrupt women; and all the failings of women should be atoned by and improved in men. For it is man who creates for himself the image of woman, and woman forms herself according to this image."
> "You are too kindhearted about women," said one of those present; "you do not know them." The sage replied: "Will is the manner of men; willingness that of women. That is the law of the sexes—truly, a hard law for women. All of humanity is innocent of its existence; but women are doubly innocent. Who could have oil and kindness enough for them?" (*GS* 126)

From reflections on being kindhearted toward women, Nietzsche's text moves on in section 69 to the ironic "kindhearted woman" of the classic Delta blues song of the same name by the legendary singer Robert Johnson:

She's a kindhearted (woman) (mama)
she studies evil all the time
She's a kindhearted woman
but she studies evil all the time
You well's to kill me (baby)
as to have it on your mind.[22]

The title of Nietzsche's equivalent comment on female treachery is *Fähigkeit der Rache* (*Capacity for revenge*), where we encounter two related rhetorical questions:

> Würde uns ein Weib festhalten (oder wie man sagt "fesseln") können, dem wir nicht zutrauten, dass es unter Umständen den Dolch (irgendeine Art von Dolch) *gegen* uns gut zu handhaben wusste? Oder gegen sich: was in einem bestimmten Falle die empfindlichere Rache wäre (die chinesische Rache). (*FW* 82)

> Would a woman be able to hold us (or, as they say, "enthrall" us) if we did not consider it quite possible that under certain circumstances she could wield a dagger (any kind of dagger) *against us*? Or against herself—which in certain cases would be a crueler revenge. (*GS* 126)

Crueler from whose point of view? The woman's? Or does Nietzsche assume that the cruelty lies in the destruction of something that belongs to (a) man? I am thinking here of Gayle Rubin's essay "The Traffic in Women,"[23] as well as Irigaray's "Les merchandises entre elles" in *Ce sexe qui n'en est pas un*.[24] An analogy from the history of slavery also suggests itself in those episodes of slaves on slave ships, still in their chains, desperately hurling themselves overboard, thus, among other things, "depriving" certain slave-owners of their chattel.

As is increasingly apparent in this sequence of examples from *Die fröhliche Wissenschaft*, it is exceedingly difficult to determine just what Nietzsche's point of view might have been. Even in the case of what certainly seems to have been a woefully preposterous attitude toward women, close examination of the text reveals a highly nuanced, shifting set of perspectives.

The remaining sections (70–75) present increasingly bizarre, murky reflections on women. *Die Herrinnen der Herren* (*Women who master the masters*) is the memorable title of section 70, where Nietzsche considers the portrayal in the theater of women of lofty, noble character. He appears to argue that these superior female characters are merely foils for ideal male characters, such as Shakespeare's Romeo, and are not to be taken literally.

Section 71, *Vor der weiblichen Keuschheit* (*On female chastity*) offers com-
plaints about the social prejudice against educating upper-class women
about "erotic matters," and scoffs at the "honor" such women seek to maintain. This section closes bluntly with "Kurz, man kann nicht mild genug
gegen die Frauen sein!" ("In sum, one cannot be too kind about women").
While the ambiguity of the English may be greater than that of the German
(and I am writing for readers who will encounter Kaufmann's English), I
respond to this somewhat in the spirit of a skeptical reader of letters of
recommendation that contain such double-edged assertions as "I cannot say
enough about this candidate's qualifications."

Depending on whether one accents the "too" or the "kind," "one cannot
be too kind about women" yields two mutually exclusive readings. In the
former case, the sense would be that women deserve as much kindness as
possible. This accords with Walter Kaufmann's observation that Nietzsche
in this sentence has switched from his use of the word *Weiber* for women to
the "more respectful" *Frauen*.[25] But in the latter case, with the accent on
"kind," the sense it takes on is that it is really not appropriate to attempt to be
kind toward women. "Too kind" thus appears to mean "very kind," i.e., one
really cannot be (does not need to be) very kind. This in turn appears to
harmonize well with the deprecating tone with which the section on "chastity" begins.

Sections 72, 74, and 75 are the remaining ones with comments on women:
first on motherhood, in which Nietzsche lapses into the kind of biologism
familiar to one-sided (masculine) commentary (e.g., "Die Schwangerschaft
hat die Weiber milder, abwartender, furchtsamer, unterwerfungslustiger
gemacht . . ." ("Pregnancy has made women kinder, more patient, more
timid, more pleased to submit . . .") (*GS* 129; *FW* 84); then on women who,
through their insecurity and uncertainty, "talk too much" ("zu viel reden")
in the company of men; and, finally, inaccurately quoting Aristotle's *Nico-
machean Ethics*,[26] Nietzsche offers his brief aphorism on "das dritte Geschlecht" ("the third sex"):

> "Ein kleiner Mann ist eine Paradoxie, aber doch ein Mann—aber die kleinen
> Weibchen scheinen mir, im Vergleich mit hochwüchsigen Frauen, von einem
> andern Geschlechte zu sein"—sagte ein alter Tanzmeister. Ein kleines Weib ist
> niemals schön—sagte der alte Aristoteles. (*FW* 85)

> "A small man is a paradox but still a man; but small females seem to me to
> belong to another sex than tall women," said an old dancing master. A small
> woman is never beautiful—said old Aristotle. (*GS* 130)

Well might we wonder what this brief observation on size and gender is doing here, or what it should mean. Kaufmann's response is to sigh wearily in a footnote to his translation: "With this absurd aphorism the pages on women reach their nadir and end," as if remarking on the antics of a beloved but exasperating relative given to rambling monologues at the dinner table.

"What a long, strange trip it's been":[27] from "artists" who necessarily find women's "natural" functions "repulsive," to women acting on men's fantasies at a distance, to women who "veil" the truth of the superficiality of existence, to women's attachment to rituals of virtue and shame, to women's manipulating men through an exaggeration of their vulnerability, to women's "cowlike" demeanor, to women conforming themselves to male-created images, to dangerous (to men and to themselves) vengeful women, to the falseness of idealized female characters in the theater, to the socially reinforced sexual naïveté of privileged women, to the beneficial effects of pregnancy on women's temperament, to excessive conversation of women who get too nervous around men, to a stated preference for tall women. The sequence begins and ends on a crude note, but we have not been brought so much full circle as around (over and under) a Möbius strip, where the underneath side of each position is always at least partly visible, as in the visual art of M. C. Escher. Much, much later, in section 361, Nietzsche offers an interesting coda to this series of meditations in a lengthy aphorism called *Von Probleme des Schauspielers* (*On the Problem of the Actor*) which closes in the following way:

> Endlich die *Frauen:* man denke über die ganze Geschichte der Frauen nach— *müssen* sie nicht zu ällerst und oberst Schauspielerinnen sein? Man höre die Ärzte, welche Frauenzimmer hypnotisiert haben; zuletzt, man liebe sie—man lasse sich von ihnen "hypnotisieren!" Was kommt immer dabei heraus? Dass sie "sich geben," selbst noch, wenn sie—sich geben . . . Das Weib ist so artistisch . . . (*FW* 235)

> Finally, *women.* Reflect on the whole history of women: do they not *have* to be first of all and above all actresses? Listen to physicians who have hypnotized women; finally, love them—let yourself be "hypnotized by them!" What is always the end result? That they "put on something" even when they take off everything. Woman is so artistic. (*GS* 317)

This passage is of enormous interest to such commentators as Derrida and Irigaray, and also cannot help but remind students of the history of psychoanalysis of the displays of hypnotized hysterics, orchestrated by

Charcot, that Freud witnessed at the Salpêtrière Clinic in Paris. The way one reads the passage depends considerably on how one would explain women's "need" to be actresses. Nietzsche's aphorism (68) in which the sage reminds his audience that women have had little choice but to fashion themselves according to the image men have imposed becomes most relevant here. Derrida and Irigaray have, of course, both seized upon that ringing last sentence: "Das Weib ist so artistisch." Given the privileged sense accorded *Künstler* (artists) throughout Nietzsche's writings, this has become one of the floating pieces of jetsam to which the drowning critic can cling in order to salvage some prospect for a feminist usage of *The Gay Science*.

Unfortunately, no one can claim this as the last word on Nietzschean sexual politics, since only a few pages later, in section 363, *Wie jedes Geschlecht über die Liebe sein Vorurteil hat* (*How each sex has its own prejudice about love*), we have a long rambling discourse that sets the way men love in opposition to the way women necessarily must love: the former by acquiring woman as a possession, the latter by giving herself as a possession. Here is a representative paragraph from this argument for the double standard:

> Das Weib will genommen, angenommen werden als Besitz, will aufgehn in der Begriff "Besitz," "besessen;" folglich will es einen, der *nimmt,* der sich nicht selbst gibt und weggibt, der umgekehrt vielmehr gerade reicher an "sich" gemacht werden soll—durch den Zuwachs an Kraft, Glück, Glaube, als welchen ihm das Weib sich selbst gibt. Das Weib gibt sich weg, der Mann nimmt hinzu— ich denke, über diesen Natur/Gegensatz wird man durch keine sozialen Verträge, auch nicht durch den allerbesten Willen zur Gerechtigkeit hinwegkommen: so wünschenswert es sein mag, dass man das Harte, Schreckliche, Rätselhafte, Un- moralische dieses Antagonismus sich nicht bestandig vor Augen stellt. Denn die Liebe, ganz, gross, voll gedacht, ist Natur und als Natur in alle Ewigkeit etwas "Unmoralisches." (*FW* 237)

> Woman wants to be taken and accepted as a possession, wants to be absorbed into the concept of possession, possessed. Consequently, she wants someone who *takes,* who does not give himself or give himself away; on the contrary, he is supposed to become richer in "himself"—through the accretion of strength, hap- piness, and faith given him by the woman who gives herself. Woman gives herself away, man acquires more—I do not see how one can get around this natural opposition by means of social contracts or with the best will in the world to be just, desirable as it may be not to remind oneself constantly how harsh, terrible, enigmatic, and immoral this antagonism is. For love, thought of in its entirety as great and full, is nature, and being nature it is in all eternity something "immoral." (*GS* 319)

Notice that the opposition is presented as natural *and* unjust, a position that would comfort the rankest sort of Social Darwinism. While Nietzsche at least admits of attempts to "get around this natural opposition by means of social contracts," he not only denies the possibility of doing so but says something more interesting and disturbing: that it is *desirable* not to be reminded of the harsh immorality of this state of things, *not* to be reminded of what he has just reminded us. Is the "real" Nietzschean message what begins to be stated in the most forceful terms in each of these aphorisms, or is it in the contradictory assertion that begins to be visible, sometimes lurking around the corner, where it is "not desirable" to look?

Most Nietzschean exegetes appear to feel that such a question is permanently suspended, or that the real Nietzschean message is one of infinite regress, i.e., that there is no Nietzschean message. A standard means of getting at this conundrum is through attention to style. The aphoristic genre itself makes for this indeterminacy according to, among others, Sarah Kofman, and she also sees this as the essence of the "gay science"—an invitation "to dance," the text as dervish, though one under no obligation to glorify a supreme deity or transcendental signified:

> L'aphorisme par sa brièveté, sa densité invite à danser: il est l'écriture même de la volonté de puissance, affirmatrice, légère, innocente. Écriture qui biffe l'opposition du jeu et du sérieux, de la surface et de la profondeur, de la forme et du contenu, du spontané et du réfléchi, du divertissement et du travail.[28]

> The aphorism by its brevity and its density invites dancing: it is the very writing of the will to power: affirming, light, innocent. Writing which eradicates the opposition between play and seriousness, surface and depth, form and content, the spontaneous and the reflective, diversion and labor. (My translation)

Kofman sees metaphor as the hallmark of Nietzsche's style, and argues that recourse to metaphor signifies aristocratic intentions, the author announcing his membership in an exclusive fraternity of refined souls who can never be comprehended by less refined readers.[29] Reading back through all the passages we have cited with metaphor in mind, we see how meaning is multiplied and complicated by a chain of metaphors that work metonymically in narrative sequence to undecide meaning.

Alexander Nehamas similarly emphasizes style in his *Nietzsche: Life as Literature,* treating him as the one Western philosopher thoroughly imbued with writerliness, to borrow and contort somewhat a term from Roland Barthes. Each of Nietzsche's texts could be seen, then, as a different experiment in style to which philosophical argument and assertion would always be subordinate. This would account for the relentless contradiction and paradox that defy attempts to generalize about the Nietzschean corpus. Unlike Walt Whitman, whose transcendentalist heritage Nietzsche, at least in its Emersonian version, admired, Nietzsche did not attempt to resolve contradictions within himself by enlarging the concept of self to "contain multitudes." Instead, according to Nehamas, he understood the persistence of contradictions to be proof of the subject's internal divisions, of the impossibility of claiming autonomous selfhood (an explanation that calls attention to the Nietzschean component in the postmodern theoretical and aesthetic assaults on the category of the subject).[30] Presumably, this would in turn explain the multiple contradictions within the series of statements about women we have just finished examining, perhaps even absolve Nietzsche (since no stable, unified entity called "Nietzsche" exists in the text) of his misogynist guilt (recall the de Man analogy).

But Nehamas insists that there is still something definably "Nietzschean" to be gleaned from this proliferation of styles, even if it is defined as an ongoing love affair with the vicissitudes of stylistic force. He also appears to define what is irreducibly "Nietzschean" as a thoroughgoing distrust of received opinions,[31] so one wonders, if only briefly, why this skepticism did not extend to received prejudices having to do with gender and sexuality. Gilles Deleuze, whom Nehamas cites as one of a host of Nietzschean commentators attentive to style, deserves credit for having inaugurated the style of interpretation that has led to the poststructuralist "new Nietzsche."[32] It should also be pointed out that Deleuze is more insistent than Nehamas on the need to define what is "Nietzschean," and for him it is the "eternal return" defined not as a cyclical philosophy of history but as a continual being as becoming, a notion that could certainly encompass acts of reading and textual interpretation.[33]

To review some of the interpretive claims that have been touched upon and to consider their implications: "Nietzsche," then, signifies style and writing. Experiments in writing style, such as the aphorism, "deconstruct" oppositions between surface and depth, form and content, etc. This takes us very close to the late work of Roland Barthes and the pleasure of surfaces that mask no hidden depth he believed he had discovered in a host of Japanese cultural forms and practices.[34] "Woman" for Nietzsche also signifies style (woman is "so artistic"). In French feminist theory "woman" signifies writing, and, in the work of Luce Irigaray, this is associated with a poetics of the female body that metaphorically suggests opposition to the "phallogocentrism" Derrida finds at work in Western metaphysics. Since Derrida has largely been interested in this concept only inasmuch as it allows him to dramatize the opposition of writing to speech, the task of demonstrating its implications for a feminist aesthetic or writing practice has been left to feminist theorists themselves.

To return for a moment to the passage concerning Lou Andréas-Salomé, horses, and whips which began this chapter, Nietzsche, at the time he wrote *Die fröhliche Wissenschaft,* was much taken with this woman whose lover Rilke would later become and with whom Freud would establish strong ties. She was every bit the intellectual, "artistic" woman targeted in *The Gay Science.* A transformed intellectual and cultural history will, one hopes, soon have us spending more time on Lou Andréas-Salomé, and less on Nietzsche or Rilke.

The photograph of the three friends with the horsecart derived its power and its "humor" less from the substitution of human beings for draft animals than from the position of the woman as the driver, the one cracking the whip. Nietzsche, who asserted the need for taking along a whip when one "goes to women," was dramatizing here his confrontation with one of the "new women" who "master the masters" ("die Herrinnen der Herren" [FW 83]). I cannot resist "reading" this famous photograph against the passage from Kundera, where Nietzsche might be understood as weeping for the ravages of a Cartesian epistemology of aloofness and objectification. Recent feminist inquiry has considered whether this is an essentially patriarchal mode of knowing.[35] Perhaps Nietzsche's gesture on the street in Turin was one of atonement for committing Descartes's error. If so, in the playful (?) photograph he had the horse before de cart.

Derrida, not one to shy away from a pun,[36] gets at the sexual politics of Nietzsche's writing (and, though he doesn't express it this way, the questions of Nietzsche's "writing like a woman") somewhat more obliquely, as usual. In *Spurs/Éperons,* one of his most convincing deconstructions (in my opinion), Derrida takes up the question of his ability to read "as a woman." It begins to look like a gesture of what Elaine Showalter has called "critical cross-dressing,"[37] but it is purely a strategic move in order to produce a symptomatic reading of moments in Nietzsche's text when "woman" is the subject. I would not wish to argue that Derrida's reading of *Die fröhliche Wissenschaft* can be improved upon in terms of sophistication. But I would certainly argue that it is possible to go further toward gender questions Derrida barely sketches out. This in particular is accomplished by Luce Irigaray in *Amante marine de Friedrich Nietzsche* (discussed below).

Derrida considers the question of Nietzsche's style(s), exploring stylistic complexities of the Nietzschean text that defy one's ability to proclaim the truth of Nietzsche. This, of course, is a kind of textual doubling maneuver, for, if Nietzsche uses style to make his challenge to truth with a capital T more formidable, then Derrida's deconstructions can convince only if they leave open and continuous the textual unraveling they set in motion, i.e., if they avoid points of closure at which a Derridean statement about the truth of Nietzsche's text appears to have been made. Much like Kofman, though less extensively than in her *Nietzsche et la métaphore,* Derrida shows how Nietzsche's aphoristic style renders his text undecidable.[38] He produces a fragment from Nietzsche's *Nachlass* ("I have forgotten my umbrella") whose meaning is impossible to explain in relation to Nietzsche's writings. Perhaps, for some readers, it will recall Lautréamont's famous passage describing a young man as being as "handsome as the fortuitous encounter upon a dissecting-table of a sewing-machine and an umbrella!"[39] but it remains an odd fragment.

To speak of fragments and fragmentation is, in the narrative tradition of psychoanalysis, to invoke the fantasy of castration, another of the subjects to which Derrida turns in *Spurs.* He does so through attention to those passages in *The Gay Science* where Nietzsche broods over the "veiled" character of female genitals in relation to other Nietzschean aphorisms about the artificiality of woman and her skeptical rejection of the truth (*GS* 64). Derrida glosses this by commenting that woman refuses the "truth" of her castration, which she knows to be but a hallucination of the man's. It is the man who persists in believing in the lack that constitutes the female genitals, just as Freud must treat the Dora case as an archeological quest to restore something that is missing and "mutilated."[40] As Cixous exclaims in "The Laugh of the Medusa,"

> Men say that there are two unrepresentable things: death and the feminine sex. That's because they need femininity to be associated with death; it's the jitters that gives them a hard-on! for themselves! They need to be afraid of us.[41]

The "laugh of the Medusa," then, is the laugh of the woman who, remembering Nietzsche's observation, has taken on the "veil" of the image constructed for her by "man." She laughs because she knows that castration is a lie but sees that man is *médusé* by regarding the "veiled" female sex at this distance. Sarah Kofman, in a move that reinforces the sense of the above quote from Cixous, associates writing with the female body and with "Medusa":

Writing, that form of the disruption of presence, is, like the woman, always put down and reduced to the lowest rung. Like the female genitalia it is troubling [one could add: *unheimlich*, i.e., "uncanny"—see Chapter 5], petrifying—it has a Medusa effect.[42]

One thing that Derrida doesn't point out is the interesting fact that both Nietzsche's German (*der Schleier*) and the French (*le voile*) words for veil—that covers this "pudendum" that worries Nietzsche so—are masculine nouns. He does call attention to the play, in French, on "veil" (*le voile*) and "sail" (*la voile*),[43] an association that figures as well for Luce Irigaray. Derrida wants to explore the "veil" in relation to metaphors of the hymen ("The Double Session")[44] and the "invaginated" text ("Living On: Border Lines"),[45] but his purpose is grammatological rather than feminist. Irigaray extends the punning series further, playing on *voiler, voler, violer* ("veil," "steal," "violate")[46] in order to examine the ways in which patriarchal logic has distorted its feminine other. French feminism has produced a rich and much-misunderstood poetics of the female body, and no one has done this in a more complicated manner than Luce Irigaray.

III.   IRIGARAY AND INDETERMINACY

If Jacques Derrida's *Glas* (1974), with its bicolumnar arrangement separated by a middle white space, mimics both phallus and hymen (as Gayatri Spivak has argued),[47] then Luce Irigaray's *Speculum de l'autre femme* (1977), much better known than *Amante marine de Friedrich Nietzsche* (1980), represents the female body presented for gynecological examination, with the middle essay, "Speculum," inserted between the "legs," respectively, of Plato and Freud, whose writings Irigaray challenges and questions in the first and third sections of the book.[48] As for "legs," keep in mind that that is also the French word for "legacy." In taking Nietzsche on, Irigaray devises another physical arrangement of the book in order to suggest the female body, conception, fertilization, and birth. Continuing the metaphor of fluids and flow deployed in her earlier work (which some readers take to be a literal comment that women's sexual pleasure is thus defined), she dramatizes her response to Nietzsche's text by posing as his aquatic lover. Thus the first essay is called "Dire d'eaux immémoriales" ("To speak of immemorial waters"). If we are right that Irigaray's reading of Nietzsche advances the feminist critique much further than that suggested by Derrida's *Spurs*, then perhaps it would not be too farfetched to read "Dire d'eaux" as composed partially of an anagram of Derrida's name. In terms of the structure of Irigaray's book, however, "Dire d'eaux immémoriales" is the scene of conception which results in the gestation and birth of the new text. The third section is duly titled "Quand naissent les dieux" ("When the gods are born"), suggesting the emergence of the *Übermenschen* who have passed through the birth canal of the book's middle essay.

For in between "Dire d'eaux immémoriales" and "Quand naissent les dieux" is the essay "Lèvres voilées" ("Veiled Lips"), forming the pivotal section of the book. It has the most to say about Nietzsche's sustained commentary on women from the sections of *The Gay Science* discussed above. Through both its title and its placement in the book, so that the reader parts it in two when the book is opened to the middle, this essay mimes the vulva, thus calling even more attention to the ways that it answers Nietzsche's absurd discussion of the "veiled" pudendum. Once we bring this text into play against this and other Nietzschean pronouncements on women, including those already made problematic by the Derridean reading, things get curiouser and curiouser.

Responding to passages such as the one in aphorism 60 of *The Gay Science* in which Nietzsche says, "Here I stand in the flaming surf whose white tongues are licking at my feet . . ." (*GS* 123), the narrator of Irigaray's text becomes the embodiment of water. Irigaray here plays on a number of oppositions, if only to deconstruct and get beyond them: Nietzsche, representing the patriarchal, is associated with solids; the "marine lover" with liquid. Irigaray has had a great deal to say in all her books about fluids, flow, and "feminine" dissolution of boundaries.[49] Jane Gallop's reading of the Lacanian sense of metaphor and metonymy,[50] along with Sarah Kofman's emphasis on Nietzsche's use of metaphor, might well encourage the association of solid (patriarchal) with metaphor and liquid (feminine) with metonymy—the "feminine" as deconstruction, as much of *l 'écriture féminine* seems to imply. Irigaray's text also associates Nietzsche with fire, and the narrator of *Amante marine* addresses him in terms of cooling water approaching his "burning lava."[51] At this point in Irigaray's performance the reader gasps in astonishment at the thought of red-hot Fred sizzling away in the cooling stream. Does this mean Nietzsche is a "churnin' urn o' burnin' funk?"[52]

Irigaray's textual flood overtakes Nietzsche at another point, again having to do with the veil. Meditating on Nietzsche's seeming fascination with and dread of the *pudendum,* she weaves a refrain of *volée, violée, voilée* ("stolen, violated, veiled"):[53] the refusal of patriarchy to allow woman to possess her own body, the "violation" that occurs through compulsory heterosexuality and rape, and the veiling and mystification that surrounds the female genitals. She speaks of "veiled lips" in order to symbolize the female body's refusal of phallocentric logic, the "diverse geography" of female pleasure, the multiplicity of "the feminine," and the unrepresentability of this undecidable "hymen." In Irigaray's writing the female body is in constant flux, these "lips" *perpétuellement en jeu*. If we remember Derrida's play on "veil" and "sail," then this *amante marine* appears always able to escape capture. At this point on our soundtrack, Muddy Waters sings "Sail on . . ."[54]

Of course this also means that Irigaray's text defies easy interpretation and categorization. She may seem to have found a convenient fluid image for the feminine, but these are very muddy waters indeed. A deliberately difficult writer, Irigaray has produced exasperation and irritation particularly in those who believe they see simply new versions of "essentialist" categories emerging out of this murky prose. This has been the complaint of Toril Moi, whose *Sexual/Textual Politics* has provided many readers with their introduction to Irigaray's work. She approvingly describes Monique Plaza's characterization of Irigaray as a "patriarchal wolf in sheep's clothing."[55]

"Essentialism" is certainly a danger to be avoided, but Moi does Irigaray's work a disservice by reducing it to this. Valuable as the book *Sexual/Textual Politics* is, its often sweeping generalizations and convenient stereotypes can work real mischief, as when they fall into the hands of male critics wishing to get "caught up" on recent feminist criticism who then conclude that feminist criticism is hopelessly infected with the essentialist plague. Their reaction to Irigaray's often baffling attempts to "write the body" may well be that Irigaray is a woman who doesn't know what she wants, doesn't know what she's saying. I allude obliquely but deliberately to some of the more infamous statements of Freud and Lacan, because Irigaray's texts are strategic interventions in patriarchal discourses from Plato to Lacan—talking back to them and resisting *their* essentialism.

Like the instructive shock of reversal that comes when we substitute a reclining male nude for the female in a classic European painting, or the exaggerated posing found in the photography of Cindy Sherman that explodes patriarchal objectifications of women from within their mise-en-scène, Irigaray's evocation of the female genitals and her description of a libidinal economy based on touch, flow, and continual play work textually to interrogate the privilege accorded the phallocentric logic of representations of the feminine.

Not content with discrediting Irigaray, Moi has more recently assailed such American feminist theorists as Alice Jardine for their mediation and adaptation of Irigaray, Cixous, Kristeva, etc. Apparently believing that taking inspiration from the stylistically innovative French writers precludes articulation with the historical materialist feminism she finds most congenial, Moi criticizes both Jardine and Jane Gallop for reducing feminism to (mere?) style, referring scornfully to Jardine's definition of "gynesis" as the "putting into discourse of women," examples of which Jardine, Moi argues, draws primarily from such male theoretical sources as Deleuze and Guattari.[56] But it is Moi's assumption that critical preoccupation with style is somehow politically suspect or self-defeating that I question. The best feminist criticism seems precisely to be that which uncovers gender ideology at the level of style; that shows the cultural construction of gender at work through aesthetics, through "science," or through a vast range of discourses. To fashion, however provisionally, an "alternative" prose style whose rhetorical flourishes respond in kind to patriarchal rhetorics of exclusion and distortion of women's realities is indeed to involve oneself politically. It seems to me to remain a vital dimension of sexual politics. If it is also "textual" politics, that need not necessarily or inevitably signal an elaborate political dodge of the urgency of contemporary feminism. Through her stylistic guerrilla raids into the territory of Western phallocentric writing, Irigaray at her rhetorical best churns up turmoil in the belly of the beast. It need not be a case of "no one here gets out alive."[57]

Do Irigaray's critics simply forget not to read her texts literally? I do not believe that she sets up oppositions to patriarchal elements in Nietzsche or other writers merely in order to argue for what is oppositional or quintessentially feminine. Her texts can show how otherness is not so "other" after all: when, in *Amante marine,* she writes of "mirroring" Nietzsche, or of reflecting him back to himself,[58] it appears to me to be a way of suggesting not a feminine essence, but the folly of masculinist attempts to regard the feminine at a distance[59] and to fail to recognize what is human in the radically projected other. Mirrors reflect back, but with a reversed image, so that the reflection is not actually "true." It is also an easy matter to multiply mirror images, and, in fact, Irigaray's writing, especially in *Amante marine,* provides a kind of horizontal version of the *mise en abyme* wherein, like one's experience in a gallery of mirrors, it becomes increasingly difficult, and ultimately futile, to locate the original "true" source of the proliferating images. Whereas Irigaray appears to posit a distinctly feminine epistemology (informed by touch, taste, movement, difference, and utopian egalitarianism) in opposition to patriarchal representation, hierarchy, and distancing, one could gain more by reading this through her own rich metaphors of multiplicity and variability. Like Derrida, she explodes binary oppositions, but, more than him, she points the way well beyond the number two. Perhaps we need to learn a positive connotation of the line "It's all done with mirrors."

IV. STYLE(S) II

But the problem of her writing style(s), like Nietzsche's style(s), remains. While it would be obviously ludicrous, in more ways than one, to claim that Nietzsche as well as Irigaray writes "like a woman," in both cases the textual displacements set in motion defy our attempts to declare with any degree of finality what the truth of these texts may be. One is tempted to say that this is the reason for Allan Bloom's discomfort. Yes, and you can't understand what they're saying in those rock 'n' roll songs, either. Do we want, following from Derrida's demonstration of Nietzsche's stylistic negations or sublations of his apparent misogyny, to celebrate an emancipatory stylistics of continual textual play and indeterminacy and to see that as somehow "feminine"? What *does* that do for a woman who wishes to write lab reports or articles in social science journals? To associate women with refusal of linear logic and objectivity is akin to associating them with madness, with "not knowing what they are saying." Remember, Nietzsche did go completely bonkers. Remember also the debate between Clément and Cixous over Dora, i.e., hysteria as tragic defeat or a desperate gesture of defiance and longed-for liberation. Some choice.

In *Reading Lacan*, Jane Gallop worries over similar problems, related to her own ability to "explain" Lacan. One of the values of her writing, I believe, is her ability to consider the argument for *l'écriture féminine* as indeterminacy, while demonstrating the drawbacks for feminism of such a view, all the while pressing the most radical implications of Lacan and cultural authority: that no one "has the phallus."[60] Put another way, men don't know what they are saying either. Lacan's remark turns back on itself. Elsewhere, Gallop refuses the equation, coming from Baudrillard, of women with style, surface, artificiality, and seduction.[61] She argues very convincingly that Baudrillard is just as foolish and destructive as Nietzsche on this score. She also avoids Toril Moi's mistake of assuming that any attempt to theorize "women's" writing as indeterminate must lead inevitably to the dead end of essentialist stereotypes.

Throughout this chapter, I have tried constantly to confront the sexual/ textual politics of my own reading of Nietzsche, of Derrida, and of Irigaray. I do not pretend that I am always capable of the necessary degree of self-criticism in this regard. I am aware that Nietzsche's text especially puts me in a contradictory position as reader; perhaps somewhere between male bonding ("Let's talk about women") and Judith Fetterley's "resisting reader."[62] I certainly recoil from what Nietzsche's text seems literally to say about women, but I still do not want to be "fettered" by any readerly stereotypes. In any case, all the deconstructions in the world still cannot escape what is most disturbing about Nietzsche's own sexual politics, however complicated and contradictory they may have been.

I think we must continue to demonstrate these complications in canonical texts: to show what is contradictory and undecidable while nevertheless demonstrating how meaning is produced in them, and how these meanings have been circulated within the cultural and pedagogical traditions that condition our assessment of them in the first place. This assessment can be shown to include unjustified assumptions and claims about the traditions these texts are thought to have inaugurated, claims having much more to do with institutional and disciplinary authority and power than with something intrinsic to the texts themselves. In opposition to those who, in recommending these texts, would return us to an imagined world of stability and order, uncontaminated by theory, we can only say that, based on the evidence of our rereading, there is a "whole lotta shakin' goin' on."[63]

"Do you wanna dance?"[64]

Constitution, we would have to pretend that structuralism, semiotics, deconstruction, feminist criticism, and psychoanalytic theory never existed. Away with all varieties of the "hermeneutics of suspicion." Since we are not about to do that, we necessarily remain alive to the ways in which even (or especially) "great" texts are decentered and thrown out of kilter as a result of a variety of factors, including the ideology of the autonomous subject and strategies of representation upon which a host of modern concepts of knowledge, truth, and aesthetic experience depend.

In particular we find that these five texts, and by extension the canon of intellectual or literary history they help to make up, are decentered by the cultural force of gender, whether gender issues are being overtly addressed or not. It is not adequate simply to demonstrate the self-deconstructing tendencies of a text like Descartes's *Méditations* with regard to the question of reason and madness. More important for a cultural criticism that would place gender at the center of its concerns, it becomes necessary to expose the ways in which Cartesian epistemology depends upon flagrantly patriarchal assumptions and strategies of representation. Similarly, the debt Marx's critique of alienation under capitalism owes to such fundamental shibboleths of patriarchal logic as the culture/nature and public/private distinctions must be faced. We have seen how the reputation of Flaubert's *Madame Bovary* is linked to misogynist assumptions, and have explored the relations between the novel's much-admired style and the contradictory sexual politics of representation in narrative discourse. In the cases of Freud and Nietzsche, we have applied similar kinds of interpretive apparatuses to, respectively, a text that appears to have little to do with gender and one that appears to have everything to do with the topic. In either case the compelling necessity of gender critique has I hope been convincingly demonstrated.

No matter how much these readings owe to Derrida or Lacan or Foucault, those theoretical perspectives are not, whatever their hermeneutical brilliance, adequate to deal with gender issues. Feminist criticism and theory, to some extent aligned with these "male" theories, is indispensable in forcing us to consider, as we reread modern texts and experience the displacements of gender woven into their fabric, the extent to which the cultural values assigned them derive from the unquestioned assumptions inscribed in them that in turn flatter the prejudices of their admirers. In Chapter 3 (Marx) we considered the view that any viable socialist position today must necessarily be a feminist one, with women's oppression, more than class oppression, being the overriding cultural and political tendency that must be combated and explained. Employing similar logic, cultural criticism primarily concerned with gender issues should be the most important way to expose ideological aspects of the texts deemed most essential to our educational and other institutions of civil society.

Obviously, this does not mean, as some readers of Michael Ryan's *Marxism and Deconstruction: A Critical Articulation* (1982) have charged, that the cultural critic imagines that each deconstructive reading makes the institutional walls come tumbling down.[1] Acts of reading, however willfully subversive, nevertheless take place within institutionally sanctioned frameworks and routinized procedures. For that matter, as this book has I hope made clear, deconstruction by itself is simply inadequate to the task. Feminist critics willing to use whatever works from Derridean thought have done far more than so-called deconstructionists to expose the "phallogocentrism" of Western texts. Still, cultural criticism can teach readers both to read against the grain of texts they encounter and to question and resist authoritative claims made for them. In the face of a right-wing demand for a return to the traditional values of the canon, the questions (paraphrased here) encouraged by Michel Foucault retain their urgent force: Who recommends these texts? Who controls their circulation? Who speaks for them?[2] Just as in the realm of theology, one must combat the fundamentalism that argues for correct interpretation and that would "canonize" (e.g., St. Descartes, St. Flaubert) great authors in order to control their reception. Instead, we must work to empower readers to examine canonical texts critically, to question reasons for their inclusion in a canon, and to question the very nature and raison d'être of canons.

This book has been somewhat in the form of a wager, i.e., to take the new right culture prophets up on their offer to lead us back into the promised land of the canon. Then, when they show us their beautiful rose garden, we can point out all the thorns. So, Bennett, Bloom, Cheney, Hirsch, et al., we'll agree to read the books on your list, but you might not like the readings we produce. You might wish you'd never recommended these books in the first place. On the one hand I feel, at this point, that we've never really read many of the authors whose names decorate our textbooks and course titles. On the other, and this is more or less my motto: I don't necessarily think we can get along without a canon,[3] but I'd like to try.

Where does that leave us? From Kate Millett's *Sexual Politics* (1970) to the present, feminist criticism and theory has proceeded through stages from feminist objections to what male authors have written to rediscovery of "lost" women writers to a theoretical exploration of *l'écriture féminine* to current debates over canons, alternative or otherwise. The important work of Sandra Gilbert and Susan Gubar has been much discussed and debated in this light. Although looking back over twenty years of feminist thought and scholarship we can discern these successive stages, it is crucial to realize that each area of activity continues to flourish.

By analogy, I believe that cultural criticism should continue to engage the canon, where, for example, there remains much to demonstrate about the central importance of gender. I also believe, and this is another reason why intellectual history should not survive in its present form, that cultural critics must shift their attention to "other" texts and traditions. Personally, I feel that moving wholeheartedly into the study of texts by women and into alternative canons, however provisional, will be a way for me to begin to repay the debt I owe feminist scholarship for what it has taught me, for helping me see the world anew. This commitment to "difference" must take place simultaneously with reexaminations of the Western canon informed by feminist theory, among others. Just as the urgent task of feminist scholarship calls us out of the ideological slumber of patriarchal thought, cultural contributions from outside Western experience must be studied and appreciated in order to defamiliarize our own tradition so that, "unlearning" our ethnocentrism, we can take steps toward a truly global outlook. Our overriding goal should be a cultural criticism and interdisciplinary education *of* and *for* difference. Themes of gender, sexual preference, race, class, and ethnicity seem best suited for such an educational credo. Anything less, any (I call it fascist) reassertion of the enduring, restoring value of one particular native tradition to the exclusion of all others is recklessly irresponsible in a late-twentieth-century world linked by electronic media, bristling with nuclear weapons, and facing almost certain ecological catastrophe if matters are left to traditional nation states and private enterprise.

It is not merely a question of setting aside one canon for another. Canonical texts could be studied in conjunction with noncanonical or alternative texts organized thematically. Even if the question of any one canon's survival remains suspended, maximum appreciation and critical awareness of difference should still be sought. As it becomes clear that writing comes from everywhere, and that academic pigeonholes like "literature" or "history" refer largely to certain kinds of writing by certain kinds of people, unwarranted distinctions (upon which such academic fields as intellectual history rest) between high culture and mass or popular culture will give way. Allan Bloom may long for an exclusive academic coterie of privileged white males, but, the more heterogeneous university populations become, the more difficult it will be to justify the traditional criteria according to which, e.g.,

Stravinsky may be labeled a "composer," but not Duke Ellington or Charles Mingus.

Those who assume that one should first become thoroughly familiar with one's own culture before attempting to appreciate others often also assume that there needs to be a careful sequence through which history or literature, e.g., is studied. If most people were really honest with themselves, they would admit that in fact this was not the pattern their education followed, and that part of the excitement of learning is its haphazard character. You develop enthusiasm for this or that local example, and experience growing pleasure over the years as you gain familiarity with a larger framework, chronological or otherwise, within which these examples might be placed. Historians, for example, may behave as if the orderly study of history should proceed through a conventional linear chronology, but in fact have themselves learned much of their history "out of order." The great majority of American historians specialize in the modern period, but this by no means precludes their developing an appreciation for earlier periods.

Certainly there are those, whatever their political predilections, who find the prospect of a radically interdisciplinary global approach to culture overwhelmingly daunting. There is too much to take in! And they fear for the well-being of students who, without the anchor of Western cultural lore, will be quite literally lost at sea. But, not to mention troubling political questions of nationalism or ethnocentrism, what evidence is there that people are truly happier as a result of being deeply rooted in one exclusive cultural tradition? That question is a variation on a theme introduced by Bruce Chatwin in his book *The Songlines,* where he speculates that human beings have always been predisposed more to live as nomads than to settle in one spot and develop civilizations.[4] This will remind readers of postmodern cultural theory of the concept of "nomad thought" adumbrated by Gilles Deleuze and Félix Guattari in their *Mille plateaux* (1980).[5] For cultural criticism, this implies a resistance to settling into any one theoretical position, a continued willingness to challenge and revise one's own critical positions and practices.

What this can produce is a sense of living in the interstices between cultures, and James Clifford's impressive book *The Predicament of Culture: Twentieth-Century Ethnography, Literature, and Art* provides some vivid examples of this sensibility from twentieth-century French ethnographers. Clifford introduces quite a range of topics, from Edward Said's writings on Palestinians in exile to the Wampanoag Indians of Mashpee, Massachusetts, and their unsuccessful suit to gain tribal status. But the book's consistent theme is twentieth-century ethnography, and the pivotal chapter, "On Ethnographic Surrealism," portrays the French ethnographers of the interwar years (i.e. 1918–39) who often allied themselves with avant-garde art and literature. Clifford's attempt to rescue the European avant-garde from Eurocentrism is convincing and refreshing, as he points out the ethnographers' fascination, admittedly from a position of considerable imperial advantage, with African aesthetic traditions especially. The introductory chapter, "The Pure Products Go Crazy," takes its title from the William Carlos Williams' work *Spring & All* (1923), with the opening lines "The pure products of America go crazy."[6]

When we are talking about literary traditions or knowledge of specific histories and specific cultures, it is indeed the pure product that goes crazy. For me, there is something warped and obsessive about cultural insularity, and, by the same token, something bracing and exhilarating about cultural diversity and, to use the term Clifford borrows affectionately from Mikhail Bakhtin, "heteroglossia,"[7] like the multiple accents heard in such recent Western pop music offerings as those by Paul Simon, Peter Gabriel, Youssou N'dour, Mahlathini, and Kate Bush. As I write these lines and bring this book to a close, I am enjoying the privilege of living in New York City, experiencing this cultural diversity (what mayor David Dinkins during his campaign liked to call the "mosaic") on a daily basis. I have been going on at some length about ethnicity, but I have not lost sight of gender. "The pure products go crazy" in terms of gender also. Living or viewing life only according to what patriarchal culture calls "masculine" or "feminine," "heterosexual" or "homosexual" is confining, and also doesn't make for very competent reading.

A more recent book that complements Clifford's multicultural perspective, but does significantly more in terms of sexual politics, is the fourth volume in the Dia Art Foundation's "Discussions in Contemporary Culture" series called *Remaking History*, edited by Barbara Kruger and Phil Mariani. Seeing contemporary "official history" as being largely what is produced for television, the editors see their task as one of bringing alternative histories along lines of gender, race, and class to light, "to allow the chorus of voices to speak, to focus on the process and not just the moment, on the scene and not just the individual, on the body and not just the figure."[8]

The topics in this provocative collection range from Edward Said's essay "Yeats and Decolonization," which manages to rescue Yeats from fascism in spite of his reputation and to establish common cause between Irish and Palestinian struggles for self-determination, to Paula Treichler on the way

Western reportage represents the AIDS crisis in the third world, to Cornel West on Black Culture and Postmodernism, to Homi Bhabha on Frantz Fanon. In addition, *Remaking History* includes essays on the sexual politics of Nazism by Alice Yaeger Kaplan, on 1988 news photographs by Carol Squiers, on the condition of being culturally and ethnically "different" by Gayatri Chakravorty Spivak, and J. Hoberman on the rewritings of history occurring in various contemporary Hollywood films about the Vietnam War (the American side of the story, that is).

All of this suggests that contemporary history is experienced through the mediation of a number of levels involving lived time, memory, and the artificial temporalities of electronic media, including the ability to experience time in terms of "fast forwarding" and "rewinding."[9] Much of postmodern cultural criticism and theory recognizes the need to apply advanced interpretive strategies developed for use with the high cultural canon to popular media and cultural practices wrongly deemed inherently inferior or debased. Among other things, this is the arena where gender construction is largely carried out. It may continue to be necessary and instructive to provide still newer interpretations of gender and representation in *Madame Bovary*, but for cultural critics or historians to argue that by definition there is nothing "intellectual" in mass or popular culture is untenable. Such distinctions rest upon assumptions that can easily be shown to be elitist, sexist, and racist, and if intellectual history, for example, must cling to these distinctions, then we should break free of its clutches. That argument is, however, the subject for another book, one in which the limits and inadequacies of postmodern cultural theories can be tested through a cultural focus that is deliberately interdisciplinary, global, popular (as in "of the people"), and affectionately sensitive to and appreciative of difference.

Notes

Chapter 1. Introduction

1. Stéphane Mallarmé, "Un coup de dés jamais n'abolira le hasard: poème," *Oeuvres complètes,* ed. Henri Mondor and G. Jean-Aubry (Paris: Gallimard/Bibliothèque de la Pléiade, 1945), 457–77.

2. See *Modern European Intellectual History: Reappraisals and New Perspectives,* ed. Dominick LaCapra and Steven Kaplan (Ithaca: Cornell UP, 1982) and, more recently, John Toews, "Intellectual History after the Linguistic Turn: The Autonomy of Meaning and the Irreducibility of Experience," *American Historical Review* 92 (1987): 879–907.

3. Catherine Belsey, *Critical Practice* (London: Methuen, 1980), 130.

4. Antonio Gramsci, *Selections from the Prison Notebooks,* ed. and trans. Quentin Hoare and G. N. Smith (New York: International Publishers, 1971), 9.

5. Robert Darnton, "Readers Respond to Rousseau: The Fabrication of Romantic Sensitivity," *The Great Cat Massacre and Other Episodes in French Cultural History* (New York: Basic Books, 1984), 216.

6. Natalie Zemon Davis, *Fiction in the Archives: Pardon Tales and Their Tellers in Sixteenth-Century France* (Stanford: Stanford UP, 1987).

7. Dominick LaCapra, *Rethinking Intellectual History: Texts, Contexts, Language* (Ithaca: Cornell UP, 1983); *History and Criticism* (Ithaca: Cornell UP, 1985); *History, Politics, and the Novel* (Ithaca: Cornell UP, 1987); *Soundings in Critical Theory* (Ithaca: Cornell UP, 1989).

8. Hayden White, *Tropics of Discourse: Essays in Cultural Criticism* (Baltimore: Johns Hopkins UP, 1978).

9. Hayden White, *Metahistory: The Historical Imagination in Nineteenth Century Europe* (Baltimore: Johns Hopkins UP, 1973).

10. See *Representing Kenneth Burke,* ed. Hayden White and Margaret Brose (Baltimore: Johns Hopkins UP, 1982).

11. White, "The Burden of History," *Tropics of Discourse,* 29. White's most recent book, *The Content of the Form: Narrative Discourse and Historical Representation* (Baltimore: Johns Hopkins UP, 1987), includes essays that refine impressively this theme of the problematic status of history and related disciplines. See especially the essay

that appeared originally in 1982 in *Critical Inquiry:* "The Politics of Historical Interpretation: Discipline and De-Sublimation," 58–82.

12. LaCapra, *History, Poltics, and the Novel; "Madame Bovary"on Trial* (Ithaca: Cornell UP, 1982).

13. The charge that so-called literary theory, deconstruction in particular, actually performs a conservative political function for the institution of literature runs throughout two books by Frank Lentricchia: *After the New Criticism* (Chicago: U of Chicago P, 1980), and *Criticism and Social Change* (Chicago: U of Chicago P, 1983).

14. Toews, "Intellectual History after the Linguistic Turn."

15. Ibid., 902.

16. Ibid., 898–99.

17. The conference was held at the University of North Carolina in Chapel Hill, September 25, 1988. The exchange took place during the final session on Sunday morning.

18. Nancy Fraser, "On the Political and the Symbolic: Against the Metaphysics of Textuality," *enclitic* 17/18 (1987), 100–114. LaCapra's response, "The Limits of Intellectual History," appears in the same issue, 141–50.

19. LaCapra, "Intellectual History and Critical Theory," *Soundings in Critical Theory* 206.

20. E. D. Hirsch, Jr., *Cultural Literacy: What Every American Needs to Know* (Boston: Houghton Mifflin, 1987).

21. Jane Gallop, *Reading Lacan* (Ithaca: Cornell UP, 1985), 13–18.

22. Gayle Rubin, "The Traffic in Women: Notes on the 'Political Economy' of Sex," in *Toward an Anthropology of Women,* ed. Rayna N. Reiter (New York: Monthly Review P, 1975), 157–210.

23. Roland N. Stromberg, *European Intellectual History Since 1789* 5th ed. (Englewood Cliffs, N.J.: Prentice Hall, 1990), 304.

24. Ibid., 320.

25. Elaine Showalter, "Critical Cross-Dressing: Male Feminists and the Woman of the Year," *Raritan* (Fall 1983): 130–49.

26. Alice Jardine and Paul Smith, eds., *Men in Feminism* (New York: Methuen, 1987).

27. Samuel Beckett, *The Unnamable* (New York: Grove Press, 1958), 179.

28. Teresa de Lauretis, "The Technology of Gender," *Technologies of Gender: Essays on Theory, Film, and Fiction* (Bloomington: Indiana UP, 1987), 3.

29. Peggy Kamuf, "Writing like a Woman," in *Women and Language in Literature and Society,* ed. Sally McConnell-Ginet et al. (New York: Praeger, 1980), quoted in Jonathan Culler, *On Deconstruction: Theory and Criticism after Structuralism* (Ithaca: Cornell UP, 1982), 57–58.

30. Friedrich Nietzsche, "Aber warum schreibst denn du?" *Die fröhliche Wissenschaft,* in *Werke* (München: Carl Hanser Verlag, 1954), 2: 99–100; "But why do you

write?" *The Gay Science,* trans. Walter Kaufmann (New York: Vintage Books, 1974), 146.

31. Bob Dylan, "From a Buick Six," *Highway 61 Revisited* (Columbia Records, 1965).

32. See Georges Bataille, *La part maudite* (Paris: Éditions de Minuit, 1949).

33. Gayatri Chakravorty Spivak, "Deconstruction in Exile," paper presented at Duke University Program in Literature conference "Convergence in Crisis: Narratives in the History of Theory," September 26, 1987.

34. Both texts are discussed in detail in Chapter 6.

35. See Chapter 4 for extended discussion of this point.

36. Michel Foucault, "Nietzsche Freud Marx," in *Nietzsche,* Cahiers de Royaumont (Paris: Éditions de Minuit, 1967), 185–87.

37. Allan Bloom, *The Closing of the American Mind: How Higher Education Has Failed Democracy and Impoverished the Souls of Today's Students* (New York: Simon and Schuster, 1987), 68.

38. James Clifford, *The Predicament of Culture: Twentieth-Century Ethnography, Literature, and Art* (Cambridge: Harvard UP, 1988). Illustrating the cross-cultural practice of *bricolage,* Clifford includes a photograph by E. T. Gilliard of a New Guinea girl sporting a necklace made of photographer's flash bulbs (211).

39. W. J. T. Mitchell, "Scholars Need to Explore Further the Links and Dissonance between Post-Colonial Culture and Post-Imperial Criticism," *Chronicle of Higher Education* 25, no. 32 (April 19, 1989): B1–3.

Chapter 2. Writing Like a Man (?)

I am indebted to Clayton Morgareidge, Karen Offen, and Winifred Woodhull for their critiques of an earlier version of this chapter.

1. René Descartes, *Méditations touchant la première philosophie,* in *Oeuvres et lettres* (Paris: Gallimard/Bibliothèque de la Pléiade, 1953), 267, and *Meditations on First Philosophy,* trans. Laurence J. Lafleur (Indianapolis: Bobbs-Merrill, 1960), 17. Hereafter, all references from these volumes will we given in the text and cited as (French) MF and (English) ME. Readers may be aware that the Latin *Meditationes de Prima Philosophia* (1641) appeared six years prior to the first French edition. Laurence J. Lafleur, who translated the edition cited above (widely used in university philosophy courses), justifies his use of the French rather than the Latin by explaining that the 1647 French edition was the only one over which Descartes had close supervision. I share Lafleur's assumption that it is thus the most reliable text. See Lafleur's "Introduction: Concerning the Translation," in ME vii–xvi.

2. T. Walter Wallbank et al., "New Dimensions of the Mind: Science, Thought,

and the Arts in the Age of Reason: 1600–1800," in *Civilization Past and Present,* 5th ed. (Glenview, Ill.: Scott, Foresman, 1978), 418.

3. Michel Foucault, "Revolutionary Action: 'Until Now'," *Language, Counter-Memory, Practice: Selected Essays and Interviews,* ed. Donald F. Bouchard (Ithaca: Cornell UP, 1977), 224.

4. Luce Irigaray, *Speculum de l'autre femme* (Paris: Éditions de Minuit, 1974), translated by Gillian C. Gill as *Speculum of the Other Woman* (Ithaca: Cornell UP, 1985); Evelyn Fox Keller, *Reflections on Gender and Science* (New Haven: Yale UP, 1985); Evelyn Fox Keller and Cristine R. Grontkowski, "The Mind's Eye," in *Discovering Reality: Feminist Perspectives on Epistemology, Metaphysics, Methodology, and Philosophy of Science,* ed. Sandra Harding and Merrill B. Hintikka (Dordrecht: D. Reidel, 1983); Christine Buci-Glucksmann, *La raison baroque: De Baudelaire à Benjamin* (Paris: Éditions Galilée, 1984) and *La folie du voir: De l'esthétique baroque* (Paris: Éditions Galilée, 1986); Susan R. Bordo, *The Flight to Objectivity: Essays on Cartesianism and Culture* (Albany: State U of New York P, 1986); and Dalia Judovitz: *Subjectivity and Representation in Descartes: The Origins of Modernity* (Cambridge: Cambridge UP, 1988).

5. Dominick LaCapra, *Rethinking Intellectual History: Texts, Contexts, Language* (Ithaca: Cornell UP, 1983).

6. Keller, *Reflections on Gender and Science* 178.

7. Elaine Showalter, "Critical Cross-Dressing: Male Feminists and the Woman of the Year," *Raritan* (Fall 1983): 130–49.

8. Elizabeth Kamarck Minnich, "From Ivory Tower to Tower of Babel?" *South Atlantic Quarterly* 89, no. 1 (Winter 1990): 184.

9. Hélène Cixous, "Sorties," in Cixous and Catherine Clément, *The Newly Born Woman,* trans. Betsy Wing (Minneapolis: U of Minnesota P, 1986), 82–83, and Cixous, "The Laugh of the Medusa," in *The Signs Reader: Women, Gender, and Scholarship,* ed. Elizabeth Abel and Emily K. Abel (Chicago: U of Chicago P, 1983), 279–83.

10. Edward W. Said, "The Problem of Textuality: Two Exemplary Positions," *Critical Inquiry* (Summer 1978): 690. A revised, expanded version of this exemplary essay appears as "Criticism between Culture and System," in Said, *The World, the Text and the Critic* (Cambridge: Harvard UP, 1983), 178–225.

11. Jacques Derrida, "Cogito et histoire de la folie," *L'écriture et la différence* (Paris: Éditions du Seuil, 1967), 51–67.

12. Michel Foucault, "Mon corps, ce papier, ce feu," appendix to *Histoire de la folie à l'âge classique* (Paris: Gallimard, 1972), 583–603.

13. Said, "Problem of Textuality"; Shoshana Felman, "Madness and Philosophy or Literature's Reason," *Yale French Studies* 52 (1975): 208; and John Frow, "Limits: The Politics of Reading," *Marxism and Literary History* (Cambridge: Harvard UP, 1986), 207–35.

14. Derrida, "Cogito," 52.

15. Frank Lentricchia, *Criticism and Social Change* (Chicago: U of Chicago P, 1984).

16. Derrida, *Spurs: Nietzsche's Styles/Éperons: Les styles de Nietzsche* (Chicago: U of Chicago P, 1978).

17. Cixous, "Sorties," and Michelle Z. Rosaldo and Louise Lamphere, Introduction, *Woman, Culture, and Society,* ed. Rosaldo and Lamphere (Stanford: Stanford UP, 1974), 1–15.

18. Luce Irigaray, *Ce sexe qui n'en est pas un* (Paris: Éditions de Minuit, 1977), 28.

19. Judovitz, *Subjectivity and Representation in Descartes,* 1–7. Judovitz argues impressively that postmodern theory, despite its intent, has not moved beyond a dependence on the categories of the subject and representation because of confusing the specifically Cartesian version of those terms with their currently conventional sense. See also Bordo, *Flight to Objectivity;* in particular, see her pages on Descartes and the "masculinization of thought," 101–5.

20. Keller, *Reflections on Gender and Science,* 63. Keller, Judovitz, and Bordo accomplish for feminism a careful historicizing of Descartes, one that has implications for the critical (à la Habermas) understanding of modernity. For more on Descartes, see especially Keller and Grontowski, "Mind's Eye," 207–24.

21. Judovitz, *Subjectivity and Representation in Descartes* 181–82.

22. Foucault, *Histoire de la folie* 57.

23. Susan Rubin Suleiman, "(Re)writing the Body: The Politics and Poetics of Female Eroticism," in *The Female Body in Western Culture: Contemporary Perspectives* (Cambridge: Harvard UP, 1986), 7–29.

24. This is not to say that Foucault was *completely* uninterested in the category of gender, as evidenced by his involvement with the publication of the memoirs of Herculine Barbin. See *Herculine Barbin: Being the Recently Discovered Memoirs of a Nineteenth-Century French Hermaphrodite,* introduced by Michel Foucault (New York: Pantheon, 1980).

25. Cixous and Clement, "The Untenable," in *Newly Born Woman* 147–60.

26. Foucault, *Histoire de la folie* 56–57.

27. Foucault, "Mon corps, ce papier, ce feu," 583–84.

28. Foucault, "What Is an Author?" *Language, Counter-Memory, Practice: Selected Essays and Interviews,* ed. Donald F. Bouchard (Ithaca: Cornell UP, 1977), 113–38. Compare Cixous: "I maintain unequivocally that there is such a thing as *marked* writing; that, until now, far more extensively and repressively than is ever suspected or admitted, writing has been run by a libidinal and cultural—hence political, typically masculine—economy; that this is a locus where the repression of women has been perpetuated, over and over, more or less consciously, and in a manner that's frightening since it's often hidden or adorned with the mystifying charms of fiction; that this locus has grossly exaggerated all the signs of sexual opposition (and not sexual difference), where woman has never *her* turn to speak—this being all the more serious and

unpardonable in that writing is precisely *the very possibility of change,* the space that can serve as a springboard for subversive thought, the precursory movement of a transformation of social and cultural structures." "Laugh of the Medusa," 283.

29. Derrida, "Cogito et histoire de la folie," 68. Cf. Angèle Kremer-Marietti, *Michel Foucault et L'archéologie du savoir* (Paris: Seghers, 1974), 122.

30. Derrida, "Cogito et histoire de la folie," 55–56.

31. Roland Barthes, "De Part et d'autre," *Essais critiques* (Paris: Éditions du Seuil, 1964), 168.

32. Derrida, "Cogito et histoire de la folie," 55–57.

33. Ibid., 95.

34. Ibid., 72.

35. Jean-Joseph Goux, "Descartes et la perspective," *L'Esprit créateur* 25, no. 1 (Spring 1985): 13–14.

36. Judovitz, *Subjectivity and Representation in Descartes* 4.

37. Bordo, *Flight to Objectivity* 106.

38. Judovitz, *Subjectivity and Representation in Descartes* 183.

39. Keller and Grontkowski, "Mind's Eye," and Martin Jay, "In the Empire of the Gaze: Foucault and the Denigration of Vision in Twentieth-Century French Thought," in *Foucault: A Critical Reader,* ed. David Couzzens Hoy (Oxford: Basil Blackwell, 1986), 174–204. See also Martin Jay, "Scopic Regimes of Modernity," in *Vision and Visuality,* ed. Hal Foster (Seattle: Bay P, 1988), 3–23.

40. Alice A. Jardine, *Gynesis: Configurations of Woman and Modernity* (Ithaca: Cornell UP, 1985), 119.

41. Goux, "Descartes et la perspective," 19.

42. See Jane Gallop, *Reading Lacan* (Ithaca: Cornell UP, 1985).

43. The Who, "I Can See for Miles," *The Who Sell Out* (Decca Records, 1967); The Police, "Every Step You Take," *Synchronicity* (A & M Records, 1983).

44. Sigmund Freud, "Femininity," *New Introductory Lectures on Psychoanalysis* (New York: Norton, 1965), 99–119.

45. Sarah Kofman, *L'énigme de la femme: La femme dans les textes de Freud* (Paris: Éditions Galilée, 1980).

46. Said, "Secular Criticism," *The World, the Text, and the Critic* 1–30.

47. Jeffrey Mehlman, "Writing and Deference: The Politics of Literary Adulation," *Representations* 15 (Summer 1986): 2.

48. Keller, *Reflections on Gender and Science* 63–64. Simone Mazauric, in an excellent and thorough introduction to a recent edition of the *Discours de la méthode,* complements this general theme, with particular emphasis on the simultaneous emergence of modern science and the material civilization of modern capitalism. Both, she argues, were in embryonic form at the time (1637) Descartes published the *Discours:* Simone Mazauric, Introduction to Descartes *Discours de la méthode* (Paris: Messidor/Éditions Sociales, 1983), 39.

49. Derrida, "La Structure, le signe et le jeu dans le discours des sciences humaines," *L'écriture et la différence* 409–28.

50. Sherry B. Ortner, "Is Female to Male as Nature Is to Culture?" in *Woman, Culture, and Society* 67–84.

51. Barbara Kruger, *We Won't Play Nature To Your Culture* (London: Institute of Contemporary Arts, 1983), 51.

52. Bordo, *Flight to Objectivity* 21.

53. Claude Lévi-Strauss, *Le cru et le cuit* (Paris: Plon, 1964).

54. Cixous, "Laugh of the Medusa," 281.

55. Descartes, *Oeuvres et lettres,* 125–265.

56. Judovitz, *Subjectivity and Representation in Descartes* ix.

57. Martin Heidegger, "The Age of the World View," *The Question Concerning Technology and Other Essays* (New York: Harper & Row, 1977), 115–54.

58. Keller, "A World of Difference," *Reflections on Gender and Science* 158–76. Cf. Keller, *A Feeling for the Organism: The Life and Work of Barbara McClintock* (New York: Freeman, 1983).

59. Buci-Glucksmann, *La folie du voir* 41. Cf. Jay, "Scopic Regimes of Modernity," 16–19.

60. Irigaray, *Speculum de l'autre femme.*

61. Jay, "In the Empire of the Gaze," 174–204.

62. Toril Moi, *Sexual/Textual Politics: Feminist Literary Theory* (London: Methuen, 1985), 127–49.

63. Luce Irigaray, *Et l'une ne bouge pas sans l'autre* (Paris: Éditions de Minuit, 1979), 10. See also Monique Plaza, " 'Phallomorphic Power' and the Psychology of 'Woman,' " *Ideology and Consciousness* 4(Autumn 1978): 26.

64. See especially Jeffrey Weeks, *Sexuality and Its Discontents: Modern Meanings, Myths, Sexualities* (London: Routledge and Kegan Paul, 1985).

65. Suleiman, "(Re)writing the Body," 24.

Chapter 3. The Persistence of the Gendered Subject

The critical comments and suggestions on this chapter provided by Thomas Mc-Laughlin, Jefferson Boyer, and A. Fuat Firat have been extremely helpful to me. Some portions of the above appeared in my essay "Foucault and Marx: A Critical Articulation of Two Theoretical Traditions," *New Orleans Review* 11, nos. 3/4 (Fall/ Winter 1984): 134–48. I am grateful for permission to reprint that material.

In this chapter, and throughout this book, the reader will notice my use of the lower-case "marxism." I have adopted this practice not to diminish marxism, but to emphasize (1) that what we call "marxism" today has been shaped by many more persons than Marx (or Engels), and (2) that marxism is of no greater political or critical value than feminism, a word I have not capitalized.

1. Louis Althusser, *For Marx,* trans. Ben Brewster (London: Verso, 1979), 51–86, 155–60.

2. Mark Poster, *Existential Marxism in Postwar France: Sartre to Althusser* (Princeton: Princeton UP, 1975).

3. Lukács first examined the newly discovered manuscripts during his trip to Moscow in 1931. See Eugene Lunn, *Marxism and Modernism: An Historical Study of Lukács, Brecht, Benjamin, and Adorno* (Berkeley: U of California P, 1982), 111.

4. Perry Anderson, "Structure and Subject," *In the Tracks of Historical Materialism* (Chicago: U of Chicago P, 1984), 32–55. See also James A. Winders, "Poststructuralist Theory, Praxis, and the Intellectual," *Contemporary Literature* 27, no. 1 (Spring 1986): 76–79.

5. See Bertell Ollman, *Alienation: Marx's Conception of Man in Capitalist Society,* 2d ed. (Cambridge: Cambridge UP, 1976).

6. Louis Althusser, "Ideology and Ideological State Apparatuses (Notes Toward an Investigation)," *Lenin and Philosophy and Other Essays,* trans. Ben Brewster (New York: Monthly Review P, 1971), 127–86.

7. Norman Geras, *Marx and Human Nature: Refutation of a Legend* (London: Verso, 1986), 81.

8. Ibid., 29–58.

9. Luce Irigaray, "Any Theory of the 'Subject' Has Always Been Appropriated by the 'Masculine,' " *Speculum of the Other Woman,* trans. Gillian C. Gill (Ithaca: Cornell UP, 1985), 133–46.

10. Harry van der Linden, *Kantian Ethics and Socialism* (Indianapolis: Hackett, 1988).

11. Sarah Kofman, *Le respect des femmes (Kant et Rousseau)* (Paris: Éditions Galilée, 1973), 13–56.

12. Jean Baudrillard, *The Mirror of Production,* trans. Mark Poster (St. Louis: Telos P, 1975). For valuable criticism of Baudrillard's ideas and the challenge they offer to contemporary marxist theory, see two articles by Mark Poster: "Technology and Culture in Habermas and Baudrillard," *Contemporary Literature* (Fall 1981): 456–77, and "Semiology and Critical Theory: From Marx to Baudrillard," *boundary 2* 8, no. 1 (Fall 1979): 275–93.

13. For an opposing view, see Jane Gallop, "French Theory and the Seduction of Feminism," in *Men in Feminism,* ed. Alice Jardine and Paul Smith (New York: Methuen, 1987), 111–15.

14. Alison M. Jaggar, *Feminist Politics and Human Nature* (Totowa, N.J.: Rowman & Allanheld, 1983), 69–79.

15. See the interesting and suggestive collection of essays in *Foucault & Feminism: Reflections on Resistance,* ed. Irene Diamond and Lee Quinby (Boston: Northeastern UP, 1988).

16. Michèle Le Doeuff, "Ants and Women, or Philosophy without Borders," in

NOTES TO PAGES 53–56

Contemporary French Philosophy, ed. A. Phillips Griffiths (Cambridge: Cambridge UP, 1987), 49.

17. Pierre Macherey, *Pour une théorie de la production littéraire* (Paris: Maspero, 1966).

18. Biddy Martin, "Feminism, Criticism, and Foucault," *New German Critique* 27 (Fall 1982): 13.

19. See Nancy S. Love, *Marx, Nietzsche, and Modernity* (New York: Columbia UP, 1986), x, and John F. Rundell, *Origins of Modernity: The Origins of Modern Social Theory from Kant to Hegel to Marx* (Madison: U of Wisconsin P, 1987), 170. Love explicitly excuses Marx for his gender-specific language, while Rundell paraphrases the arguments of the *EPM* about the worker's existence to read "his or her."

20. Heidi Hartmann, "The Unhappy Marriage of Marxism and Feminism: Towards a More Progressive Union," in *Women and Revolution,* ed. Lydia Sargent (Boston: South End P, 1981), 1–43.

21. Hélène Cixous, "Sorties," in Cixous and Catherine Clément, *The Newly Born Woman,* trans. Betsy Wing (Minneapolis: U of Minnesota P, 1986), 63–72.

22. Cf. Fredric Jameson, *The Political Unconscious: Narrative as a Socially Symbolic Act* (Ithaca: Cornell UP, 1981), 114.

23. Jackson Browne, "The Pretender," *The Pretender* (Asylum Records, 1976).

24. Cf. Karen Sacks, "Engels Revisited: Women, the Organization of Production, and Private Property," in *Toward an Anthropology of Women,* ed. Rayna N. Reiter (New York: Monthly Review P, 1975), 211–34.

25. Joan Kelly, "The Doubled Vision of Feminist Theory: Postscript to the 'Women and Power' Conference," *Women, History, and Theory* (Chicago: U of Chicago P, 1984), 51–64.

26. Natalie J. Sokoloff, *Between Money and Love: The Dialectics of Women's Home and Market Work* (New York: Praeger, 1980), 124.

27. Karl Marx, *Capital: A Critique of Political Economy,* Vol. 1: *The Process of Capitalist Production* (New York: International Publishers, 1967), 395–96. Marx complains that factory labor for women "usurped the place . . . of free labour at home within moderate limits for the support of the family." Despite the fact that, elsewhere, Marx and Engels appear to welcome the historical necessity of this transformation, one still detects in this passage a hint of regret. For an excellent overview of recent social theory pertaining to women's employment that surveys the changing patterns of job segregation by sex during the historical periods Marx concerned himself with in the *Grundrisse* and *Capital,* see Heidi Hartmann, "Capitalism, Patriarchy, and Job Segregation by Sex," *Signs* 1, no. 3 (1976): 137–69. Hartmann's essay helps to place the above passage by Marx within a contemporary feminist framework.

28. Sherry B. Ortner, "Is Female to Male as Nature Is to Culture?" in *Woman, Culture, and Society,* ed. Michelle Z. Rosaldo and Louise Lamphere (Stanford: Stanford UP, 1974), 67–87.

29. One essay that brilliantly synthesizes the diverse currents—feminist, marxist, psychoanalytic, structuralist, and poststructuralist—of theory that figure in much of the preceding discussion is Gayle Rubin's "The Traffic in Women: Notes on the 'Political Economy' of Sex," in *Toward an Anthropology of Women* 157–210.

30. Karl Marx, "Ökonomisch-philosophische Manuskripte," *Werke/Artikel/Entwürfe/März 1843 bis August 1844: Text*, in *Marx-Engels Gesamtausgabe* (Berlin: Dietz Verlag, 1982), 2:363–75; *The Economic and Philosophic Manuscripts of 1844*, trans. Martin Milligan (New York: International Publishers, 1964), 147–64. Hereafter, these will be cited in the text as (German) *MEGA* and (English) *EPM*, respectively.

31. John Berger, *Ways of Seeing* (New York: Penguin Books, 1972).

32. Jacques Derrida, "Le structure, le signe, et le jeu dans le discours des sciences humaines," *L'écriture et la différence* (Paris: Éditions du Seuil, 1967), 409–28.

33. Le Doeuff, "Ants and Women," 49.

34. Jacques Derrida, "La brisure," in *De la grammatologie* (Paris: Éditions de Minuit, 1967), 96–108.

35. Ollman, "With words that appear like bats," *Alienation* 3–11.

36. Jeffrey Weeks, *Sexuality and Its Discontents: Meanings, Myths, and Modern Sexualities* (London: Routledge & Kegan Paul, 1985), 160–170.

37. Quoted in Ollman, *Alienation* 159.

38. Luce Irigaray, "The Blind Spot of an Old Dream of Symmetry," *Speculum of the Other Woman* 13–129.

39. Edward W. Said, *The World, the Text and the Critic* (Cambridge: Harvard UP, 1983).

40. Marx, *Capital*, 1: 351.

41. Wallace Stevens, "The Man Whose Pharynx Was Bad," *The Palm at the End of the Mind: Selected Poems and a Play*, ed. Holly Stevens (New York: Vintage Books, 1972), 51–52.

42. See Griselda Pollock, "Modernity and the Spaces of Femininity," *Vision and Difference: Femininity, Feminism, and the Histories of Art* (New York: Routledge, 1988), 50–90.

43. Jaggar, *Feminist Politics and Human Nature* 75.

44. John Sayles, "The Shooting Script," *Thinking in Pictures: The Making of the Movie "Matewan"* (Boston: Houghton Mifflin, 1987), 4.

45. See Mark Poster, *Foucault, Marxism, and History: Mode of Production versus Mode of Information* (London: Polity P, 1984).

46. Frank Lentricchia, "Reading Foucault (Punishment, Labor, Resistance): Part Two," *Raritan* (Summer 1982): 46. Also see part 1 of the same essay in *Raritan* (Spring 1982): 5–32, and James A. Winders, "Foucault and Marx: A Critical Articulation of Two Theoretical Traditions," *New Orleans Review* 11, nos. 3/4 (Fall/Winter 1984): 134–48.

47. Most notably in Michael Ryan, *Marxism and Deconstruction: A Critical Articulation* (Baltimore: Johns Hopkins UP, 1982).

48. Martin, "Feminism, Criticism and Foucault," 15.

49. Terry Eagleton, "Capitalism, Modernism and Postmodernism," *Against the Grain: Essays 1975–1985* (London: Verso, 1986), 132.

50. Winders, "Foucault and Marx," 145–48.

51. Ibid., p. 146.

52. Georg Lukács, "Reification and the Consciousness of the Proletariat," *History and Class Consciousness: Studies in Marxist Dialectics,* trans. Rodney Livingstone (Cambridge: MIT P, 1971), 83–222.

53. Martin Jay, "In the Empire of the Gaze: Foucault and the Denigration of Vision in Twentieth-Century French Thought," in *Foucault: A Critical Reader,* ed. David Couzzens Hoy (Oxford: Basil Blackwell, 1986), pp. 174–204; and "Scopic Regimes of Modernity," in *Vision and Visuality,* ed. Hal Foster (Seattle: Bay P, 1988), 3–23.

54. Michel Foucault, *The History of Sexuality, Vol. 1: Introduction,* trans. Robert Hurley (New York: Vintage Books, 1980), 100–102.

55. Rosalind Coward, *Female Desires: How They Are Sought, Bought, and Packaged* (New York: Grove P, 1985).

56. Quoted in Marshall Berman, *All That Is Solid Melts into Air: The Experience of Modernity* (New York: Simon and Schuster, 1982), 59.

57. Weeks, *Sexuality and Its Discontents.*

58. Rosalind Pechetsky, "Dissolving the Hyphen: A Report on Marxist-Feminist Groups 1–5," in *Capitalist Patriarchy and the Case for Socialist Feminism,* ed. Zillah R. Eisenstein (New York: Monthly Review P, 1979), 373–89.

59. *Technologies of the Self: A Seminar with Michel Foucault,* ed. Luther H. Martin et al. (Amherst: U of Massachusetts P, 1988).

60. Gilles Deleuze and Félix Guattari, *Anti-Oedipus: Capitalism and Schizophrenia,* trans. Robert Hurley et al. (Minneapolis: U of Minnesota P, 1983), 1–50.

61. Nancy Chodorow, *The Reproduction of Mothering: Psychoanalysis and the Sociology of Gender* (Berkeley: U of California P, 1978). For a critique that finds in Chodorow an overly ahistorical conceptual framework, see Jacqueline Rose, *Sexuality and the Field of Vision* (London: Verso, 1986).

62. Luce Irigaray, *Et l'une ne bouge pas sans l'autre* (Paris: Éditions de Minuit, 1979), 10.

63. Marx, *Capital, Volume 1,* quoted in Berman, *All That Is Solid Melts into Air* 97.

64. Félix Guattari, "The Group and the Person," in *Molecular Revolution: Psychiatry and Politics* trans. Rosemary Sheed (Harmondsworth: Penguin Books, 1984), 24–44.

65. Gilles Deleuze and Félix Guattari, "November 28, 1947: How Do You Make Yourself a Body without Organs?" in *A Thousand Plateaus: Capitalism and Schizophrenia,* trans. Brian Massumi (Minneapolis: U of Minnesota Press, 1987), 149–66.

66. Ibid., 3–4.

Chapter 4. Modernism, Postmodernism, and Writing

1. Naomi Schor and Henry F. Majewski, eds., *Flaubert and Postmodernism* (Lincoln: U of Nebraska P, 1984).

2. Percy Lubbock, *The Craft of Fiction* (New York: Viking, 1957), 60.

3. Jonathan Culler, "The Uses of *Madame Bovary*," in *Flaubert and Postmodernism* 1–12.

4. Lubbock, *Craft of Fiction* 69.

5. Allan Bloom, *The Closing of the American Mind* (New York: Simon and Schuster, 1987).

6. See remarks on Bloom in Chapter 6.

7. See Mario Vargas Llosa, *The Perpetual Orgy: Flaubert and Madame Bovary* (New York: Farrar, Straus and Giroux, 1986), 213. Vargas Llosa is much more reliable as a critic of Flaubert than he is as an interpreter of contemporary Latin American politics.

8. Bakhtin's studies of Rabelais and Flaubert's use of Rabelais interest Dominick LaCapra considerably in *"Madame Bovary" on Trial* (Ithaca: Cornell UP, 1982). See also Arthur Mitzman, "Roads, Vulgarity, Rebellion, and Pure Art: The Inner Space in Flaubert and French Culture," *Journal of Modern History* 51, no. 3 (September 1979): 504–24.

9. Dominick LaCapra, *History, Politics, and the Novel* (Ithaca: Cornell UP, 1987).

10. LaCapra, *"Madame Bovary" on Trial* 10.

11. For a careful theorization of what might be meant by "field," see Pierre Bourdieu, "Flaubert's Point of View," *Critical Inquiry* 14, no. 3 (Spring 1988): 541–45.

12. Roland Barthes, "Flaubert et la phrase," *Le degré zéro de l'écriture suivi de nouveaux essais critiques* (Paris: Éditions du Seuil, 1972), 135–44. In this characteristically graceful, intelligent essay, Barthes writes of Flaubert's stylistic quest as one of immense labor and ceaseless correction and revision ("le dur travail du style, la fatigue des corrections incessantes"), and quotes claims from the author's correspondence of having spent five days on a single page, or devoting two days' research to a single line! (135). This "infinite" labor of correction, Barthes suggests, gives the lie to any notion that the Flaubertian sentence is perfectly realized or "finished": "parce que la phrase est libre, l'écrivain est condamné non à chercher la meillure phrase, mais à assumer toute phrase . . ." (because the sentence is free, the writer is condemned not to search for the best sentence, but to assume every sentence) (143; translation mine).

13. John J. O'Connor, "When the Sun Set on the Nixon Presidency," *New York Times,* October 29, 1989, 33.

14. Elizabeth Wilson, "Rewinding the Video," *Hallucinations: Life in the Postmodern City* (London: Hutchinson Radius, 1988), 191–209.

15. Julio Cortazar, "Blow-up," *Blow-up and Other Stories* (New York: Collier Books, 1968), 100–115.

16. Jane Gallop, "French Theory and the Seduction of Feminism," in *Men in Feminism*, ed. Alice A. Jardine and Paul Smith (New York: Methuen, 1987), pp. 111–15.

17. See, among many other sources, Laura Mulvey, "Visual Pleasure and Narrative Cinema," *Screen* (Autumn 1975): 6–18; Annette Kuhn, *Women's Pictures: Feminism and Cinema* (London: Routledge & Kegan Paul, 1982); and Teresa de Lauretis, *Technologies of Gender: Essays on Theory, Film, and Fiction* (Bloomington: Indiana UP, 1987).

18. Gérard Genette, "Les silences de Flaubert," *Figures I* (Paris: Éditions du Seuil, 1966), 228.

19. Pierre Danger, *Sensations et objets dans le roman de Flaubert* (Paris: Librairie Armand Colin, 1973), 186.

20. Mieke Bal, "Théorie de la description: L'exemple de *Madame Bovary*," in *Flaubert: La dimension du texte*, ed. P. M. Wetherill (Manchester: Manchester UP, 1982), 187–88.

21. Ibid., 188.

22. Nathaniel Wing, *The Limits of Narrative: Essays on Baudelaire, Flaubert, Rimbaud and Mallarmé* (Cambridge: Cambridge UP, 1986), 57.

23. Gustave Flaubert, *Madame Bovary: Moeurs de province*, in *Oeuvres I*, ed. Albert Thibaudet and René Dumésnil (Paris: Gallimard/Bibliothèque de la Pléiade, 1951), 461. Hereafter, this will be cited as MBF.

24. Cf. Winifred Woodhull, "Configurations of the Family in 'Un Coeur simple,' " *Comparative Literature* 39, no. 2 (Spring 1987): 141. Woodhull argues that this text of Flaubert "problematizes" the opposition between public and private spheres.

25. Mary Ann Caw, "Ladies Shot and Painted: Female Embodiment in Surrealist Art," in *The Female Body in Western Culture*, ed. Susan R. Suleiman (Cambridge: Harvard UP, 1986), 262–87.

26. Gustave Flaubert, *Madame Bovary: Moeurs de province* (Paris: Éditions Garnier Frerès, 1961).

27. Gustave Flaubert, *Madame Bovary*, trans. Paul de Man (New York: Norton, 1969), 11. Hereafter cited as MBE.

28. Stéphane Mallarmé, "Ses purs ongles très haut dédiant leur onyx," *Selected Poetry and Prose*, ed. Mary Ann Caws, trans. Mary Ann Caws et al. (New York: New Directions, 1982), 48.

29. John Berger, *Ways of Seeing* (New York: Penguin Books, 1977), 47.

30. Jean-Paul Sartre, *Being and Nothingness* (New York: Washington Square P, 1966), 340–400.

31. James Joyce, *Ulysses: The Corrected Text*, ed. Hans Walter Gabler et al. (New York: Vintage Books, 1987), 643–44.

32. Wallace Stevens, "The Poems of Our Climate," *The Palm at the End of the Mind: Selected Poems and a Play*, ed. Holly Stevens (New York: Vintage Books, 1972), 158. Here is a four-line passage, containing the phrase just quoted, that might comment sadly on Emma's longings: "The imperfect is our paradise. / Note that, in this

bitterness, delight, / Since the imperfect is so hot in us, / Lies in flawed words and stubborn sounds."

33. See the interesting comments on this passage in Hazel E. Barnes, *Sartre & Flaubert* (Chicago: U of Chicago P, 1981), 352.

34. Michal Peled Ginsburg, *Flaubert Writing: A Study in Narrative Strategies* (Stanford: Stanford UP, 1986), 2–3. Alice Jardine, in *Gynesis: Configurations of Woman and Modernity* (Ithaca: Cornell UP, 1985), makes representation a central problematic for (post)modernism.

35. De Lauretis, "Calvino and the Amazons: Reading the (Post) Modern Text," *Technologies of Gender* 82.

36. LaCapra, *"Madame Bovary" on Trial* 129. For extensive examples of the workings of free indirect style and the overall "uncertainty" this gives *Madame Bovary* and other texts of Flaubert, see Jonathan Culler, *Flaubert: The Uses of Uncertainty,* rev. ed. (Ithaca: Cornell UP, 1985).

37. Flaubert, *The Letters of Gustave Flaubert, 1830–1857,* selected, edited, translated by Francis Steegmuller (Cambridge: Belknap/Harvard UP, 1980), 154.

38. Vaheed K. Ramazani, *The Free Indirect Mode: Flaubert and the Poetics of Irony* (Charlottesville: UP of Virginia, 1988), 122.

39. Wallace Stevens, "Anecdote of the Jar," *The Palm at the End of the Mind* 46.

40. Fredric Jameson, "Flaubert's Libidinal Historicism: *Trois contes,*" in *Flaubert and Postmodernism* 76–83.

41. Quoted in Ramazani, *Free Indirect Mode* 111.

42. Friedrich Nietzsche, "But why do you write?" *The Gay Science,* trans. Walter Kaufmann (New York: Vintage Books, 1974), 146.

43. Barnes, *Sartre and Flaubert* 2–5.

44. Ramazani, *Free Indirect Mode* 45.

45. Walter Benjamin, *Illuminations* (New York: Schocken, 1969), 257–58.

46. See Lisa Phillips, *Cindy Sherman* (New York: The Whitney Museum, 1987).

47. Dalia Judovitz, *Subjectivity and Representation in Descartes: The Origins of Modernity* (Cambridge: Cambridge UP, 1988). See Chapter 2 for detailed discussion of her argument.

48. Cf. Wing, *Limits of Narrative* 47.

49. Marcie Blane, "Bobby's Girl" (Seville Records, 1962).

50. Rainer Warning, "Irony and the 'Order of Discourse' in Flaubert," *New Literary History* 13, no. 2 (Winter 1982): 269.

51. Rosalind Coward, *Female Desires: How They Are Sought, Bought, and Packaged* (New York: Grove, 1985).

52. Ginsburg, *Flaubert Writing* 85.

53. The Rolling Stones, "We Are Waiting," *Aftermath* (London Records, 1966).

54. Michael Danahy, "Le roman est-il chose femelle?" *Poétique: Revue de théorie et d'analyse littéraires* 25 (1976): 93.

55. Ibid., 89–90.

56. Fredric Jameson, "Postmodernism, or the Cultural Logic of Late Capitalism," *New Left Review* 146(1984): 53–92.

57. Woody Allen, "The Kugelmass Episode," *Side Effects* (New York: Random House, 1980), 41–55.

58. Bo Diddley, "You Can't Judge a Book by Its Cover," *Got My Own Bag of Tricks* (Chess Records, 1977).

59. Tony Tanner, *Adultery in the Novel: Contract and Transgression* (Baltimore: Johns Hopkins UP, 1979), 306.

60. See Gayle Rubin, "The Traffic in Women: Notes on the 'Political Economy' of Sex," in *Toward an Anthropology of Women*, ed. Rayna N. Reiter (New York: Monthly Review P, 1975), 157–210.

61. Eugenio Donato, "Qui signe 'Flaubert'?" *MLN* 98, no. 4 (May 1983): 579–93.

62. Michel Foucault, "What Is an Author?" *Language, Counter-Memory, Practice: Selected Essays and Interviews*, ed. Donald F. Bouchard (Ithaca: Cornell UP, 1977), 113–38.

Chapter 5. Gender and Temporality

An earlier much shorter draft of this chapter was published as "Politics of Gender and Temporality in *Beyond the Pleasure Principle*," *Critical Exchange* 25 (Spring 1988). The author gratefully acknowledges permission to reprint this material.

1. These lines, spoken by Woody Allen in his film *Sleeper,* are not to be found in any copy of the screenplay that I have been able to locate.

2. Wayne Weiten, *Psychology: Themes and Variationns* (Pacific Grove, Cal.: Brooks/Cole Publishing Co., 1989), 9, 435. I am indebted to Joan Walls for locating this material for me.

3. Sigmund Freud, *Beyond the Pleasure Principle* (New York: Norton, 1961), 49. Cited hereafter as *BPP.* Freud, "Jenseits des Lustprinzips," *Gesammelte Werke: Chronologisch Geordnet* (Frankfurt am Main: S. Fischer Verlag, 1976), 13: 59. Cited hereafter as *JLP.* For background on Spielrein see Aldo Carotenuto, *A Secret Symmetry: Sabina Spielrein between Freud and Jung* (New York: Pantheon Books, 1982).

4. Frank J. Sulloway, *Freud, Biologist of the Mind: Beyond the Psychoanalytic Legend* (New York: Basic Books, 1983), 415.

5. Harold Bloom, "Freud and the Poetic Sublime," *Antaeus* 30/31 (1978): 365–66.

6. See Juliet Mitchell, *Psychoanalysis and Feminism* (New York: Pantheon Books, 1974); Jacques Lacan and the école freudienne, *Feminine Sexuality,* ed. Juliet Mitchell and Jacqueline Rose (New York: Norton, 1985); Luce Irigaray, *Speculum de l'autre femme* (Paris: Éditions de Minuit, 1974), *Ce sexe qui n'en est pas un* (Paris: Éditions de Minuit, 1977); and Hélène Cixous and Catherine Clément, *The Newly Born Woman* (Minneapolis: U of Minnesota P, 1986).

7. Sarah Kofman, *The Enigma of Woman: Woman in Freud's Writings*, trans. Catherine Porter (Ithaca: Cornell UP, 1985), 122.

8. Freud, "The Transformations of Puberty," *Three Essays on the Theory of Sexuality*, trans. James Strachey (New York: Basic Books, 1975), 85–86.

9. Steven Marcus, Introduction, in ibid., xix.

10. Jacques Lacan, "The Mirror Stage as Formative of the Function of the I," *Ecrits: A Selection* (New York: Norton, 1977), 3–4. Cf. Samuel Weber, *The Legend of Freud* (Minneapolis: U of Minnesota P, 1982), 137.

11. Quoted by Carl Pletsch in "Freud's Case Studies," *Partisan Review* (Winter 1982): 104.

12. Fredric Jameson, *The Political Unconscious: Narrative as a Socially Symbolic Act* (Ithaca: Cornell UP, 1981).

13. Gayle Rubin, "The Traffic in Women: Notes on the 'Political Economy' of Sex," in *Toward an Anthropology of Woman*, ed. Rayna N. Reiter (New York: Monthly Review P, 1975), 157–210. Her *autocritique* came in 1982 in "Thinking Sex: Notes for a Radical Theory of the Politics of Sexuality," in *Pleasure and Danger: Exploring Female Sexuality*, ed. Carole S. Vance (Boston: Routledge & Kegan Paul, 1984), 267–319. The latter essay is equally as substantial and significant as the much more often cited "The Traffic in Women."

14. See, for example, Bruno Bettelheim, *Freud and Man's Soul* (New York: Vintage Books, 1984).

15. Jean Laplanche et J.-B. Pontalis, *Vocabulaire de la psychanalyse* (Paris: Presses Universitaires de France, 1967), 67–70.

16. Michel de Certeau, "Psychoanalysis and Its History," *Heterologies: Discourse on the Other* (Minneapolis: U of Minnesota P, 1986), 6.

17. See Weber, *Legend of Freud* 160.

18. One of the most uncompromising, and certainly influential, arguments for the sociological determination of gender attributes is found in Nancy Chodorow, *The Reproduction of Mothering: Psychoanalysis and the Sociology of Gender* (Berkeley: U of California P, 1978). For a recent critique of Chodorow's failure sufficiently to historicize her analysis of the cultural production of mothering, see Jacqueline Rose, *Sexuality in the Field of Vision* (London: Verso, 1986), 90.

19. Elizabeth Wilson, *Hallucinations: Life in the Postmodern City* (London: Hutchinson Radius, 1988), 169.

20. Alison M. Jaggar, *Feminist Politics and Human Nature* (Totowa, N.J.: Rowman & Allanheld, 1983).

21. Linda Alcoff, "Cultural Feminism versus Post-Structuralism: The Identity Crisis in Feminist Theory," in *Feminist Theory in Practice and Process*, ed. Micheline R. Malson et al. (Chicago: U of Chicago P, 1989), 320.

22. Hélène Cixous, "Sorties," in *The Newly Born Woman*.

23. Jean Laplanche, *Life and Death in Psychoanalysis*, trans. Jeffrey Mehlman (Baltimore: Johns Hopkins UP, 1985), 119–20. For a detailed and fascinating account of the

currents in biological science that nurtured Freud's thought see Sulloway, *Freud*. Pp. 403–15 are especially relevant to Freud's biological musings in *Beyond the Pleasure Principle*. Sulloway wants to rescue Freud from psychoanalysis and reclaim him for biological science, but this polemical bent does not diminish the rich contribution his book makes to intellectual history.

24. Kofman, *Enigma of Woman* 18. Cf. Freud, "Femininity," *New Introductory Lectures on Psychoanalysis* (New York: Norton, 1965), 99–119.

25. Chodorow, *Reproduction of Mothering* 50.

26. Freud, "The Ego and the Id," *The Standard Edition of the Complete Psychological Works of Sigmund Freud,* trans. James Strachey, Anna Freud, et al., Vol. 19 (1923–25) (London: Hogarth Press and Institute of Psychoanalysis, 1961), 3–66.

27. Michel Foucault, *Les mots et les choses: Une archéologie des sciences humaines* (Paris: Gallimard, 1966); *The Order of Things: An Archaeology of the Human Sciences,* trans. A. M. Sheridan-Smith (New York: Vintage Books, 1974).

28. Bertell Ollman, *Alienation: Marx's Conception of Man in Capitalist Society* (New York: Cambridge UP, 1976).

29. Georges Bataille, *La part maudite* (Paris: Éditions de Minuit, 1949); Jean-François Lyotard, *Économie libidinale* (Paris: Éditions de Minuit, 1977).

30. Jean-Joseph Goux, *Économie et symbolique: Freud, Marx* (Paris: Éditions du Seuil, 1973), 36.

31. Rosalind Coward and John Ellis, *Language and Materialism: Developments in Semiology and the Theory of the Subject* (London: Routledge & Kegan Paul, 1977).

32. Karl Marx, "Die entfremdete Arbeit," *Ökonomisch-philosophische Manuskripte aus dem Jahre 1844,* in *Marx-Engels Gesamtausgabe, Erste Abteilung* (Berlin: Marx-Engels Verlag, 1932), 3: 72, 83–84. Cf. James A. Winders, "Foucault and Marx: A Critical Articulation of Two Theoretical Traditions," *New Orleans Review* 11, nos. 3/4 (Fall/Winter 1984): 134–48, as well as Chapter 3 of this book.

33. Elisabeth Bronfen, "The Lady Vanishes: Sophie Freud and *Beyond the Pleasure Principle,*" *South Atlantic Quarterly* 88, no. 4 (Fall 1989): 966.

34. Jacques Derrida, "Spéculer—sur 'Freud,' " in *La Carte postale de Socrate à Freud et au-delà* (Paris: Flammarion, 1980), 327–49. Derrida returns to this biographical emphasis on Freud at the time of his *fort/da* insight in his reply to Patrick Mahony's "Play, Work, and Beyond" in the "Roundtable on Autobiography" in *The Ear of the Other: Texts and Discussions with Jacques Derrida: Otobiography, Transference, Translation,* ed. Christie McDonald, trans. Peggy Kamuf and Avital Ronell (Lincoln: U of Nebraska P, 1988), 70.

35. Derrida, "Spéculer—sur 'Freud,' " 327–49.

36. Serge Leclaire, *On tue un enfant: Un essai sur le narcissisme primaire et la pulsion de mort/suivi d'un texte de Nata Minor* (Paris: Éditions du Seuil, 1975).

37. Jane Gallop, *Reading Lacan* (Ithaca: Cornell UP, 1985), 102.

38. Weber, *Legend of Freud* 96.

39. Toril Moi, "Representation of Patriarchy: Sexuality and Epistemology in Freud's Dora," in *In Dora's Case: Freud—Hysteria—Feminism,* ed. Charles Bernheimer and Claire Kahane (New York: Columbia UP, 1985), 181–99. Moi frames this and other arguments about Freud's failings in terms of the problem of fragment versus whole (184–87). In a brilliant long passage on p. 198, she demonstrates Freud's use of "feminine" as a projection or negative opposite of "masculine."

40. Jacques Lacan, "Le stade du miroir comme formateur de la fonction du Je: telle qu'elle nous est révélée dans l'expérience psychanalytique," in *Écrits I* (Paris: Éditions du Seuil, 1966), 90.

41. David Macey, *Lacan in Contexts* (London: Verso, 1988).

42. See Georges Bataille, "Sacrificial Mutilation and the Severed Ear of Vincent Van Gogh" and "Sacrifices," *Visions of Excess: Selected Writings, 1927–1939,* ed. and trans. Allan Stoekl (Minneapolis: U of Minnesota P, 1985), 61–72, 130–36.

43. Weber, *Legend of Freud* 96. Cf. Lacan, "Tuché and Automaton," *The Four Fundamental Concepts of Psycho-analysis,* trans. Alan Sheridan (New York: Norton, 1981), 62–63.

44. Lacan, "Of the Subject Who Is Supposed to Know," *Four Fundamental Concepts* 239.

45. Lacan, "Tuché and Automaton," 62–63.

46. Moustapha Safouan, *La sexualité féminine dans la doctrine freudienne* (Paris: Éditions du Seuil, 1976), 143.

47. Lacan, "Le séminaire sur 'La Lettre volée,' " *Écrits I* 24.

48. Eugénie Lemoine-Luccioni, *Partage des femmes* (Paris: Éditions du Seuil, 1976), 85.

49. Jane Flax, "Postmodernism and Gender Relations in Feminist Theory," in *Feminist Theory in Practice and Process* 60.

50. Kate Millett, *Sexual Politics* (Boston: Little, Brown, 1970). Cf. Catherine Clément, *Les fils de Freud sont fatiqués* (Paris: Éditions Grasset et Fasquelle, 1978); *The Weary Sons of Freud,* trans. Nicole Ball (London: Verso, 1987).

51. Macey, *Lacan in Contexts.*

52. Shoshana Felman, "Psychoanalysis and Education: Teaching Terminable and Interminable," *Yale French Studies* 63 (1982): 42–43.

53. Jane Marie Todd, "The Veiled Woman in Freud's 'Das Unheimliche,' " *Signs: Journal of Women in Culture and Society* 11, no. 3 (1986): 520, 524, 527.

54. Leclaire, *On tue un enfant* 69.

55. Weber, *Legend of Freud.*

56. Tom Paxton, "The Marvelous Toy" (Cherry Lane Music, 1961).

57. Samuel Beckett, *Watt* (New York: Grove P, 1953), 30. Here is the memorable beginning of Beckett's description of Watt's means of locomotion: "Watt's way of advancing due east, for example, was to turn his bust as far as possible towards the north and at the same time to fling out his right leg as far as possible towards the south, and then to turn his bust as far as possible toward the south and at the

same time to fling out his left leg as far as possible toward the north, and then
again to turn his bust as far as possible towards the north and to fling out his right
leg as far as possible towards the south and to fling out his left leg as far as
possible towards the north, and so on, over and over again, many many times,
until he reached his destination, and could sit down." A vidid cartoon illustration
of Watt in motion, by writer and illustrator Guy Davenport, accompanies Hugh
Kenner's *The Stoic Comedians: Flaubert, Joyce and Beckett* (Berkeley: U of California P, 1962), 79.

58. Cf. Susan Buck-Morss, *Negative Dialectics: Theodor W. Adorno, Walter Benjamin and the Frankfurt Institute* (New York: Free Press, 1977).

59. de Certeau, "Psychoanalysis and Its History," 3–16.

60. Stephen Hawking, *A Brief History of Time: From the Big Bang to Black Holes*
(New York: Bantam Books, 1988), 143–53.

61. Walter Benjamin, "Theses on the Philosophy of History," *Illuminations* (New
York: Schocken Books, 1969), 257–58.

62. See n. 39.

63. Freud, "The Dissection of the Psychical Personality," *New Introductory Lectures* 71.

64. Clément, *Weary Sons of Freud*, 82.

65. Catherine Clément, *The Lives and Legends of Jacques Lacan*, trans. Arthur
Goldhammer (New York: Columbia UP, 1983).

66. Freud, "Transformations of Puberty," 85–87.

67. Michèle Montrelay, "Recherches sur la fémininité," *Critique* 26 (1970): 654.

68. Jane Gallop, *The Daughter's Seduction: Feminism and Psychoanalysis* (Ithaca:
Cornell UP, 1982), 3.

69. Cixous, "Sorties," 79.

70. Luce Irigaray, "Women's Exile: Interview with Luce Irigaray," *Ideology and
Consciousness* 1 (1977): 67. Cf. Irigaray, *Speculum of the Other Woman* (Ithaca: Cornell
UP, 1985), 98–99, and Naomi Segal, "Freud and the Question of Women," in *Freud
in Exile: Psychoanalysis and Its Vicissitudes*, ed. Edward Timms and Naomi Segal (New
Haven: Yale UP, 1988), 246.

71. Luce Irigaray, *Et l'une ne bouge pas sans l'autre* (Paris: Éditions de Minuit,
1979). Cf. Chodorow, *Reproduction of Mothering*.

72. Monique Plaza, " 'Phallomorphic Power' and the Psychology of 'Woman,' "
Ideology and Consciousness 4 (Autumn 1978): 31–32, cited in Toril Moi, *Sexual/Textual
Politics: Feminist Literary Theory* (London: Methuen, 1985), 146–47.

73. Felman, "Psychoanalysis and Education," and Gallop, *Reading Lacan*.

Chapter 6. Writing Like a Woman(?)

I am indebted to Thomas McLaughlin and to Dale Bauer for their critical suggestions and comments on an earlier version of this chapter.

1. Cf. Peggy Kamuf, "Writing like a Woman," in *Women and Language in Litera-ture and Society,* ed. Sally McConnell-Ginet, Ruth Borker, and Nelly Furman (New York: Praeger Books, 1980), 298, cited in *Men in Feminism,* ed. Alice Jardine and Paul Smith (New York: Methuen Books, 1987), 266.

2. The texts I am using in this essay are Friedrich Nietzsche, *Die fröhliche Wissenschaft,* in *Werke in Drei Bänden; Zweiter Band* (München: Carl Hanser Verlag, 1954), and, in English translation: Friedrich Nietzsche, *The Gay Science: with a prelude in rhymes and an appendix of songs,* trans. Walter Kaufmann (New York: Vintage Books, 1974). Hereafter, I refer to them, respectively, as *FW* and *GS.*

3. Cf. Christine Delphy, "Protofeminism and Antifeminism," in *French Feminist Thought: A Reader,* ed. Toril Moi (Oxford: Basil Blackwell, 1987), 80–109; and Monique Plaza, " 'Phallomorphic Power' and the Psychology of 'Woman'," *Ideology and Consciousness* 4 (Autumn 1978): 4–36.

4. Most notably, *Sexual/Textual Politics: Feminist Literary Theory* (London: Me-thuen, 1985). Like so many of the books in the "New Accents" series, this is no impartial introduction.

5. Frank Lentricchia, "Patriarchy against Itself—The Young Manhood of Wal-lace Stevens," *Critical Inquiry* 13, no. 4 (Summer 1987): 742–86. The fallout from this blast can be found in the "Critical Response" section of *Critical Inquiry* 14, no. 2 (Winter 1988): 379–413.

6. William Gass, "The Polemical Philosopher," *New York Review of Books* (Febru-ary 4, 1988): 37.

7. Jacques Derrida, *Spurs: Nietzsche's Styles/Éperons: Les Styles de Nietzsche,* En-glish Translation by Barbara Harlow (Chicago: U of Chicago P, 1979).

8. Michel Foucault, "Nietzsche, Genealogy, History," in *Language, Counter-memory, Practice: Selected Essays and Interviews,* ed. Donald F. Bouchard (Ithaca: Cor-nell UP, 1977), 142.

9. Allan Bloom, *The Closing of the American Mind: How Higher Education Has Failed Democracy and Impoverished the Souls of Today's Students* (New York: Simon and Schuster, 1987), pp. 217–26. This representative passage, in which rock 'n' roll is seen as wreaking cultural havoc through disguised or unacknowledged influences from decadent German culture, gives some indication of the strangeness of Bloom's argu-ment: "Our stars are singing a song they do not understand, translated from a Ger-man original and having a huge popular success with unknown but wide-ranging consequences, as something of the original message touches something in American souls. But behind it all, the master lyricists are Nietzsche and Heidegger" (152). Not quite Tipper Gore's argument, and certainly not her language, but she would proba-bly welcome Bloom as an ally.

10. Walter Kaufmann, "Translator's Introduction," in *GS* 19–20.

11. Paul de Man quotes this passage from *Der Wille zur Macht:* "Der Text bejaht und verneint nicht ein und dasselbe sondern er verneint das Bejahen," which he translates as: "The text does not simultaneously affirm and deny identity but it denies

affirmation." Paul de Man, *Allegories of Reading: Figural Language in Rousseau, Nietzsche, Rilke, and Proust* (New Haven: Yale UP, 1979), 124.

12. Jacques Derrida and Christie V. McDonald, "Choreographies: Interview," *diacritics* 12 (Summer 1982): 66–76.

13. Derrida's citations of Sarah Kofman, whose work has been most closely linked to his own, are exceptions to this general rule.

14. Gustave Flaubert, *Madame Bovary,* in *Oeuvres complètes,* ed. A. Thibaudet and R. Dumesnil (Paris: Éditions Gallimard/Bibliothèque de la Pléiade, 1951), 500 (translation mine).

15. *GS* 124n.

16. Jacques Derrida, "Like the Sound of the Sea Deep within a Shell: Paul de Man's War," *Critical Inquiry* 14, no. 3 (Spring 1988): 590–652, and "Biodegradables: Seven Diary Fragments," *Critical Inquiry* 15, no. 4 (Summer 1989): 812–73.

17. Alexander Nehamas, "The Most Multifarious Art of Style," *Nietzsche: Life as Literature* (Cambridge: Harvard UP, 1985), 13–41.

18. Jacques Derrida, "Otobiographies: The Teaching of Nietzsche and the Politics of the Proper Name," *The Ear of the Other: Texts and Discussions with Jacques Derrida: Otobiography, Transference, Translation,* ed. Christie McDonald, trans. Peggy Kamuf and Avital Ronell (Lincoln: U of Nebraska P, 1988), 1–38.

19. Barbara Kruger, "Your Comfort Is My Silence," *We Will Not Play Nature to Your Culture* (London: Institute for Contemporary Arts, 1983), unpag.

20. Friedrich Nietzsche, "Thus Spoke Zarathustra: First Part," *The Portable Nietzsche,* ed. and trans. Walter Kaufmann (New York: Penguin Books, 1976), 169.

21. Jerzy Kosinski, *Being There* (New York: Bantam Books, 1972).

22. Robert Johnson, "Kindhearted Woman Blues," *King of the Delta Blues Singers* (Columbia Records, n.d.).

23. Gayle Rubin, "The Traffic in Women: Notes on the Political Economy of Sex," in *Toward an Anthropology of Women,* ed. Rayna N. Reiter (New York: Monthly Review P, 1975).

24. Luce Irigaray, "Les marchandises entre elles," *Ce sexe qui n'en est pas un* (Paris: Éditions de Minuit, 1977).

25. *GS* 128n.

26. Ibid., 130n.

27. The Grateful Dead, "Truckin," *American Beauty* (Warner Brothers Records, 1970).

28. Sarah Kofman, *Nietzsche et la métaphore* (Paris: Éditions Galilée, 1983), 167.

29. Ibid., 169.

30. Nehamas, *Nietzsche* 13–41, 180.

31. Ibid., 74.

32. See *The New Nietzsche: Contemporary Styles of Interpretation,* ed. David Allison (New York: Delta Books, 1977); *Why Nietzsche Now?,* ed. Daniel T. O'Hara (Bloomington: Indiana UP, 1985).

33. Ronald Bogue, *Deleuze and Guattari* (London: Routledge, 1989), 29–31.

34. See Roland Barthes, *The Empire of Signs,* trans. Richard Howard (New York: Hill and Wang, 1982).

35. See Susan R. Bordo, *The Flight to Objectivity: Essays on Cartesianism and Culture* (Albany: State U of New York P, 1987).

36. Something Derrida denies as far as his text *Glas* is concerned in "Proverb: 'He That Would Pun . . .'," in *Glassary,* ed. John P. Leavey, Jr. (Lincoln: U of Nebraska P, 1987), 17–20.

37. Elaine Showalter, "Critical Cross-Dressing: Male Feminists and the Woman of the Year," *Raritan* (Fall 1983): 130–49.

38. Derrida, *Spurs* 130–39.

39. Lautréamont, *Maldoror* (*Les Chants de Maldoror*), trans. Guy Wernham (New York: New Directions, 1965), 263.

40. Toril Moi, "Representation of Patriarchy: Sexuality and Epistemology in Freud's Dora," in *In Dora's Case: Freud—Hysteria—Feminism,* ed. Charles Bernheimer and Claire Kahane (New York: Columbia UP, 1985), 186.

41. Hélène Cixous, "The Laugh of the Medusa," in *The Signs Reader: Women, Gender, and Scholarship,* ed. Elizabeth Abel and Emily K. Abel (Chicago: U of Chicago P, 1983), 289.

42. Sarah Kofman, "Un philosophe 'unheimlich,'" *Écarts: Quatre essais à propos de Jacques Derrida* (Paris: Fayard, 1973), quoted in Patrick Mahony, "Transformations and Patricidal Deconstruction," in *The Ear of the Other* 97.

43. Derrida, *Spurs* 46–55.

44. Jacques Derrida, "The Double Session," *Dissemination,* trans. Barbara Johnson (Chicago: U of Chicago P, 1981), 173–286.

45. Jacques Derrida, "Living On: Border Lines," trans. James Hulbert, in *Deconstruction and Criticism,* ed. Harold Bloom et al. (New York: Continuum/Seabury P, 1979), 97–102.

46. Luce Irigaray, "Lèvres voilées," *Amante marine de Friedrich Nietzsche* (Paris: Éditions de Minuit, 1980), 112, 120.

47. Gayatri Chakravorty Spivak, "*Glas*-Piece: A *Compte-rendu*," *diacritics* 7 (1977).

48. Luce Irigaray, *Speculum de l'autre femme* (Paris: Éditions de minuit, 1974).

49. See Luce Irigary, "La Mécanique des fluides," *Ce sexe qui n'en est pas un* (Paris: Editions de Minuit, 1977), 103–16.

50. Jane Gallop, *Reading Lacan* (Ithaca: Cornell UP, 1985), 127.

51. Irigaray, *Amante marine* 59.

52. James Taylor, "Steam Roller," *Sweet Baby James* (Warner Brothers Records, 1970).

53. Irigaray, *Amante marine* 120.

54. Muddy Waters, "Honey Bee," *Muddy Waters/Chess Blues Masters Series* (Chess Records, 1976).

55. Moi, *Sexual/Textual Politics* 146.

56. Toril Moi, "Feminism, Postmodernism, and Style: Recent Feminist Criticism in the United States," *Cultural Critique* (Spring 1988): 3–22.

57. The Doors, "When the Music's Over," *Strange Days* (Elektra Records, 1967).

58. Irigaray, *Amante marine* 12.

59. See Nietzsche, "Women and Their Action at a Distance," in *GS* 123. Nietzsche's attitude toward viewing from a distance is a complicated and somewhat contradictory one, as Kofman especially demonstrates in *Nietzsche et la métaphore* 149–57.

60. Gallop, *Reading Lacan*, passim.

61. Jane Gallop, "French Theory and the Seduction of Feminism," in *Men in Feminism* 111–15.

62. Judith Fetterley, *The Resisting Reader: A Feminist Approach to American Fiction* (Bloomington: Indiana UP, 1978).

63. Jerry Lee Lewis, "Whole Lotta Shakin' Goin' On," *The Original Jerry Lee Lewis* (Sun Records, 1978).

64. Bobby Freeman, "Do You Wanna Dance?" (Josie Records, 1958).

Chapter 7. Conclusion

1. Nancy Fraser, "On the Political and the Symbolic: Against the Metaphysics of Textuality," *enclitic* 17/18 (1987): 102.

2. Michel Foucault, "What Is an Author?" *Language, Counter-Memory, Practice: Selected Essays and Interviews,* ed. Donald F. Bouchard (Ithaca: Cornell UP, 1977), 113–38.

3. Martin Jay makes a strong case for the point of view that canon formation of some kind is inevitable in his "Hierarchy and the Humanities: The Radical Implications of a Conservative Idea," *Telos* 62 (Winter 1984–85): 131–44.

4. Bruce Chatwin, *The Songlines* (New York: Viking P, 1987).

5. Gilles Deleuze and Félix Guattari, *A Thousand Plateaus: Capitalism and Schizophrenia,* trans. Brian Massumi (Minneapolis: U of Minnesota P, 1987).

6. James Clifford, *The Predicament of Culture: Twentieth-Century Ethnography, Literature, and Art* (Cambridge: Harvard UP, 1988), 1–17.

7. Ibid., 23.

8. Barbara Kruger and Phil Mariani, Introduction, *Remaking History,* ed. Barbara Kruger and Phil Mariani (Seattle: Bay Press, 1989), xi.

9. Elizabeth Wilson, "Rewinding the Video," *Hallucinations: Life in the Postmodern City* (London: Hutchinson Radius, 1988), 191–209.

Bibliography

Allen, Woody. "The Kugelmass Episode." In his *Side Effects*, pp. 41–55. New York: Random House, 1980.

Allison, David, ed. *The New Nietzsche: Contemporary Styles of Interpretation*. New York: Delta Books, 1977.

Althusser, Louis. *For Marx*, trans. Ben Brewster. London: Verso, 1979.

Althusser, Louis. *Lenin and Philosophy and Other Essays*, trans. Ben Brewster. New York: Monthly Review P, 1971.

Anderson, Perry. *In the Tracks of Historical Materialism*. Chicago: U of Chicago P, 1984.

Barbin, Herculine. *Herculine Barbin: Being the Recently Discovered Memoirs of a Nineteenth-Century French Hermaphrodite*. Introduced by Michel Foucault. New York: Pantheon Books, 1980.

Barnes, Hazel E. *Sartre & Flaubert*. Chicago: U of Chicago P, 1981.

Barthes, Roland. *Le degré zéro de l'écriture suivi de nouveaux essais critiques*. Paris: Éditions du Seuil, 1972.

Barthes, Roland. *The Empire of Signs*, trans. Richard Howard. New York: Hill and Wang, 1982.

Barthes, Roland. *Essais critiques*. Paris: Éditions du Seuil, 1964.

Bataille, Georges. *La part maudite*. Paris: Éditions de Minuit, 1949.

Bataille, Georges. Visions of Excess: Selected Writings, 1927–1939, ed. and trans. Allan Stoekl. Minneapolis: U of Minnesota P, 1985.

Baudrillard, Jean. *The Mirror of Production*, trans. Mark Poster. St. Louis: Telos P, 1975.

Beckett, Samuel. *The Unnamable*. New York: Grove P, 1958.

Beckett, Samuel. *Watt*. New York: Grove P, 1953.

Belsey, Catherine. *Critical Practice*. London: Methuen, 1980.

Benjamin, Walter. *Illuminations*, ed. Hannah Arendt, trans. Harry Zohn. New York: Schocken, 1969.

Berger, John. *Ways of Seeing*. New York: Penguin Books, 1972.

Berman, Marshall. *All That Is Solid Melts Into Air: The Experience of Modernity*. New York: Simon and Schuster, 1982.

Bettelheim, Bruno. *Freud and Man's Soul*. New York: Vintage Books, 1984.

Bloom, Allan. *The Closing of the American Mind: How Higher Education Has Failed Democracy and Impoverished the Souls of Today's Students*. New York: Simon and Schuster, 1987.

Bloom, Harold. "Freud and the Poetic Sublime." *Antaeus* 30/31 (1978): 355–77.

Bloom, Harold, et al. *Deconstruction and Criticism*. New York: Seabury P, 1979.

Bogue, Ronald. *Deleuze and Guattari*. New York: Routledge, 1989.

Bordo, Susan R. *The Flight to Objectivity: Essays on Cartesianism and Culture*. Albany: State U of New York P, 1986.

Bourdieu, Pierre. "Flaubert's Point of View," trans. Priscilla Parkhurst Ferguson. *Critical Inquiry* 14, no. 3 (Spring, 1988): 539–62.

Bronfen, Elisabeth. "The Lady Vanishes: Sophie Freud and *Beyond the Pleasure Principle*." *South Atlantic Quarterly* 88, no. 4 (Fall, 1989): 961–91.

Buci-Glucksmann, Christine. *La folie du voir: De l'esthétique baroque*. Paris: Éditions Galilée. 1986.

Buci-Glucksmann, Christine. *La raison baroque: De Baudelaire à Benjamin*. Paris: Éditions Galilée, 1984.

Buck-Morss, Susan. *Negative Dialectics: Theodor W. Adorno, Walter Benjamin and the Frankfurt Institute*. New York: Free Press, 1977.

Carotenuto, Aldo. *A Secret Symmetry: Sabina Spielrein between Freud and Jung*. New York: Pantheon Books, 1982.

Caws, Mary Ann. "Ladies Shot and Painted: Female Embodiment in Surrealist Art." In *The Female Body in Western Culture*, ed. Susan Rubin Suleiman, pp. 262–87. Cambridge: Harvard UP, 1986.

Chatwin, Bruce. *The Songlines*. New York: Elisabeth Sifton Books/Viking P, 1987.

Chodorow, Nancy. *The Reproduction of Mothering: Psychoanalysis and the Sociology of Gender*. Berkeley: U of California P, 1978.

Cixous, Hélène. "The Laugh of the Medusa," trans. Keith and Paula Cohen. In *The Signs Reader: Women, Gender, and Scholarship*, ed. Elizabeth Abel and Emily K. Abel, pp. 279–99. Chicago: U of Chicago P, 1983.

Cixous, Hélène, and Catherine Clément. *The Newly Born Woman*, trans. Betsy Wing. Minneapolis: U of Minnesota P, 1986.

Clément, Catherine. *Les fils de Freud sont fatigués*. Paris: Éditions Grasset et Fasquelle, 1978.

Clément, Catherine. *The Lives and Legends of Jacques Lacan*, trans. Arthur Goldhammer. New York: Columbia UP, 1983.

Clément, Catherine. *The Weary Sons of Freud*, trans. Nicole Ball. London: Verso, 1987.

Clifford, James. *The Predicament of Culture: Twentieth-Century Ethnography, Literature, and Art*. Cambridge: Harvard UP, 1988.

Cortázar, Julio. *Blow-up and Other Stories*, trans. Paul Blackburn. New York: Collier Books, 1968.

Coward, Rosalind. *Female Desires: How They Are Sought, Bought, and Packaged*. New York: Grove P, 1985.

Coward, Rosalind, and John Ellis. *Language and Materialism: Developments in Semiology and the Theory of the Subject*. London: Routledge & Kegan Paul, 1977.

Culler, Jonathan. *Flaubert: The Uses of Uncertainty*, rev. ed. Ithaca: Cornell UP, 1985.

Culler, Jonathan. *On Deconstruction: Theory and Criticism after Structuralism*. Ithaca: Cornell U P, 1982.

Danahy, Michael. "Le roman est-il chose femelle?" *Poétique: Revue de théorie et d'analyse littéraires* 25 (1976): 85–106.

Danger, Pierre. *Sensations et objets dans le roman de Flaubert.* Paris: Librairie Armand Colin, 1973.

Darnton, Robert. *The Great Cat Massacre and Other Episodes in French Cultural History.* New York: Basic Books, 1984.

Davis, Natalie Zemon. *Fiction in the Archives: Pardon Tales and Their Tellers in Sixteenth-Century France.* Stanford: Stanford UP, 1987.

de Certeau, Michel. *Heterologies: Discourse on the Other,* trans. Brian Massumi. Minneapolis: U of Minnesota P, 1986.

De Lauretis, Teresa. *Technologies of Gender: Essays on Theory, Film, and Fiction.* Bloomington: Indiana UP, 1987.

Deleuze, Gilles, and Félix Guattari. *Anti-Oedipus: Capitalism and Schizophrenia,* trans. Robert Hurley et al. Minneapolis: U of Minnesota P, 1983.

Deleuze, Gilles, and Félix Guattari. *A Thousand Plateaus: Capitalism and Schizophrenia,* trans. Brian Massumi. Minneapolis: U of Minnesota P, 1987.

de Man, Paul. *Allegories of Reading: Figural Language in Rousseau, Nietzsche, Rilke, and Proust.* New Haven: Yale UP, 1979.

Derrida, Jacques. "Biodegradables: Seven Diary Fragments," trans. Peggy Kamuf. *Critical Inquiry* 15, no. 4 (Summer, 1989): 812–73.

Derrida, Jacques. *La carte postale de Socrate à Freud et au-delà.* Paris: Flammarion, 1980.

Derrida, Jacques. *Dissemination,* trans. Barbara Johnson. Chicago: U of Chicago P, 1981.

Derrida, Jacques. *De la grammatologie.* Paris: Éditions de Minuit, 1967.

Derrida, Jacques. *L'écriture et la différence.* Paris: Éditions du Seuil, 1967.

Derrida, Jacques. *Glas.* Paris: Éditions Galilée, 1974.

Derrida, Jacques. "Like the Sound of the Sea Deep within a Shell: Paul de Man's War," trans. Peggy Kamuf. *Critical Inquiry* 14, no. 3 (Spring, 1988): 590–652.

Derrida, Jacques. *Spurs: Nietzsche's Styles/Éperons: Les Styles de Nietzsche,* trans. Barbara Harlow. Chicago: U of Chicago P, 1979.

Derrida, Jacques and Christie V. McDonald. "Choreographies: Interview." *diacritics* 12 (Summer, 1982): 66–76.

Descartes, René. *Discours de la méthode.* Introduction by Simone Mazauric. Paris: Messidor/Éditions Sociales, 1983.

Descartes, René. *Meditations on First Philosophy,* trans. Laurence Lafleur. Indianapolis: Bobbs-Merrill, 1960.

Descartes, René. *Oeuvres et lettres.* Paris: Gallimard/Bibliothèque de la Pléiade, 1953.

Diamond, Irene, and Lee Quinby, eds. *Foucault & Feminism: Reflections on Resistance.* Boston: Northeastern UP, 1988.

Donato, Eugenio. "Qui signe 'Flaubert'?" *MLN* 98, no. 4 (May, 1983): 579–93.

Eagleton, Terry. *Against the Grain: Essays 1975–1985*. London: Verso, 1986.

Eisenstein, Zillah R., ed. *Capitalist Patriarchy and the Case for Socialist Feminism*. New York: Monthly Review P, 1979.

Felman, Shoshana. "Madness and Philosophy *or* Literature's Reason." *Yale French Studies* 52 (1975): 206–28.

Felman, Shoshana. "Psychoanalysis and Education: Teaching Terminable and Interminable." *Yale French Studies* 63 (1982): 21–44.

Fetterley, Judith. *The Resisting Reader: A Feminist Approach to American Fiction*. Bloomington: Indiana UP, 1978.

Flaubert, Gustave. *The Letters of Gustave Flaubert, 1830–1857*, ed. and trans. Francis Steegmuller. Cambridge: Belknap/Harvard UP, 1980.

Flaubert, Gustave. *Madame Bovary: Moeurs de province*. Paris: Éditions Garnier Frères, 1961.

Flaubert, Gustave. *Madame Bovary*, trans. Paul de Man. New York: Norton, 1969.

Flaubert, Gustave. *Oeuvres I*, ed. Albert Thibaudet and René Dumesnil. Paris: Gallimard/Bibliothèque de la Pléiade, 1951.

Foucault, Michel. *Histoire de la folie à l'âge classique*. Paris: Gallimard, 1972.

Foucault, Michel. *History of Sexuality*, vol. I: *Introduction*, trans. Robert Hurley. New York: Vintage Books, 1980.

Foucault, Michel. *Language, Counter-Memory, Practice: Selected Essays and Interviews*, ed. Donald F. Bouchard. Ithaca: Cornell UP, 1977.

Foucault, Michel. *Les mots et les choses: Une archéologie des sciences humaines*. Paris: Gallimard, 1966.

Foucault, Michel. "Nietzsche Freud Marx." In his *Nietzsche,* pp. 183–200. Cahiers de Royaumont. Paris: Éditions de Minuit, 1967.

Fraser, Nancy. "On the Political and Symbolic: Against the Metaphysics of Textuality." *enclitic* 17/18 (1987): 100–114.

Freud, Sigmund. *Beyond the Pleasure Principle,* trans. James Strachey. New York: Norton, 1961.

Freud, Sigmund. *Gesammelte Werke: Chronologisch Geordnet,* vol. 13. Frankfurt am Main: S. Fischer Verlag, 1976.

Freud, Sigmund. *New Introductory Lectures of Psychoanalysis,* trans. James Strachey. New York: Norton, 1965.

Freud, Sigmund. *The Standard Edition of the complete Psychological Works of Sigmund Freud,* trans. James Strachey, Anna Freud, et al, vol. 19 (1923–25). London: Hogarth Press and Institute of Psychoanalysis, 1961.

Freud, Sigmund. *Three Essays on the Theory of Sexuality,* trans. James Strachey. Introduction by Steven Marcus. New York: Basic Books, 1975.

Frow, John. *Marxism and Literary History*. Cambridge: Harvard UP, 1986.

Gallop, Jane. *The Daughter's Seduction: Feminism and Psychoanalysis*. Ithaca: Cornell UP, 1982.

Gallop, Jane. *Reading Lacan*. Ithaca: Cornell UP, 1985.

Gass, William. "The Polemical Philosopher." *New York Review of Books* (February 4, 1988): 35–41.

Genette, Gérard. *Figures I*. Paris: Éditions du Seuil, 1966.

Geras, Norman. *Marx and Human Nature: Refutation of a Legend*. London: Verso, 1986.

Gilbert, Sandra M., and Susan Gubar. "The Man on the Dump versus the United Dames of America; or, What Does Frank Lentricchia Want?" *Critical Inquiry* 14, no. 2 (Winter, 1988): 386–406.

Ginsburg, Michal Peled. *Flaubert Writing: A Study in Narrative Strategies*. Stanford: Stanford UP, 1986.

Goux, Jean-Joseph. "Descartes et la perspective." *L'esprit créateur* 25, no. 1 (Spring, 1985): 10–20.

Goux, Jean-Joseph. *Économie et symbolique: Freud, Marx*. Paris: Éditions du Seuil, 1973.

Gramsci, Antonio. *Selections from the Prison Notebooks,* ed. and trans. Quentin Hoare and G. N. Smith. New York: International Publishers, 1971.

Guattari, Félix. *Molecular Revolution: Psychiatry and Politics,* trans. Rosemary Sheed. Harmondsworth: Penguin Books, 1984.

Hartmann, Heidi. "The Unhappy Marriage of Marxism and Feminism: Towards a More Progressive Union." In *Women and Revolution,* ed. Lydia Sargent, pp. 1–43. Boston: South End P, 1981.

Hawking, Stephen. *A Brief History of Time: From the Big Bang to Black Holes*. New York: Bantam Books, 1988.

Heidegger, Martin. "The Age of the World View." In *The Question Concerning Technology and Other Essays,* trans. William Lovitt, pp. 115–54. New York: Harper & Row, 1977.

Hirsch, E. D., Jr. *Cultural Literacy: What Every American Needs to Know*. Boston: Houghton Mifflin, 1987.

Irigaray, Luce. *Amante marine de Friedrich Nietzsche*. Paris: Éditions de Minuit, 1980.

Irigaray, Luce. *Ce sexe qui n'en est pas un*. Paris: Éditions de Minuit, 1977.

Irigaray, Luce. *Et l'une ne bouge pas sans l'autre*. Paris: Éditions de Minuit, 1979.

Irigaray, Luce. *Speculum de l'autre femme*. Paris: Éditions de Minuit, 1974.

Irigaray, Luce. *Speculum of the Other Woman,* trans. Gillian C. Gill. Ithaca: Cornell UP, 1985.

Irigaray, Luce. "Woman's Exile: Interview with Luce Irigaray." *Ideology and Consciousness* I (May, 1977): 62–76.

Jaggar, Alison M. *Feminist Politics and Human Nature*. Totowa, N.J.: Rowman & Allanheld, 1983.

Jameson, Fredric. *The Political Unconscious: Narrative as a Socially Symbolic Act*. Ithaca: Cornell UP, 1981.

Jameson, Fredric. "Postmodernism, or the Cultural Logic of Late Capitalism." *New Left Review* 146 (1984): 53–92.

Jardin, Alice. *Gynesis: Configurations of Woman and Modernity.* Ithaca: Cornell UP, 1985.

Jardine, Alice, and Paul Smith, eds. *Men in Feminism.* New York: Methuen, 1987.

Jay, Martin. "Hierarchy and the Humanities: The Radical Implications of a Conservative Idea." *Telos* 62 (Winter 1984–85): 131–44.

Jay, Martin. "In the Empire of the Gaze: Foucault and the Denigration of Vision in Twentieth-Century French Thought." In *Foucault: A Critical Reader,* ed. David Couzzens, pp. 174–204. Oxford: Basil Blackwell, 1986.

Jay, Martin. "Scopic Regimes of Modernity." In *Vision and Visuality,* ed. Hal Foster, pp. 3–23. Seattle: Bay P, 1988.

Joyce, James. *Ulysses: The Corrected Text,* ed. Hans-Walter Gabler et al. New York: Vintage Books, 1987.

Judowitz, Dalia. *Subjectivity and Representation in Descartes: The Origins of Modernity.* Cambridge: Cambridge UP, 1988.

Kamuf, Peggy. "Writing Like a Woman." In *Woman and Language in Literature and Society,* ed. Sally McConnell-Ginet et al, pp. 284–99. New York: Praeger, 1980.

Keller, Evelyn Fox. *A Feeling for the Organism: The Life and Work of Barbara McClintock.* New York: Freeman, 1983.

Keller, Evelyn Fox. *Reflections on Gender and Science.* New Haven: Yale UP, 1985.

Keller, Evelyn Fox, and Christine R. Grontkowski. "The Mind's Eye." In *Discovering Reality: Feminist Perspectives on Epistemology, Metaphysics, Methodology, and Philosophy of Science,* ed. Sandra Harding and Merrill B. Hintikka, pp. 207–24. Dordrecht: D. Reidel, 1983.

Kelly, Joan. *Woman, History, and Theory.* Chicago: U of Chicago P, 1984.

Kenner, Hugh. *The Stoic Comedians: Flaubert, Joyce and Beckett.* Berkeley: U of California P, 1962.

Kofman, Sarah. *The Enigma of Woman: Woman in Freud's Writings,* trans. Catherine Porter. Itahca: Cornell UP, 1985.

Kofman, Sarah. *L'énigme de la femme: La femme dans les textes de Freud.* Paris: Éditions Galilée, 1980.

Kofman, Sarah. *Nietzsche et la métaphore.* Paris: Éditions Galilée, 1983.

Kofman, Sarah. *Le respect des femmes (Kant et Rousseau).* Paris: Éditions Galilée, 1973.

Kosinski, Jerzy. *Being There.* New York: Bantam Books, 1972.

Kremer-Marietti, Angèle. *Michel Foucault et l'archéologie du savoir.* Pairs: Seghers, 1974.

Kruger, Barbara. *We Won't Play Nature to Your Culture.* London: Institute of Contemporary Arts, 1983.

Kruger, Barabra, and Phil Mariani, eds. *Remaking History.* Seattle: Bay P, 1989.

Kuhn, Annette. *Women's Pictures: Feminism and Cinema.* London: Routledge & Kegan Paul, 1982.

Lacan, Jacques. *Écrits I.* Paris: Éditions du Seuil, 1966.

Lacan, Jacques. *Écrits: A Selection,* trans. Alan Sheridan. New York: Norton, 1977.

Lacan, Jacques. *The Four Fundamental Concepts of Psycho-Analysis,* trans. Alan Sheridan. New York: Norton, 1981.

Lacan, Jacques, and the école freudienne. *Feminine Sexuality,* ed. Juliet Mitchell and Jacqueline Rose. New York: Norton, 1985.

LaCapra, Dominick. *History and Criticism.* Ithaca: Cornell UP, 1985.

LaCapra, Dominick. *History, Politics, and the Novel.* Ithaca: Cornell UP, 1987.

LaCapra, Dominick. "The Limits of Intellectual History." *enclitic* 17/18 (1987): 141–50.

LaCapra, Dominick. *"Madame Bovary" On Trial.* Ithaca: Cornell UP, 1982.

LaCapra, Dominick. *Rethinking Intellectual History: Texts, Contexts, Language.* Ithaca: Cornell UP, 1983.

LaCapra, Dominick. *Soundings in Critical Theory.* Ithaca: Cornell UP, 1989.

LaCapra, Dominick, and Steven Kaplan, eds. *Modern European Intellectual History: Reappraisals and New Perspectives.* Ithaca: Cornell UP, 1982.

Laplanche, Jean. *Life and Death in Psychoanalysis,* trans. Jeffrey Mehlman. Baltimore: Johns Hopkins UP, 1985.

Laplanche, Jean, and J.-B. Pontalis. *Vocabulaire de la psychanalyse.* Paris: Presses Universitaries de France, 1967.

Lautréamont. *Maldoror (Les Chants de Maldoror),* trans. Guy Wernham. New York: New Directions, 1965.

Leavey, John P., Jr., ed. *Glassary.* Lincoln: U of Nebraska P, 1987.

Leclaire, Serge. *On tue un enfant: Un essai sur le narcissisme primaire et la pulsion de mort/suivi d'un text de Nata Minor.* Paris: Éditions du Seuil, 1975.

Le Doeuff, Michèle. "Ants and Women, or Philosophy Without Borders." In *Contemporary French Philosophy,* ed. A. Phillips Griffiths, pp. 41–54. Cambridge: Cambridge UP, 1987.

Lemoine-Luccioni, Eugénie. *Partage des femmes.* Paris: Éditions du Seuil, 1976.

Lentricchia, Frank. *After the New Criticism.* Chicago: U of Chicago P, 1980.

Lentricchia, Frank. *Criticism and Social Change.* Chicago U of Chicago P, 1983.

Lentricchia, Frank. "Patriarchy Against Itself—The Young Manhood of Wallace Stevens." *Critical Inquiry* 13, no. 4 (Summer, 1987): 742–86.

Lentricchia, Frank. "Reading Foucault (Punishment, Labor, Resistance)." *Raritan* (Spring, 1982): 5–32.

Lentricchia, Frank. "Reading Foucault (Punishment, Labor, Resistance): Part Two." *Raritan* (Summer, 1982): 41–70.

Lévi-Strauss, Claude, *Le cru et le cuit.* Paris: Plon, 1964.

Love, Nancy S. *Marx, Nietzsche, and Modernity.* New York: Columbia UP, 1986.

Lubbock, Percy. *The Craft of Fiction.* New York: Viking, 1957.

Lukács, Georg. *History and Class Consciousness: Studies in Marxist Dialectics,* trans. Rodney Livingstone. Cambridge: MIT P, 1971.

Lunn, Eugene. *Marxism and Modernism: An Historical Study of Lukács, Brecht, Benjamin, and Adorno.* Berkeley: U of California P, 1982.

Lyotard, Jean-François. *Économie libidinale.* Paris: Éditions de Minuit, 1977.

McDonald, Christie V., ed. *The Ear of the Other: Texts and Discussions with Jacques Derrida: Otobiography, Transference, Translation,* trans. Peggy Kamuf and Avital Ronell. Lincoln: U. of Nebraska P, 1988.

Macey, David. *Lacan in Contexts.* London: Verso, 1988.

Macherey, Pierre. *Pour une théorie de la production littéraire.* Paris: Maspero, 1966.

Mallarmé, Stéphane. *Oeuvres complètes,* ed. Henri Mondor and G. Jean-Aubry. Paris: Gallimard/Bibliothèque de la Pléiade, 1945.

Mallarmé, Stéphane. *Selected Poetry and Prose,* ed. Mary Ann Caws, trans. Mary Ann Caws et al. New York: New Directions, 1982.

Malson, Micheline R. et al., eds. *Feminist Theory in Practice and Process.* Chicago: U of Chicago P, 1989.

Martin, Biddy. "Feminism, Criticism, and Foucault." *New German Critique* 27 (Fall, 1982): 3–30.

Martin, Luther H. et al., eds. *Technologies of the Self: A Seminar with Michel Foucault.* Amherst: U of Massachusetts P, 1988.

Marx, Karl. *Capital: A Critique of Political Economy,* vol. I: *The Process of Capitalist Production.* New York: International Publishers, 1967.

Marx, Karl. *The Economic and Philosophic Manuscripts of 1844,* ed. Dirk J. Struik, trans. Martin Milligan. New York: International Publishers, 1964.

Marx, Karl. *Werke/Artikel/Entwürfe/März 1843 bis August 1844: Text.* In *Marx-Engels Gesamtausgabe.* Berlin: Dietz Verlag, 1982.

Mehlman, Jeffrey. "Writing and Deference: The Politics of Literary Adulation." *Representations* 15 (Summer, 1986): 1–14.

Millett, Kate. *Sexual Politics.* Boston: Little, Brown, 1970.

Minnich, Elizabeth Kamarck. "From Ivory Tower to Tower of Babel?" *South Atlantic Quarterly* 89, no.1 (Winter, 1990): 181–94.

Mitchell, Juliet. *Psychoanalysis and Feminism.* New York: Pantheon Books, 1974.

Mitchell, W. J. T. "Scholars Need to Explore Further the Links and Dissonance between Post-Colonial Culture and Post-Imperial Criticism." *Chronicle of Higher Education* 25, no. 32 (April 19, 1989): B1–3.

Mitzman, Arthur. "Roads, Vulgarity, Rebellion, and Pure Art: The Inner Space of Flaubert and French Culture." *Journal of Modern History* 51, no. 3 (September, 1979): 504–24.

Moi, Toril. "Feminism, Postmodernism, and Style: Recent Feminist Criticism in the United States." *Cultural Critique* (Spring, 1988): 3–22.

Moi, Toril. "Representation of Patriarchy: Sexuality and Epistemology in Freud's Dora." In *In Dora's Case: Freud—Hysteria—Feminism,* ed. Charles Bernheimer and Claire Kahane. New York: Columbia UP, 1985: 181–99.

Moi, Toril. *Sexual/Textual Politics: Feminist Literary Theory.* London: Methuen, 1985.

Moi, Toril, ed. *French Feminist Thought: A Reader.* Oxford: Basil Blackwell, 1987.

Montrelay, Michèle. "Inquiry into Femininity," trans. Parveen Adams. *m/f* 1 (1978): 83–101.

Montrelay, Michèle. "Recherches sur la fémininité." *Critique* 278 (1970): 654–74.

Mulvey, Laura. "Visual Pleasure and Narrative Cinema." *Screen* (Autumn, 1975): 6–18.

Nehamas, Alexander. *Nietzsche: Life as Literature.* Cambridge: Harvard UP, 1985.

Nietzsche, Friedrich. *The Gay Science: With a Prelude in Rhymes and an Appendix of Songs,* trans. Walter Kaufmann. New York: Vintage Books, 1974.

Nietzsche, Friedrich. *The Portable Nietzsche,* ed. and trans. Walter Kaufmann. New York: Penguin Books, 1976.

Nietzsche, Friedrich. *Werke in Drei Bänden: Zweiter Band.* München: Carl Hanser Verlag, 1954.

O'Connor, John J. "When the Sun Set on the Nixon Presidency." *New York Times* (October 29, 1989): 33.

O'Hara, Daniel T., ed. *Why Nietzsche Now?* Bloomington: Indiana UP, 1985.

Ollman, Bertell. *Alienation: Marx's Conception of Man in Capitalist Society,* 2nd edition. Cambridge: Cambridge UP, 1976.

Ortner, Sherry B. "Is Female to Male as Nature Is to Culture?" In *Woman, Culture, and Society,* ed. Michelle Z. Rosaldo and Louise Lamphere, pp. 67–84. Stanford: Stanford U P, 1974.

Phillips, Lisa. *Cindy Sherman.* New York: The Whitney Museum, 1987.

Plaza, Monique. " 'Phallomorphic Power' and the Psychology of Woman." *Ideology and Consciousness* 4 (Autumn, 1978): 4–36.

Pletsch, Carl. "Freud's Case Studies." *Partisan Review* (Winter, 1982): 101–18.

Pollock, Griselda. *Vision and Difference: Femininity, Feminism, and Histories of Art.* New York: Routledge, 1988.

Poster, Mark. *Existential Marxism in Postwar France: Sartre to Althusser.* Princeton: Princeton UP, 1975.

Poster, Mark. *Foucault, Marxism, and History: Mode of Production versus Mode of Information.* London: Polity P, 1984.

Poster, Mark. °Semiology and Critical Theory: From Marx to Baudrillard." *boundary 2* 8, no. 1 (Fall, 1979): 275–93.

Poster, Mark. "Technology and Culture in Habermas and Baudrillard." *Contemporary Literature* (Fall, 1981): 456–77.

Ramazani, Vaheed K. *The Free Indirect Mode: Flaubert and the Poetics of Irony.* Charlottesville: UP of Virginia, 1988.

Rosaldo, Michelle Z., and Louise Lamphere, eds. *Woman, Culture, and Society.* Stanford: Stanford UP, 1974.

Rose, Jacqueline. *Sexuality and the Field of Vision.* London: Verso, 1986.

Rubin, Gayle. "Thinking Sex: Notes for a Radical Theory of the Politics of Sexuality." In *Pleasure and Danger: Exploring Female Sexuality,* ed. Carole S. Vance, pp. 267–319. Boston: Routledge & Kegan Paul, 1984.

Rubin, Gayle. "The Traffic in Women: Notes on the 'Political Economy' of Sex." In Rayna N. Reiter, ed. *Toward an Anthropology of Women,* pp. 157–210. New York: Monthly Review P, 1975.

Rundell, John F. *Origins of Modernity: The Origins of Modern Social Theory from Kant to Hegel to Marx.* Madison: U of Wisconsin P, 1987.

Ryan, Michael. *Marxism and Deconstruction: A Critical Articulation.* Baltimore: Johns Hopkins UP, 1982.

Sacks, Karen. "Engels Revisited: Women, the Organization of Production, and Private Property." In *Toward an Anthropology of Women,* ed. Rayna N. Reiter, pp. 211–34. New York: Monthly Review P, 1975.

Safouan, Moustapha. *La sexualité féminine dans la doctrine freudienne.* Paris: Éditions du Seuil, 1976.

Said, Edward W. "The Problem of Textuality: Two Exemplary Positions." *Critical Inquiry* (Summer, 1978): 673–714.

Said, Edward W. *The World, The Text, and the Critic..* Cambridge: Harvard UP, 1983.

Sartre, Jean-Paul. *Being and Nothingness,* trans. Hazel E. Barnes. New York: Washington Square P, 1966.

Sayles, John. *Thinking in Pictures: The Mkaing of the Movie "Matewan."* Boston: Houghton Mifflin, 1987.

Schor, Naomi, and Henry F. Majewski, eds. *Flaubert and Postmodernism.* Lincoln: U of Nebraska P, 1984.

Showalter, Elaine. "Critical Cross-Dressing: Male Feminists and the Woman of the Year." *Raritan* (Fall, 1983): 130–49.

Sokoloff, Natalie J. *Between Money and Love: The Dialectics of Women's Home and Market Work.* New York: Praeger, 1980.

Spivak, Gayatri Chakravorty. "Deconstruction in Exile." Unpublished paper presented at Duke University Program in Literature conference "Convergence in Crisis: Narratives in the History of Theory." September 26, 1987.

Spivak, Gayatri Chakravorty. "*Glas*-Piece: A *Compte-rendu.*" *diacritics* 7, no. 3 (1977): 22–43.

Stevens, Wallace. *The Palm at the End of the Mind: Selected Poems and a Play,* ed. Holly Stevens. New York: Vintage Books, 1974.

Stromberg, Roland N. *European Intellectual History Since 1789,* 5th ed. Englewood Cliffs, N.J.: Prentice-Hall, 1990.

Suleiman, Susan Rubin. "(Re)writing the Body: The Politics and Poetics of Female Eroticism." In *The Female Body in Western Culture: Contemporary Perspectives,* ed. Susan Rubin Suleiman, pp. 7–29. Cambridge: Harvard UP, 1986.

Sulloway, Frank. *Freud, Biologist of the Mind: Beyond the Psychoanalytic Legend.* New York: Basic Books, 1983.

Tanner, Tony. *Adultery in the Novel: Contract and Transgression.* Baltimore: Johns Hopkins UP, 1979.

Timms, Edward, and Naomi Segal, eds. *Freud in Exile: Psychoanalysis and Its Vicissitudes.* New Haven: Yale UP, 1988.

Todd, Jane Marie. "The Veiled Woman in Freud's 'Das Unheimliche'." *Signs: Journal of Women in Culture and Society* 11, no. 3 (1986): 519–28.

Toews, John E. "Intellectual History After the Linguistic Turn: The Autonomy of Meaning and the Irreducibility of Experience." *American Historical Review* 92 (1987): 879–907.

van der Linden, Harry. *Kantian Ethics and Socialism*. Indianapolis: Hackett, 1988.

Vargas Llosa, Mario. *The Perpetual Orgy: Flaubert and Madame Bovary*, trans. Helen Lane. New York: Farrar, Straus and Giroux, 1986.

Wallbank, T. Walter, et al. *Civilization Past and Present*, 5th ed. Glenview, IL: Scott, Foresman, 1978.

Warning, Rainer. "Irony and the 'Order of Discourse' in Flaubert." *New Literary History* 13, no. 2 (Winter, 1982): 253–86.

Weber, Samuel. *The Legend of Freud*. Minneapolis: U of Minnesota P, 1982.

Weeks, Jeffrey. *Sexuality and Its Discontents: Modern Meanings, Myths, Sexualities*. London: Routledge and Kegan Paul, 1985.

Weiten, Wayne. *Psychology: Themes and Variations*. Pacific Grove, CA; Brooks/Cole Publishing Co., 1989.

Wetherill, P. M., ed. *Flaubert: La dimension du texte*. Manchester: Manchester UP, 1982.

White, Hayden. *The Content of the Form: Narrative Discourse and Historical Representation*. Baltimore: Johns Hopkins UP, 1987.

White, Hayden. *Metahistory: The Historical Imagination in Nineteenth Century Europe*. Baltimore: Johns Hopkins UP, 1973.

White, Hayden. *Tropics of Discourse: Essays in Cultural Criticism*. Baltimore: Johns Hopkins UP, 1978.

White, Hayden, and Margaret Brose, eds. *Representing Kenneth Burke*. Baltimore: Johns Hopkins UP, 1982.

Wilson, Elizabeth. *Hallucinations: Life in the Postmodern City*. London: Hutchinson Radius, 1988.

Winders, James A. "Foucault and Marx: A Critical Articulation of Two Intellectual Traditions." *New Orleans Review* 11, nos. 3/4 (Fall/Winter, 1984): 134–48.

Winders, James A. "Poststructuralist Theory, Praxis, and the Intellectual." *Contemporary Literature* 27, no. 1 (Spring, 1986): 73–84.

Wing, Nathaniel. *The Limits of Narrative: Essays on Baudelaire, Flaubert, Rimbaud and Mallarmé*. Cambridge: Cambridge UP, 1986.

Woodhull, Winifred. "Configurations of the Family in 'Un Coeur simple'." *Comparative Literature* 39, no. 2. (Spring, 1987): 139–61.

Index